The Adulterer's Daughter

The Adulterer's Daughter

THE LIFE, LOVES AND LONGINGS OF A GIRL WHOSE FATHER STRAYED

Patricia Weiss Levy

ISBN-13: 9781537514246
ISBN-10: 1537514245
Library of Congress Control Number: 2016918042
CreateSpace Independent Publishing Platform
North Charleston, South Carolina

To my mother, Bernice,
who was a much better parent
than she may appear to be in this book
and my husband, Harlan.
Wish I were a better wife.

Contents

Acknowledgments

～

MEMOIR IS A FUNNY WORD, and not just because it is fundamentally French, and therefore a little pretentious and a little hard to pronounce. ("MEM-wahr?" Or, as my mother used to say, "mem-WAHHH?") But unlike biography, which aims to present the story of a life, memoir is simply stories *from* a life, more often than not pivotal stories that focus on turning points. And as pretentious as it may sound, after spending decades as a journalist, always telling other people's stories and turning points, I felt that it was time to tell my own.

I cannot say that what you are about to read is the whole truth, but I would like to believe it is nothing but. I have done my best to recollect and recapture details from the somewhat checkered events that constitute my past. Most of them took place long ago, though. In fact, most of these stories were *written* long ago. It took me a full ten years to finish them, then another decade to get them where they are today: in print. So it might be fair to say that this manuscript has a rather checkered past itself.

At one point in that history, a friend far savvier about the publishing industry asked why I insisted on remaining faithful to fact. Why not juice it up a bit to make it more marketable – introduce a murder or two, an unhealthy dose of substance abuse, maybe even a bit of incest, and call it fiction?

The answer, I explained as calmly as I could, was that I had spent years (OK, a decade) trying to document exactly what had happened and precisely how it had. My mother and brother, the only two people who had been there through most of these events with me, had already read it and not disputed one word. Besides, to me, any intrinsic value these tales offer lies mostly in their truth. Why muck them up with fabricated nonsense now in order to make them more titillating?

After all, as a journalist, I have devoted my entire career not just to headlines and deadlines, but the pursuit of accuracy. How can I possibly let go of that now and simply start making sh-t up?

In the interests of not only getting it right, but giving credit where it rightfully goes, I have many people to thank. I am grateful to my literary agent, Russell Galen, who read most of these stories as they were hatched and encouraged me to hatch more. I would like to express my deepest appreciation to my good friends Elizabeth Roth, Patricia Kazakoff, Stacey Savin, Suzanne Eagle, Kathy Arnold and Paul Wade, who read many of these stories at various stages and offered their own input, insights, and most of all moral support. Infinite thanks go to Roxanne Stachelek for her prolonged efforts in designing the cover, as well as to Rafael Wurzel for shooting that shirt with the snapshot tucked into the pocket. I am also deeply indebted to my daughter Allegra and to JP Sistenich for lending their time and expertise to resolve technical difficulties and bring that cover to life.

Most of all, thanks to my husband Harlan, children Aidan and Allegra, and daughter-in-law Kaitlin for continuing to cheer me on, egg me on, and believe in me, even when I no longer believed in myself. Here is one thing I know to be true: No family anywhere could be better, or better loved.

The Adulterer's Daughter

I FIRST LAID EYES ON my father's mistress in Women's Coats at Bloomingdale's. God only knows why she and my father had gone for outerwear. Clearly, she was already set in that department, decked out as she was in a knee-length mink — one of three furs, I would learn, that were hers, all hers, all supplied, little doubt, by him. As I approached, she extended a stiff, bony hand to me, palm down, her long, slim fingers with their fiery red nails like cigarettes with burning tips. "Hoy," she said, her nasal, Brooklyn accent conjuring to me an American Eliza Doolittle from Prospect Park, pre-Professor Higgins. "Oy'm Elaine."

This was no chance encounter. No mere coincidence or deliberate ambush amid the racks of Burberrys and sensible woolen pea coats in my favorite store. Now 23, I had agreed with a sound mind and free will to set aside my moral compass and lingering dread and at long last meet the mystery woman whose decade-plus-long liaison with my father had decapitated my family and made emotional mincemeat of my childhood.

My father, eager to mitigate the tension of this real-life melodrama, had chosen to stage our first confrontation in the most innocuous public setting he could find. Why not defuse its emotional wallop with the frivolity of a little shopping trip? Maybe, in his usual materialistic mode of expressing love, he actually figured that he could offset any pain that the meeting might cause by letting us each pick out a new blouse or purse. I could only hope it wasn't the baldly crass alternative: that he believed he could buy me off.

It was a scene I'd had countless years to rehearse in my mind and a day or two to debate. Yet seeing her posed there before me now, in the flesh, I realized that I wasn't ready. I wanted my mother. I wanted to flee. I wanted to drop to the floor and seek refuge beneath the clothing racks, like a runaway toddler playing hide and seek, or to turn and sprint at breakneck speed down the Up escalator on which I'd just risen. Yet as a timid young woman, I wanted even more to act like an adult, or at least be taken for one. I also wanted to end the icy war that I'd long been waging with my father, and to exterminate the dark little secrets that had infested our home like bedbugs. So instead of leaving, I swallowed hard, reached out to clasp that fistful of fire, and dutifully shook hands with The Devil.

Although my father had wandered off for the moment, I'd recognized her almond-shaped eyes instantly from a painted portrait I'd once seen hanging in the apartment they shared. My mother had first learned of this secret hideaway more than a dozen years earlier, when he had carelessly left a mysterious parking ticket lying on top of his dresser in our suburban house. The license plate number listed on the ticket wasn't his. It wasn't hers, either. This discovery only lent credence to her longstanding suspicions. My parents were already in marriage counseling. Confidentially, she consulted their therapist for advice.

"Write to the Department of Motor Vehicles in Albany," the doctor advised. "They'll tell you everything."

She did, and soon received back by mail what she believed to be solid evidence that my father was seeing another woman. A married mother of two. She confronted him head-on. "I know what you're up to," she said. "I know who she is. I even know her name."

Rather than retaliating with threats to wring her neck – words that customarily flew off his tongue as casually as his order for chicken chow mein at our favorite Chinese restaurant – he vowed to give up his secret life and never stray again. Lies on both counts. Or so we would soon learn.

To convince my mother that he was sincere, my father resorted to a strange tactic. He handed over a key to his trysting place, insisting that he needed to keep it for business purposes. My mother would never understand why he offered her that key. "Did he think I was such a mouse?" she later asked me. "Or did he psychologically want me to stop them?" Either way, she tried to believe his promise. Tried hard. But the next time she visited their therapist in the city, she took a detour. It ended at my father's apartment building on East 46th Street.

Inside, she found a studio apartment all set up, or so she said, for a rendezvous that night. There was dinner in the fridge, and a window was wide open. "You don't leave a window open," she insisted, "unless you're planning to be back soon." To her horror, she noticed a framed collage of photographs combining pictures of my father, his girlfriend, and their respective children — her son and daughter, and my brother and me. As if they had one big family together. Or hoped to someday.

Her incensed response was immediate. Finding four pairs of feminine sunglasses on a night table, she smashed them all and scattered the broken glass all over the bed. Then she stormed into the small kitchenette, where she was amazed to discover a large box of kosher salt. At home, this was something she routinely used not just for cooking, but also to cleanse things. She scattered its contents everywhere, thoroughly covering the kitchen counters, sink, and floor. Then she dumped everything else she could quickly get her hands on into the incinerator chute. Down flew his lover's toiletries, along with every last bottle from their well-stocked liquor cabinet and the fancy dinner they apparently planned to share that night.

Then she drove to see her therapist... who insisted that she go back and clean it all up again. The doctor feared that her actions would send my temperamental father into a rage. Reluctantly, my mother complied. It was a move she would always regret. "I'm so angry at myself for doing that," she said. "Because he went into a rage anyway."

I still try to picture her returning to the scene of the crime that harrowing day, slowly turning the doorknob in fear that my father and his lover might now be within. I try to picture her sweeping up every single grain of spilled salt, then collecting every last shard of shattered glass from the bed — the bed that her husband shared with his mistress. I try to imagine all this, but I can't. I also can't help hoping that when she was done, a few fragments of glass were left.

My father, indeed, came home and exploded at my mother that night. Although she had tidied up the mess, the doorman had tipped him off. He actually demanded to know what she'd done with all the food and liquor. "I gave them to a poor person," she lied. Then he packed his bags and moved into the city. It was neither the first nor the last time he would abandon our family. I had just turned 15.

⁓

These ceaseless separations came as anything but a shock to me. They were more like someone acknowledging that it was time to pull the plug on a terminally ill patient. The problem was that the patient – my parents' diseased marriage – would still refuse to die a natural death. Instead, it remained on life support for nearly three decades, while my father returned home repeatedly and then departed anew.

Elaine was not the first woman he ever saw on the sly. She was merely the only one we knew about for sure, or actually knew by name.

Their affair had apparently begun during the Big Blackout of 1965, when he got stuck in the city overnight, and it continued extra-maritally for nearly15 years. Throughout that time, my mother remained convinced, all signs to the contrary, that my father would eventually give his girlfriend up. Our lives would return to normal, and no one need ever know the truth. But ours was a small town in Westchester, and too many people knew the terrible truth. News would get back to her from well-meaning acquaintances that my father had been spied dining out with another woman, or even vacationing with her in the Bahamas. Those people, no doubt, didn't just tell my mother. In a small town, there's always talk.

And if worrying about rumors weren't enough, there was the constant evidence of my father's philandering flung cavalierly in her face. Never mind that it had long become the norm in our house that Thursday was official boys' night out, meaning that during the times he was living at home, he was allowed to stay out *all* night. There were countless other evenings when he would call home to say, "Sorry, gotta work late," or would wander in after 9 or 10, shrug a hasty *mea culpa,* and mutter, "Sorry, I missed my train."

Yet still my mother held fast to her failing marriage, like a castaway clutching the remains of a rot-ridden, sinking raft. The message I got from this was that the alternative was far too shameful. That if and when my parents resolved to split up permanently, we were doomed to become instant outcasts. Never mind that by the late 1960s, the wholesome milieu of *Leave It to Beaver* had long been replaced by the salacious TV soap opera *Peyton Place*, and half the human race was flagrantly going haywire. It was as though we were on the verge of becoming the Only Divorced Family in America.

All this while, I hung around the guidance office at my high school, pretending to plumb through countless college manuals. All I really was seeking was some adult who might suddenly notice how unbearably sad I was. It took awhile, but eventually one did. At the time, there was a girl in the next class up from mine dying from some virulent disease. One day, one of the secretaries could stomach watching me mope no longer.

"Some of you kids feel so damned sorry for yourselves," she seethed to me. "How would you like to trade places with poor Melissa Wood?"

I stared back silently, my cheeks aflame with shame, then gathered my books and left. I didn't dare reply with the honest answer: that, in at least one respect, I would.

One Friday night a few months later, I went to visit my father for the first time. It was on this weekend that I first glimpsed that painted portrait of Elaine hanging in the apartment they shared. At least the woman herself, as he had promised, was nowhere in sight. The plan was that I'd stay until Sunday. Noticing decidedly feminine toiletries as intimate as the razor with which she shaved her legs, though, I began to feel queasy. This sensation only worsened on Saturday when my father pulled me into a posh boutique so I could try on a bracelet he had admired in the window.

"Do you think your boyfriend's going to buy it for you?" gushed the young Asian salesgirl breathlessly when he had wandered across the shop to examine another bauble.

"He's not my boyfriend," I shot back, mortified. Then I insisted I didn't like it, after all. On the way back to his apartment, I announced that I felt sick and wanted to go home. Both were true, and I soon left. I didn't have the heart to tell my mother why.

My parents remained separated throughout that year, but I never visited again. They astonished me by getting back together again briefly the summer before I left for college. The reconciliation didn't last for long, however, to no one's surprise, least of all mine. And by the time I had agreed to play Meet the Mistress at Bloomingdale's, to everyone's relief – most of all mine – legal proceedings were underway.

⎯⎯ᦔ⎯⎯

Although I suffered through every second of that store encounter, I walked away inclined to laugh. It wasn't just that it felt safer to make light of the situation than to let myself cry – much like it was easier to blame Elaine for the dissolution of my family than to actually condemn my father. The situation seemed so pathetic that it verged on humor (which, unlike coffee, I tend to take black).

I would like to look back now and say that my father was the charismatic and charming man that to most outsiders he appeared to be, but that was only part of the story – the part that made me cringe inside when he flirted so flagrantly with waitresses and other women right in front of my mother that I was embarrassed for us all.

In public, he had the brand of brash self-assurance and sharp-tongued aplomb that made him the life of many a party. But this bore little resemblance to the private persona that planted terror in our hearts at home. For behind closed doors he was a tyrant, so short-fused and apt to explode at the slightest provocation that we learned to tiptoe around him. Often literally. I will never forget the time that my mother enlisted me to slip out the back door surreptitiously and hurriedly borrow a tomato from a friend. She had already offered my father a couple of slices on his tuna sandwich and didn't dare risk his wrath by informing him that she had discovered we didn't have any tomatoes, after all.

This is not to say he wasn't a family-oriented man... up to a point. He no doubt fancied himself a loving dad. But back in those days mothers were in charge of most things domestic, and he had little patience for parenting. So when my brother and I were young, we were shipped off to visit my maternal grandparents nearly every weekend. And once we grew older, my father found solitude instead by spending Saturdays and Sundays at an exclusive tennis club to which he maintained a solo membership. The game was his passion, and on the rare occasions that he deigned to play it with us, he quickly grew short-tempered if my energy started to flag and began to hit at me rapid-fire, sending the ball from one side to the other as he hollered loudly enough for all within earshot to hear, "MOVE YOUR FAT ASS!"

That my derriere was relatively diminutive then did nothing to soften the blow.

Yet this was nothing compared to the gut-wrenching anxiety I felt as a teenager, when I would lie in bed at night listening to the rhythmic pounding emanating from my parents' bedroom down the hall, trying desperately to decipher the sounds. Was Dad was slamming Mom's head against the wall again, or were they merely having sex?

As sickened as I was by the repeated assaults I saw inflicted on my mother, both physical and verbal, I tried to keep a sliver of an open mind about my father's affair. I could only begin to imagine how excruciating it might feel to be a married adult and then encounter your so-called soul mate — someone brilliant, poetic, witty, and kind (my personal preferences), who got all of your jokes and didn't mind or even seem to notice your annoying idiosyncrasies.

Still, as I stepped out of that upscale department store that fateful day, I shuddered at the chilling reality that had just come to light. *She* was the irresistible magnet that had lured my father to put us all through a living hell? Nominally educated, coarse, and decidedly common, Elaine may have possessed a wealth of wicked feminine wiles, but she was no match for my witty and successful father on any level. Whatever earthy strategies she'd used to entice him over all those years, this woman was sorely lacking in intellect and civility. How could she be his or anyone's soul mate? She was a mate who had no soul. She wasn't an uncut diamond like Eliza Doolittle. To me, she was just an aging slut.

Whatever had happened to the unofficial creed that once American businessmen became successful, they dumped their starter wives in favor of younger "trophy" models? Elaine may have been sexy, if you preferred your women tart instead of sweet, but at three years beyond my father's prematurely stodgy 52, she was no spring chicken. My mother once heard that my father envisioned

Elaine, with her dark bouffant hair and almond-shaped eyes, as a Semitic version of Sophia Loren. Yeah, right! Maybe she was a mediocre knock-off of the Italian sex symbol… minus the *zaftig* curves and bee-stung lips… if Sophia was having a really bad day… and you had misplaced your glasses.

And yet, as I gradually got to know Elaine, that harsh first assessment would soften. I would get used to her trashy, skintight clothes and nasal twang. I would even come to recognize, although never to accept, what my father might have seen in her.

The absolute antithesis of my caring, cultured, and intellectually competitive mother, who'd graduated at the top of her high school class and gone on to get multiple advanced degrees, Elaine could be crude, undignified, and ditzy to the point of hilarity. Yet unlike my parents, who behaved like two sea captains vying to steer the same ship, Elaine readily capitulated to her domineering spouse's every demand and recognized him as the undisputed leader. And although she joked, mostly in private, about his tyrannical nature, she realized how lucky she was to have him, and she often let him know it.

That is not to say that her flirtatious, overt subservience to men didn't make me squirm. (Years later, I'd shudder when she always greeted my husband with the coy and weirdly lascivious salutation, "Hello, *sexy!*") Yet I desperately craved the years of warm, personal contact with my father that I'd missed. Craved, more than anything, the normal life that my mother had promised would someday be ours. So, as easy as it would have been to hold a grudge against my father – and surely "grudge" is way too trite or trivial a word – my only chance at having any relationship with him was to simply accept her. And so I did.

I didn't merely tolerate her with a closed-mouth smile gift-wrapping clenched teeth. I behaved as if the past were genuinely past. When her birthday arrived, I bought her pretty things. When she met me at the door of their flat, I let her kiss my cheek and even kissed hers back. Afterwards, rubbing the imprint of her dark lipstick like dirt from my skin, I would feel like a traitor to my mother, and myself. But that was, to me, my best option. So I smiled.

My father and Elaine were married at home on a Tuesday night, about a year after my parents' divorce came through. Personally, I would never agree to wed anyone on a Tuesday or any other ordinary weeknight. But given the seedy circumstances of their courtship, they may have wanted to keep the celebration low-key. Or maybe my father harbored unresolved reservations about marrying her, after all. Think about it: Had he ever seen her as a suitable wife, would he have strung her along for 15 years and then waited another year to seal the deal? My mother herself had delayed all of about six weeks after their divorce became final before making it official with my stepfather. Then she had scheduled their wedding so abruptly that I hadn't even had time to buy a new dress.

My father's midweek nuptials were too small and low-key to require new attire. The ceremony was performed by a clergyman whom I believe they found in the Yellow Pages through an organization that might as well have been called Rent-a-Rabbi. Arriving a little past the appointed hour, this portly fellow proceeded to remove a black judicial-style robe from a bowling bag and slip it over his business suit.

"When you travel around like I do, performing rituals for strangers," he began, "you never know quite what to expect. For all you know, the couple could be anyone. They could turn out to be two pigs in a poke. But you look like very nice people."

Indeed, from appearances alone, who would have guessed that they'd been carrying on a flagrant adulterous affair that spanned four presidential terms of office?

The reception, at least, many months later, was a festive Saturday night party. What I remember most clearly about it is that Elaine's daughter was accompanied by a red-haired fellow named Rusty, who professed to be able to read people's futures by feeling their elbows. "Maura" had been forbidden to bring her real live-in boyfriend, whom Elaine referred to far from affectionately as "The Beast" and who Maura claimed could see through walls. All this only helped reinforce, if possible, my longstanding reluctance to gain these new relatives. But the fact is that you don't get to choose your stepparents any more than you get to choose your actual parents. You just have to take what you get.

—❧—

And so my father's former mistress became a permanent fixture in my life, present on all important occasions, from major holidays to, eventually, my children's birthday parties. Never exactly the maternal type, she actually admitted to me once that she had resented having little children of her own and been a mediocre mother. She fared somewhat better in the grandparent department, always fussing over my kids with what seemed like genuine affection. Still, it felt strange to me to hear them call her "Grandma," as though she were in any possible way on a par with my own mother.

The two women had finally come face to face years earlier, at my brother's wedding. My mother and I had been stationed in a closet-sized powder room before the ceremony began when her former rival burst in and uttered the same three words she'd once said to me. "Hoy! Oy'm Elaine."

My mother had responded as cordially as she could. Then I'd seized her arm and steered her out before either of us might faint. After that, I'd taken great pains to prevent them from ever meeting again unless absolutely unavoidable, such as at my own wedding, at which my mother and father agreed to be civil and walk me down the aisle together. (This spared Elaine from taking a stab at stepmother-of-the-bride style. Instead, she showed her true colors, in a slinky, hot pink polka dot slip dress with spiky heels dyed to match.)

Otherwise, we carefully alternated, inviting only one set of grandparents at a time. On the one hand, it was a relief to see my formerly irascible father mellow, as my mother had always predicted he would someday. Who's to say whether this composure was due to the maturity engendered by advancing age or his having finally found harmony at home?

On the other hand – the ugly, gnarled one – Elaine seemed like an unlikely source of domestic solace. Quite the contrary; she could be wildly tactless and cruel. And she often unleashed these two untamed qualities, like large, vicious guard dogs, on me.

The worst examples of this torment began soon after my father died. Typical was the time she called to say that she'd been cleaning out my father's closet and had come across a box in which he'd chosen to save every picture my children had drawn for him since they were small. You know – the ones showing stick figures with arms akimbo, the capital "D" invariably scrawled backwards in "I LOVE YOU, GRANDPA."

"Really? That's so sweet!" I'd exclaimed, my eyes already beginning to brim with tears. "I'd love to have them back."

"You would?" she replied, clearly mystified. "Too bad. I already threw them out."

More agonizing was a lethal weapon she began to deploy every time we spoke. "Your father loved you, you know," she would concede, a little too half-heartedly. "But you know who he *really* loved? Your brother. He was the prince. Your father expected him to be governor one day. He could do no wrong."

After hearing this heartless rhetoric many times, I gradually began to believe it.

I recognized that my father had been a man's man who preferred the company of other men and relished masculine pastimes like watching football and going fishing. I even knew that he had, in many ways, openly favored my older sibling. But the less-than-subtle message embedded in Elaine's repeated barbs was that he hadn't really loved *me*.

Then one day, I came across my own box of faded letters in my old bedroom. Opening them, one by one, I discovered something I had somehow managed to forget.

After I'd gone to college, my father had written to me religiously. I'm not talking about occasional letters. He wrote me *every day*. And in keeping with his habit of using money to express feelings, most of these missives had arrived containing some amount of currency. Whether it was a ten-dollar bill or just a paltry penny, his messages were invariably laden with cash – as good as being sealed with a kiss.

Even so, at the time I'd resented this relentless attention. When you're 17, having your father insinuate himself so incessantly into your life feels like an intrusion about as welcome as a mammoth pimple on your chin that won't go away.

That's all I had remembered about his barrage of letters, in retrospect – how I had felt all those years ago about receiving them, rather than what they had said. Then I slid open those yellowed sheaves and began reading, and my heart severed in two.

Several letters are as much as two pages long, others barely two sentences. At times, they merely natter on about the weather, and whether I was managing to stay warm, cool, or dry now that I was on my own. Other days, he succumbed to his fatherly tendency to lecture, doling out kernels of paternal wisdom about dealing with everything from too much homework to unrequited love. Still, what struck me above all else was the valiant efforts to which he went to find a topic or tidbit of news that might interest me. Or made up for a lack of either one by resorting to private jokes and baby talk.

Typical is this hand-written note, scrawled in the fall of my junior year:

Mz Pattie Soupy:

Why are you spending so much time in the library?
Play a little bit of tennis.
Get more fresh air.
Call your Mr. D., for heaven's sake.
Here's some lunch $.

> *Love,*
> *Dada*

That final salutation was typical of the many mushy endearments with which most of these letters conclude. These ranged from the intimate informality of his childhood nickname to the above-mentioned Mr. D. (short for Mr. Daddy) to the universally tender "Papa."

That's when I had one of those "Ah-ha!" moments. Forget everything Elaine had ever said to the contrary. At the risk of sounding like Sally Field accepting her Academy Award, he had loved me. He'd really loved me.

And despite anything I'd ever felt to the contrary, and everything he'd done to deserve the contrary, underneath it all I had to admit that I had continued to love him.

From then on, I began to take every insidious thing that Elaine found to say to me with several grains of salt. Make that a whole boxful of kosher salt.

And then, finally, without warning, I got an easy shot at revenge a few years later. My brother phoned one night in late December to say that he had some news.

Elaine had been ill for quite some time. In fact, she had missed my daughter's bat mitzvah the month before, insisting that she was "in no shape to travel." A few weeks later, my husband and I had called and offered to stop in for a quick visit. She'd adamantly declined, insisting that she was "in no shape for company." I had assumed that this might simply mean that her hair had not been done.

Evidently, the problem wasn't just on her head. Or *in* her head. Elaine had grown so sick and frail that she had slipped into a coma. She wouldn't last the night.

The funeral was held the very next day. It was December 24th, and her son, a practicing "Jew for Jesus," was eager to get home to his children for Christmas Eve. My brother, who had married a Gentile himself, was scheduled to fly out to spend Christmas with his in-laws. Rescheduling flights is hard over the holidays, and he had decided against trying to do it. Someone, I felt, had to represent our family at the funeral, if only for my dead father's sake. That someone would have to be me.

I was the first to arrive at the cemetery for the graveside service. It had distressed me to hear that her son had asked his family priest to officiate.

Elaine, like my father, had been a Jew. She was to be buried beside my father in a Jewish cemetery. The whole thing just wasn't kosher. The sheer *chutzpah* was sure to make my father roll over in his grave.

To mitigate these matters, I had asked to participate in the short service that they planned by saying *Kaddish*, the traditional Jewish mourner's prayer. But when Elaine's children arrived, her son informed me that an old friend of the family who was a Holocaust survivor was there, and that he wanted to lead this prayer himself.

The last thing I'd ever do was begrudge anything to a Holocaust survivor, I said. I was happy to relinquish the duty.

"That's wonderful," the son's wife piped up, stepping forward to kiss me. "Because what we'd like you to do instead is say a few words about my mother-in-law."

Say a few words… about Elaine?

I looked at her aghast. Were they insane? Surely, attending my father's former mistress's funeral was indignity enough. Did they really expect me to give a eulogy?

"Oh, no. I'm sorry, I just can't," I replied. "I didn't prepare anything to say." The unfortunate thing was that I hadn't prepared an excuse any more persuasive than that.

"Don't worry," the wife replied, undeterred. "That's fine. All we really want you to do is speak straight from the heart, just like you did at your father's funeral."

I continued to protest feebly, but was interrupted by the unexpected arrival of one of my uncles. Although it had been over 20 years since Elaine had married my father, I was convinced that most of my father's family detested her and far preferred my mother. My Uncle Julie was foremost among my mother's fans. Yet, to my surprise, there he was.

Moments later, we all crowded into a limousine together and set off for the grave. This might have been the time to decisively announce that I was just unwilling to speak. But I had come to the conclusion that nothing I said would get me off the hook. Besides, I had endured the deaths of my father, stepfather, and grandmother within the few preceding years. I knew what it felt like to lose a loved one, and far be it from me to insult anyone at their own mother's funeral. Even the children of my father's mistress.

And so I chose to use the few minutes remaining instead to try to assemble some remarks in my mind that were reasonably articulate and that I would be willing to say. Rather than resorting to what I couldn't say: "Elaine gave my father 30 good years. It's too bad half of them happened to coincide with the 30 years he gave to my mother."

It turned out – by act of God, perhaps? – that the priest had been unable to make it after all, due to an impending snowstorm. Instead, Elaine's son read a few comments that he had prepared. Then the Holocaust survivor said his prayer, and, before I knew it, I was up. Taking a gulp big enough to swallow my pride, I opened my mouth and began to speak.

"If there's one thing you can say about Elaine, it's that she was unpretentious," I began. "She was someone who never pretended to be someone she was not. Born and raised in Brooklyn, New York, she came from humble roots. When she met my father, her fortunes changed. But she never did."

Although she could have lived extravagantly at this point, I continued, that was not her style. They could afford to eat out every night, but she preferred her own cooking. She could have shopped at the finest stores, but old habits die hard, and she had chosen to keep hunting for bargains. How often she had regaled me with her favorite bit of fashion advice: "If you have a good figure, all you need is a pair of jeans and a few cheap tops."

"A few *tight* cheap tops!" her daughter, Maura, corrected. Everyone laughed, including me.

"You're right. *Tight* cheap tops," I agreed. Whereupon the eulogy devolved into an informal, often comic free-for-all, with the daughter of the deceased chiming in repeatedly to spice up my self-censored recollections with candid outbursts of her own.

As I continued speaking, I found myself studying my uncle. When you stand beside a casket that's about to be lowered into an open grave, there's an innate human tendency to whitewash your true sentiments and speak reverently of the dead, no matter how defective, disappointing, or downright skuzzy the dead may have been in life. With no one from my own camp present, I might have succumbed too fervently to this urge. My uncle was there to serve as my external conscience. He'd hear me. He would know.

Still, I heard myself begin to wax eloquent about how much Elaine had loved her children and grandchildren, sensing that this was the one thing at this moment that they truly needed to hear. Her two grown offspring had been feuding since I could remember. Yet at this juncture, to my amazement, they put their arms around each other and hugged.

Maybe that's why I later drove away shell-shocked, but with an unexpected sense of satisfaction. I had managed not only to rise to the occasion, but also to rise above it.

—☙—

Sadly, this momentary sense of closure didn't last. For my inner turmoil hadn't ceased with the termination of my parents' terrible marriage. Neither did it come to an end along with my father's and his mistress's lives. It's been years now since we buried them both, but I can't seem to bury my pain. I carry the residue of their secret relationship with me everywhere. It's in my blood. In my bones. As much a part of me as my own name.

The result is that I grew up determined to be totally different from my parents, but still ended up very much like them. I don't expect happiness. I don't expect peace. I expect to be abandoned. I expect to be betrayed. Despite my best efforts and intentions, I find myself re-enacting many of their marital missteps – not to the extent of engaging in extramarital escapades myself, but by compulsively butting heads with my husband. I make sure every spark of domestic friction flares into a raging fire.

For in the end, you can't forget the past. And the best you can do to fix it, as far as I can tell, is to try to do better the next time. So I'm intent on setting a better example for my kids. The jury's still out on that one. At least my own marriage is now older than my parents' was when it died. And I'm not saying any eulogies over it just yet.

The Ninety-Dollar Secret

MY YOUNG DAUGHTER MAY BE the joy of my life, but she is clearly her father's child. She has his straight dark hair and hazelnut eyes. Her complexion, like his, is bronzer in January than mine ever gets in July. Even her physique, beyond the obvious contrasts in anatomy and size, is almost a mirror image of her dad's, from the soft, full-moon shape of her face to the funny curve of her second toe.

The resemblance, however, runs more than skin-deep. The two of them are as spontaneous and outgoing as I am deliberate and shy. One of my daughter's early teachers used to remark that Allegra was "all heart." That heart was so light that she used to break into a skip when she walked. When alone, which was rare, she would sing.

The odd thing is that when I was little, my mother said, I was just like her. Bursting with confidence, I babbled incessantly to strangers on the street. I didn't have a self-conscious cell in my body. Then something happened to make me clam up.

I would reply to my mother that if there were ever such a "something," it wasn't a single incident. It was my parents' many years of unabated bickering. It was the muffled sounds of malice emanating from behind their bedroom door. It was the icy contempt with which my father glared at her almost any time she spoke.

Still, the notion that something could happen to dull my daughter's radiant eyes frightens me. How terrifying to think that I could make one thoughtless comment and turn her into . . . me.

Of course, in my case, my mother didn't just utter one remark. There actually was a huge blunder I once made that she considered unforgivable, and she harped on the matter incessantly. This episode happened decades ago, when I was just a small child, yet even long after I grew up, she wouldn't let a month go by without dredging it up again. And each time she did, I felt shame anew. In many families, particularly Jewish ones like mine, no statute of limitations exists on either inflicting or feeling pain.

And so one day I dared to bring it up myself and discuss it, one adult with another. At the same time, I began to wonder: Do I do anything comparable, quite unknowingly, to my own two children? I can't believe I'm capable of such torment. Neither do I imagine that the human spirit, especially that of my indefatigable daughter, is quite so easily crushed. But my mother insisted otherwise. She traced my reticence and stultifying reserve to her own wrath and the ninety-dollar dress.

～ぅ

The story dates back to 1961. Our country was still swathed in innocence, and so was I. JFK had just become president – still alive! – and I was no longer a wide-eyed 5. So my parents deemed me old enough to attend my Cousin David's bar mitzvah.

This bar mitzvah wasn't going to be your customary, run-of-the-mill affair, a Saturday morning religious service followed by a lavish luncheon. It would be an entire weekend of feasting and celebration: a Saturday lunch, Sunday brunch, and evening ball straight out of *Gone With the Wind*. For one thing, my cousin's family lived down in Virginia. They'd be entertaining countless out-of-town guests who, like my family in New York, would have to travel far. For another, Cousin David was Aunt Gloria's son. Nothing usual was good enough for them.

Gloria, my mother's older sister and only sibling, had always demanded the best. Both girls had grown up in Brooklyn, born to a struggling Jewish family of Russian immigrants in Borough Park. Their father, my Grandpa Charlie, was an erudite, educated man who shunned "the family business." He refused

18

to become a rabbi like his father and brothers before him. Instead, he questioned everything and read voraciously, indulging a passion for literature, science and philosophy. But he was driven to study, not to succeed. After floundering in a series of unsuitable careers, he eked out a living selling life insurance. This generated little income, but left plenty of time to sneak off to the library.

Into this household of limited means, my mother and aunt were born. It is said that wars begin between adjacent countries when there aren't enough resources to go around. So began a lifelong rivalry between the Lichtenstein sisters.

My mother, to this day, believes that my aunt was favored overtly by their mother. There is no question that she was widely admired for her looks. Despite struggling continuously with her weight, honey-blonde Gloria was considered a beauty. My mother was far better known for her brains, not a priority for women in her day.

My aunt, as the family's first-born child, was not only the first sibling to receive many privileges, but often the only one. In those days, my mother explained, daughters were treated as second-class citizens. "The boy got everything and the girl got nothing. Since we were two girls, and she was the eldest, she was treated like the boy."

My Aunt Gloria attended Sunday school and learned to read and write Hebrew. My mother received no formal religious training of any kind. My aunt was always dressed in exquisite, brand-new clothes. My mother didn't even get second dibs on these garments, since they were too roomy to fit her far scrawnier frame. My aunt was treated to summer camp, and enriched by cultural lessons in everything from piano to elocution. My mother was permitted none of these advantages. By the time her turn came around, there was never enough money left.

"Once," she recalls, "when she felt guilty, Grandma Mary took me down to the basement in our building, where there was an old piano, and tried to teach me to play herself." The experiment was never repeated, however. My mother continued trying to "play by ear," as she called it, picking out popular tunes herself, but never approached the refined skills that her sister displayed at recitals.

To top things off, my aunt married young – before she hit 20 – to my Uncle Walter, a brilliant man of considerable means. This was, perhaps, no coincidence. She had grown up poor, but with a taste for all things luxurious. Soon after, they chose to move down South, to Newport News, Virginia, where money stretched like Silly Putty. Here, my aunt was finally able to afford the finery for which she had always hankered. She set up house as an aristocrat, in a stately mansion teeming with servants.

Her life, at least as we observed it, was one long and extravagant spending spree. When she traveled by airplane, she sat in first class. When she visited New York, she booked a suite in the posh Waldorf-Astoria. We could only imagine the luxury that was planned for the day her first-born became a man.

My mother harbored her own secret lust for grandeur, but had far from the means to indulge it. My father was still in his early thirties and the fledgling stages of his career. We lived in a modest starter house in a working-class town on Long Island. But like Cinderella, she longed to go to the ball wearing a dress with a fairy godmother label.

Throughout her life, she defended that lofty aspiration as a matter of family honor. It was something, she claimed, that she owed to my aunt. "She had invited her whole town. She had invited her whole temple. She was a very big wig," she explained. "And I, as my sister's sister – her *only* sister – really had to look elegant."

Lacking fairy-tale connections, though, my mother had only one hope of attaining adequate style. She put me into our bulbous, aquamarine Plymouth sedan and drove to Miracle Mile.

Long before anyone had ever heard the word "mall," this mammoth shopping strip haunted the heart of fashion-conscious Long Island. Though perhaps not an actual mile in length, it was long enough to encompass every store imaginable, from discount chains to specialty shops. Usually, we only gazed at the mannequins in the windows of the ritzier stores. But this trip was different from all other trips. My mother took me firmly by the hand, strode straight into B. Altman and up the escalator to Better Dresses.

Within minutes, we were escorted into a dressing room with an armful of slinky designs. I scrunched into a corner on the floor of this cubby, my tiny fingers probing the carpet for stray straight pins while my mother squeezed her panty-girdled frame into half a dozen chic prospects.

Some were embroidered with sequins or caviar beads, others trimmed with ruffles and lace. But the one that suited her best, by far, was a simple, elegant, black velvet shift. This dress had no frills. It didn't need them. Though lacking an actual designer pedigree, it was eminently tasteful: a knock-off of The Little Black Dress, that soon-to-be classic that French couturier Hubert de Givenchy had just created for Audrey Hepburn to wear in the movie *Breakfast at Tiffany's*.

My mother turned to face the mirror, then swiveled to check her profile. The dress fit her like a black leather glove. She grinned at her svelte reflection, then grimaced when she surveyed the price tag.

"Daddy's going to love it," I crooned as she straightened up and smoothed the shimmering cloth over her hips.

"No, Daddy's going to kill me," she said with a sigh. "Ninety dollars! It's much too much."

For most people in today's economy, that figure would not have been a splurge, especially for a special occasion. Ninety bucks then, however, was a very different story. Spending so much on a single dress was hardly within the realm of a middle-class budget.

My mother maintains that my father could have afforded to let her buy it anyway. He simply wouldn't have wanted to. "He was doing pretty well," she says. "He just wasn't a spender yet." There was no way on earth that he would have allowed such a purchase. If he knew about it, that is.

And so it was that, inside this compact dressing room, my mother hatched a plan. Actually, it wasn't much of a plan. The plan was that she would buy the dress, but under no circumstances let my father find out how much it cost.

This, luckily for her, was long before the popularity of credit cards. My father would receive no tattletale bill from MasterCard or American Express. My mother had gone on this shopping expedition armed with actual cash. Only she would know how much she'd plunked down for a measly few yards of cloth.

There was only one potential flaw in this scheme: She had already told me how much it cost. She had to make sure I didn't squeal.

All the way home in the car, we rehearsed what I would say. It was a dramatic role that even a 6-year-old could handle. After all, it involved no lines. I was to say absolutely *nothing*.

"Not one word," my mother repeated at home as she prepared dinner. "Do you understand?" She was counting on me. What my father didn't know wouldn't hurt him. We would keep our entire shopping trip a secret.

Even at 6, I knew about secrets. I had simply never possessed such a juicy one before. "Don't tell Daddy," my mother had ordered. I rolled the words around on my tongue, savoring a flavor far sweeter than any Sugar Daddy, Tootsie Roll or other candy I'd ever eaten. I knew something my own father didn't know. It was my first taste of trust and true power.

The thrill of being caught in such intrigue was almost more than I could bear. I was privy to classified information about which my older brother, a worldly and superior 8, hadn't the slightest inkling. While he sat upstairs, a slave to ignorance and the rigors of third-grade homework, I took up my usual evening post peering out the front door. Watching for my father to return from work, I practiced silence, my head resounding with all the words I had promised not to say.

My father, unlike my mother's father, was a deeply ambitious man. He valued hard work almost as much as its intended result, material gain. Commuting to and from New York City each day, he worked long hours as a salesman at a firm that he would eventually buy. On good nights, he returned home late from the office. On bad nights, he came home *very* late. This, it turned out, was not a particularly good night. I had a long time to wait and think.

By the time his black Thunderbird had rounded the corner, an eternity had passed. Slowly, carefully, my father pulled into our driveway. He inched down the blacktop at a leisurely pace, then let his car idle in neutral while he stepped out and bent to lift the heavy garage door. Then he returned to the car, stepped back inside, and let the T-bird glide into the one-car garage attached to our house by a breezeway. I listened as he paused momentarily, perhaps catching the end of a report on the radio before shutting the engine.

By the time he had slammed the car door shut, pulled down the garage door and ambled up the walk to our house, I was ready to burst with the words.

When he opened the front door, I did.

"Guess what Mommy did today!"

"What?"

"Mommy bought a ninety-dollar dress!"

"*WHAT?*"

By the time my mother had dashed out from the kitchen, it was already too late.

———— ❧ ————

He looked at the dress, but wasn't impressed. It went back the very next day.

To replace it, my mother was put on a very strict budget. She could spend up to $45, tops – no more than half as much.

With such restraints, she didn't dare venture into Altman's. She was reduced to shopping in the lowly, bargain-rate Alexander's. The best she could find there was a tight black sheath with a low-cut, ruffled neckline. Though somewhat similar in cut to the first dress, it was the opposite of refined. It was flashy. "It enhanced my figure," she recalls, "but it wasn't the proper dress to wear. I didn't feel elegant in it. I felt cheap."

My Cousin David's bar mitzvah turned out, indeed, to be an affair to remember. Being only 6, I was sent to bed early on Saturday evening, long before the dancing began. But my mother remembers that at the party, a man at my parents' table admired her dress, noting that she reminded him of Paris. My father laughed, she recalls, and remarked, "Yes, the Left Bank." She is convinced that this was a reference to the French prostitutes who congregated alongside the Seine to ply their wares. She felt utterly mortified.

I cringe now thinking of the humiliation she suffered because of my loose young lips. I sorely wish she had gotten her chance to measure up at last, after decades of being overshadowed by her own ever-superior sibling. Instead, she was the poor relation, shown up once again.

Her anguish, however, lasted for only one night of a weekend long forgotten by everyone else. My punishment endures to this day.

From the moment I blurted out my mother's little secret, I was branded for life. Never would she dare to confide in me again. I was untrustworthy. A stool pigeon.

Nothing I could do would convince her otherwise. A few years later, when I was 9, I was visiting a friend when the girl's mother accidentally struck her little brother with her car in their driveway. While we waited for the ambulance, the frantic woman ordered me not to tell anyone. And I didn't. My mother was shocked when news of the incident finally reached her days later. What astounded her most was that I'd witnessed the whole thing and hadn't breathed a word to her. Yet she still told everyone not to trust me.

The problem was that my family life was riddled with secrets. Not just silly secrets about overpriced dresses, but dark, dirty ones. Most of these related to my parents' troubled marriage. And most were secrets that, despite their best efforts, I knew.

—6—

Although there must have been some moments of relative calm during the 29 years that they remained legally bound, I can't recall one when they were visibly content. My earliest memory of any kind dates back to when I was 4. I'm sitting in the hallway outside their bedroom, listening to them talk. Their voices aren't raised, for once. The conversation, in a distinctly minor key, is conducted *sotto voce*. Yet I can easily make out what they're saying. My father says he doesn't love her any more. My mother says almost nothing. All I hear from her are muffled sobs.

The mind plays tricks on us all, of course; it's perfectly possible that I have mixed this discourse up with other exchanges very much like it that I overheard over the years. But about the next part, I am certain. Suddenly, the door to their room flies open and my mother is running toward me. As she passes, she hoists me into her arms, and half-pulls, half carries me down the stairs and outside. Now we are sprinting across the front lawn, my father charging after us in hot pursuit. Just as we reach her car, which is parked out front alongside the curb, he catches up at last and tries to rip me from her grasp.

My mother won't let go, however. Never a quitter, she clutches me by one arm. My father latches onto the other. They proceed to have a tug of war, using me as the rope.

"Let go of her!" my mother shrieks at him. "Stop it! You're hurting the child!" She doesn't refer to me by name. I am an object. I am the child.

Her frantic warning works, however. He releases me instantly, and my mother and I clamber into the car. She fumbles with the key, then jams it into the ignition and pumps the gas. I look back as we race down the block. My father is still standing there watching, his face red as raw meat. I don't make a sound until we reach the first stoplight. Then I begin to cry.

"What's the matter?" my mother demands. I don't answer. I try to stop, but can't.

By the time that my father left, though, many years later, I could control myself. Perfectly. At least, I didn't dare cry.

⟶—☾

Throughout my adolescence, my father repeatedly left my mother, moving in and out of our house to go live with Elaine, his mistress, in the city, often for months at a time. I knew where he was and whom he was with because he took little care to disguise his behavior. I knew because my mother, having no one else to confide in, discussed it with me regularly. Discussed it in excruciating detail. My mother, though, remained convinced that my father would eventually settle down from what she called his "mid-life crisis." For that reason, she didn't want other people to know what was happening in our house. I was forbidden to tell anyone – even my closest friends. And I didn't for almost a decade.

The hardest test came when I was 17 and my parents separated for nearly a year. They hadn't yet decided whether to actually divorce, though, and didn't want anyone to know of their rift – not even my own brother.

He had just returned to school for his sophomore year at a state university, and they feared that this news would shatter him. The problem was that he was dating one of my friends, a hometown girl, and journeyed home almost every weekend. To avoid distressing him with the harrowing truth, we engaged in an elaborate charade.

On Friday evenings, shortly before my brother arrived, my father would return from the city and quickly unpack his suitcase. After my brother departed on Sunday night, my father would pack and leave again. I was sworn to secrecy and didn't divulge this peculiar arrangement to my sibling until years later, after they finally had divorced.

My sadness about this sick situation, though, and the relentless pressure to keep it under wraps, grew so unbearable that one afternoon I truly could stand it no longer. Overwrought and unable to think clearly, I removed the inner screen from one of the windows in my bedroom, pulled out all the glass jalousie slats, and crawled outside. And there I hung, head in, body out, clutching the window frame while I tried to decide what to do. It didn't cross my mind that my room was only on the second floor, and that falling would probably just break my legs or back. I had little doubt that the impact of a fall would hurt like hell, but I didn't really care. I just wanted the inner pain to stop.

I hung there that way for about ten or fifteen minutes, letting my body slip lower and lower, until I realized that I was about to lose my grip and fall. I must have cried out then, because my mother suddenly appeared in my bedroom, screamed, and pulled me in. Whether or not it was her preference or mine, I never told anyone about that day, either.

The result is that I grew up to be something of a professional confidante. Friends and relatives call me daily to divulge their heartbreaks and other troubles. I think their eagerness to seek my counsel stems largely from the fact that I'm a sympathetic listener.

The main reason I think people confide in me, though, is that they sense that they can truly trust me. If they reveal something private and potentially embarrassing, it's like putting that information into a vault. Having learned my lesson the hard way, I like to imagine that I'd actually stand up well to torture.

There are even secrets I know that might devastate my mother. **But she** needn't worry. I'll never tell. Thanks to the ninety-dollar dress, I learned **my** lesson well.

—⟨⟩—

It was only when I became a parent myself that I began to realize that my one unfortunate confession wasn't really my fault. I started conducting occasional, informal experiments with my own children. I wanted to prove to my mother that I had merely done what any 6-year-old would do. But mostly, I wanted to prove this to myself.

In one such instance, when my daughter was 6, she begged to know what I'd bought her older brother for his birthday. Plaintively, she pleaded for me to whisper it in her ear. Having poignant memories, I murmured an answer that was false. Yet that's not the only reason I sighed with relief when she blurted out the news to my son instantly.

More recently, I've begun to think about what the dress incident meant to my mother. It wasn't about her needing to impress other people. It wasn't about fashion, or foolish pride. It was that, for once, I think, she wanted her own mother to love her as much as she seemed to love her sister. She didn't dare hope to be the favored child. She just wanted to appear equal. More important, she wanted to feel worthy of such love.

If so, then she finally got her wish, although – isn't it always the case? – not as she ever would have wished it. For my poor Aunt Gloria, always the first at everything, died long before her time, too. She passed away in her mid-sixties, after an agonizing battle with breast cancer. Meanwhile, my grandmother continued to live on. Dear Grandpa Charlie had passed away nearly nine years earlier. Only my mother remained to be Grandma's family and tend to her many needs.

And tend to them she did. Although Grandma Mary had long ago moved to Florida, my mother took over her affairs. It wasn't merely a matter of seeing that the bills got paid. She flew down often to pay Grandma extended visits.

She hired women to care for her when she wasn't there, yet still made sure to telephone her five or six times a day.

When Grandma approached 90, my mother moved her to a fancy assisted living facility. But she took care to make her quarters there look the way her old apartment had: filled with family photos, with a larger-than-life-size portrait of my aunt, painted in her glory days, gazing down regally from over the living room couch.

It was here that my mother, who worked as a teacher, spent school vacations, most major holidays and at least a month each summer. She carted her mother to doctors, administered her medications and read to her aloud. She was so busy with Grandma that she rarely got to see her own children or grandchildren. It nearly consumed her life.

Then, one afternoon, something changed. Grandma woke up from a nap, looked at my mother and seemed startled.

"I dreamt that Gloria was here," she said, talking as though still in a dream. "She drove me to a store, and then we came home and she went to find my shoes. But it wasn't her, was it?" Grandma asked. "You're the one. It was you all along."

Ever the pragmatist, I took this at face value. Grandma had simply had a dream about my aunt. But in her words of sudden recognition, my mother gleaned much more.

"She knows!" my mother exclaimed. "Everything I've been doing for her all this time? She finally realized it wasn't my sister. It was me."

In this light, the load she'd been carrying for so many years suddenly looked less like a burden than a privilege. "I love Grandma!" my mother declared in the same breath. "I hope she lives forever."

If only it could have been so. Meanwhile, I should know better than to give away any secrets. But if she can forgive her mother after all those years, then surely I can forgive mine.

Fragile

HOW DO YOU TAKE THE measure of a man, woman or child? Like many people, we did it in pencil slashes with initials and dates scrawled on the jamb of our bathroom door. We began tabulating this vertical family history as soon as our firstborn could stand. Every time my husband would add another line, on birthdays, holidays or whenever it crossed his mind, our children would strain eagerly upward, hoping to stretch another smidgen. Meanwhile, we'd marvel aloud at their remarkable gains. But my secret hope, I must confess, was always that they would be merely normal. In intellect, talent, and character, I wanted them to be exceptional, of course. Height is the one area about which I always prayed, "Please, God, let them be average!"

I feared that deviating too far in either direction could make a kid self-conscious. Haven't we all rubbed elbows with some domineering little Napoleon, or a towering Titan who's tired of hearing, "How's the air up there?" As for girls, as useful as extra inches might prove on the basketball court, many a tall woman seems to have trouble finding dates who measure up to her height in heels, let alone her personal expectations.

Neither is it any picnic for a girl to be short, even if you cutesy it up by calling her build "delicate." I know that, although my own dimensions are comfortably commonplace, because I was once friends with "Joanie Steiner."

In junior high school, Joanie, as I'll call her, was the shortest girl in my class by a long shot. She was what, if you're looking on the bright side, or shopping in the women's department, is commonly called "petite." But in her eyes there could be no doubt about it. She felt like the runt of the litter.

She was half a head shorter than most other girls in our class and barely shoulder-height to the boys. Although she was slender and delicately pretty, with short, dark brown hair and huge mahogany eyes, it was agonizingly obvious that she felt like she never measured up.

Maybe that's how we became friends.

Our association started as a matter of convenience. Our fathers were longtime tennis partners. This meant that we were often thrown together, expected to keep each other company while our dads slugged it out on the court. The reason it clicked was that our friendship began when I was in the throes of what was then called an "identity crisis." Hovering on the cusp of adolescence, I was becoming painfully aware of the opposite sex. And learning what it meant to be cool.

In my case, I was medium cool at best. More, in fact, like tepid. On the outermost fringes of my school's "in" crowd, I managed to get invited to most of the popular kids' boy-girl parties. Once I arrived at them, though, I rarely got asked to dance. For a shy, sensitive self-loather like me, this was like being stuck in social purgatory.

In 1967, the rage among my suburban seventh-grade classmates was slam books. These were notebooks that would be passed around surreptitiously during or after class. At the top of each page would be written the name of a boy or girl in our grade. Beneath it, kids would pass judgment on the youngster in question by scrawling a single word.

All the popular girls were typically termed "stacked," "cool" or "bitch." Most other girls would be damned with faint praise as "nice," or dismissed altogether as "flat," which had nothing to do with having a lack of emotional affect or one-dimensional personality. My page, when they bothered to include me at all, would be a tapestry of pencil marks mixing the two latter words. The only notable exception is a mystery I've been mulling for much of my life. Once, a cute, relatively nice boy named Luke whom I had a huge crush on wrote a very different word: "fragile."

Why any 12-year-old would think of that word, let alone use it in this otherwise crude, rubber-stamp context, was beyond me. But the fact was that he was right.

I was as vulnerable as a dandelion after it has turned to a puff of wispy seeds, ready to be scattered in the wind by the slightest gust of mean-spirited gossip. I was as defenseless as a tiny green inchworm dangling precariously on a gossamer thread from a swaying tree. I was certainly far too self-conscious and emotionally frail to withstand interminable evenings sitting all alone on a couch in someone's living room watching other girls dance, giggle, or endure the probing paws of future junior-varsity athletes.

As gratifying as it was to be invited to these evenings of prepubescent carousing, attending them left me feeling awkward and desolate. And as thrilling as it was to be privy to the gossip of the pretty girls – which happened regularly, provided that I was willing to grovel in their presence and feed them breathless compliments – the fact was that those slam books were right. Most of these girls were stacked, cool bitches. They were vain, selfish, catty, and capable of extreme, wanton cruelty. In short, I didn't like them any more than any of them seemed to like me.

As much as I've since overcome most of their personal slights, I still cringe at the memory of one. A girl named Susie's birthday party that year was scheduled the week after mine. She refused my invitation, it was reported widely enough to get back to me – even though this predated Facebook by nearly four decades – because her mother had decreed that if she attended my party she had to invite me to hers, and over her dead body would she include a drip like me.

I don't remember how I veered off-track from my short-lived life in the fast lane. Did I actually summon the courage to refuse a coveted party invitation or two? Or did I simply stop following the popular girls around and forcing myself to howl at their half-witted comments, invariably made at someone else's expense? In any case, by the start of eighth grade I found myself abandoned, alone at school and on Saturday nights, left to either sink into the abyss of adolescent loneliness or finally make some real friends.

It was around this time that I discovered Joanie.

She was always called "Joanie," never Joan. She was too tiny and perky for that. Joanie was upbeat and fun to hang out with, just hypersensitive about her height. She once persuaded her parents to take her for medical tests to make sure she'd eventually grow to normal size. This girl was no pushover. You were either with her or against her. Usually, I was with her.

And on one important evening, she came to be with *me*.

I was supposed to go to the high school play, a student production of Arthur Miller's *The Crucible*. It was a Saturday night in 1967, and my parents, as usual, were out for the evening. My older brother had gone out, too. I had arranged to hitch a ride to school from a nice girl named Holly, but her parents showed up early to get me. I was just stepping out of the shower when I heard the doorbell ring. Frantically, I tried to pull on my clothes, but I couldn't do it fast enough, and Holly, standing outside on the front steps, couldn't hear me calling to her to wait. I reached the door just in time to see her family drive away. I was going to be stuck at home, I realized, all alone for hours.

That was the first time I ever thought about suicide. I wasn't going to kill myself because I was alone for an evening. I was just incredibly sad about everything in my life. My paternal grandparents had each died the year before, within six months of each other. My father, having just lost both his parents, was depressed and seeking solace elsewhere – with Elaine. He was rarely home anymore, and when he was, he often burst into tears.

Occasionally, I'd hear him crying aloud in his room. Never mind that under normal circumstances he was often a belligerent bully who could make people cower. These were manly yet barely muffled sobs. And almost nightly, lying awake, I'd hear my parents arguing in their bedroom. Whenever my father was home, they fought like fiends.

So my reaction to facing a whole evening alone had little to do with petty, preteen concerns. This was not a case of your typical youngster's allergy to boredom. I felt hopeless and self-destructive. It wasn't a rationally considered, specific plan: I'm going to kill myself and this is how I'll do it. I was simply overcome with anguish and a desperate desire to escape it. There was only one way I could think of to make the pain stop.

I walked into the kitchen, slid open the silverware drawer and lifted out a long, sharp knife. Running my fingertips along the blade, I carefully tested the edge. Was it sharp enough? And if it was, what then? I had never used a knife on anything but food. Where, exactly, would I stick it? How much would it hurt? How quickly would it work?

Whatever I was about to do, another more sensible voice inside my head told me I shouldn't have a few more hours in which to possibly accomplish it. I needed to call someone right away. I needed to get out of the house. That's when I thought of Joanie.

This was a cold, blustery night in late fall, and Joanie lived more than a mile away. The houses in our neighborhood were spread far apart alongside long, winding roads. But when she heard that I was alone and frightened – although I didn't tell her of what – she immediately invited me over and offered to meet me halfway. She was home baby-sitting her younger brother, but was willing to risk her parents' wrath by bringing him along for the walk.

I still remember the wind hissing through the woods that night, and the gnarled trees along the road writhing angrily in the darkness as though their branches were trying to reach out and snatch me. I was so terrified that I almost turned back several times. Then Joanie appeared with her brother around a bend, her shyly brave grin trying hard to conceal how frightened she was, too. I was so relieved to reach them that I cried.

Although my troubles weren't over that night, her loyalty cemented our friendship. She was no longer just someone to do things with; she was some-one to do things *for*. I figured we would remain friends for life. Then two other people unwittingly collaborated to come between us: Leanne Kuntzler and Donny Goldman.

Leanne was the only girl I knew whose parents were divorced. I know I have no right to cast aspersions, since my parents eventually divorced, too. So, for that matter, did Joanie's. But Leanne's had split up when she was very young. Is that what made her so hair-trigger nasty? Her father, a successful TV sports producer, was a former quarterback of a prominent college football team. Her mother looked and acted like she had once been a hot number. Now she was just an aging divorcée, her heavy hand with makeup and her form-fitting clothes mouthing the unmistakable message that she was none too pleased to be serving her current tour of duty as a single parent in the stultifying suburbs.

Leanne was a feisty, blond, athletic tomboy who delighted, when we were little, in calling me vicious names. In middle school, she took our rivalry up a notch. She stole the heart of my would-be heartthrob, Ricky Miller, when I foolishly introduced them at a school football game. "He must really like you," she cooed disingenuously when he kept finding excuses to wander by the two of us. But it turned out to be her sassy disposition, wheat-colored waves, and limber frame that he liked. By the time I entered high school, I loathed Leanne with a vengeance. Ricky, however, had long been replaced in my heart by the decidedly worthier Donny.

Donny, a shy, studious junior who was two years my senior, was unquestionably my perfect match. At least he would have been had he possessed the nerve to say hello. Every day, I would gaze longingly at him across the school cafeteria. And every day – it was not just wishful thinking or my fertile imagination – I would catch him staring timidly back. All fall, we indulged in this dangerous game, exchanging distant, furtive glances over boiled, rubbery hot dogs or Salisbury steak with gravy and canned peas.

Occasionally, when we passed each other unexpectedly in the hallway, our eyes would meet at closer range for a single, heart-stopping instant. But that was the closest we ever came to personal contact. In fact, that was about as close as he ever got to any girl, according to my brother, who was a classmate of Donny's, although they were not good friends. Listening to me moon wistfully over my knight in shy armor, my elder, worldlier sibling offered minimal encouragement.

"Give up, he'll never call you," he would say. "He doesn't have the guts."

―ᕬ―

All that changed when the posters went up at school announcing The Snow Ball, the December holiday dance.

My only hope, my brother was convinced, was that Donny would somehow summon the nerve to approach me at the dance. Although the Women's Liberation Movement was then vociferously under way, thanks to Gloria

Steinem et al, it was unthinkable to me – and socially unacceptable at that time – to consider approaching him.

I had so many fantasies about that ball, you would have thought I was Cinderella. Thank God, I didn't need an invitation from the king, merely to purchase a ticket. But, of course, I would need a new outfit to wear and to do something special to poof up my hair.

Then, suddenly, my fairy-tale dreams crashed and shattered like a glass slipper. Joanie was turning 14 that week and scheduled her party for the same night. She had no interest in attending the dance or doing anything involving boys. Her modest celebration would consist of going out for pizza and bowling with only two female guests: the dreaded Leanne and me.

As unlikely a duo as Joanie and Leanne were, in both physique and temperament, their close bond had also been forged by family circumstances; their mothers were best friends. Somehow, Joanie remained curiously blind to Leanne's vindictive tendencies, and realizing that few people are open to the defamation of their dearest friends, I chose to refrain from pointing them out. Instead, I did my best to avoid joining them for group activities. On the rare occasions that the three of us were thrown together, Leanne would hurl insults at me whenever Joanie was out of earshot, just as my much bigger brother had once twisted my arm behind my back when he knew our mother wasn't watching.

Now I faced an excruciating moral dilemma. Should I go to the dance and fall blissfully, perchance, into the arms of my reticent Romeo? Or need I give up my only decent chance at teenage romance in order to endure an evening of tongue-lashing and other torture inflicted by my archenemy and facilitated unwittingly by my best friend?

I knew what the right thing to do was, and I was the kind of nice kid who habitually did it. But my brother, hovering devilishly over my shoulder, kept tempting me to choose heaven over hell. "There isn't another dance until March," he would taunt me. "This is your last chance."

I couldn't summon the nerve to approach Joanie until the middle of that week. Perhaps I could get her to understand my urgent need to go to the dance, or so I hoped. But she didn't yet share my fascination with boys. I barely got a chance to explain.

"You'd rather go to the dance than my party?" she asked indignantly. "Oh, great. Thanks for ruining my birthday. I don't ever want to speak to you again!"

It was too late to take my own words back. The damage was already done.

The new outfit I bought for the dance, although no ballgown, was trendy for 1968. But as I pulled on this faux pony-skin miniskirt, gold satin blouse, and tapestry vest, my stomach churned wildly, not with breathless anticipation but a sickening sense of guilt.

Arriving alone at the dimly lit school cafeteria, which had been decorated with giant cardboard snowflakes and tiny blinking lights to resemble a winter wonderland, I found myself a safe corner in which to wait. I stood in that corner for the entire evening. No one ever asked me to dance. As for Donny? He never even showed up.

The next day, my father drove me to Lord & Taylor, where we purchased a peace offering – a long, red, plaid flannel nightgown with white lace trim at the neck. No one was home at Joanie's house, so I left the elegantly wrapped package inside her front door. She handed it back to me at school on Monday, the gift wrapping, including ribbon and bow, still intact. "I can't accept this," was all she said. Then she turned and walked away.

And, true to her word, she didn't speak to me again for years.

Although I eventually made other friends, I was the one left feeling small. Meanwhile, Joanie began to grow. She shot up a few inches, at least. More important, she filled out the way young women do. She also fell in with the popular crowd and actually made the cheerleading squad, which was then considered the height of social status.

As for Donny, he was back in the lunchroom the Monday after the dance, peering wistfully at me from afar. Our soulful exchange of glances continued all year, but he never called. Late that spring, however, he cornered my brother after school one day.

"I have this problem," Donny told him, almost stammering. "It's just – well, um, I really want to go to the junior prom, but I have no one to ask. Do you have any ideas?"

My brother looked at him curiously, paused in brief thought, then shook his head. "No," my brother later told me he calmly replied. "Sorry. Can't help you there."

There's no telling if, with one small change, things might have gone differently. Had Joanie been a few crucial inches taller, might she have been less sensitive, or understood my longing for love? Might our friendship have been less fragile?

I also used to wonder what might have happened if, the day that Donny approached my brother about finding a prom date, my brother had chosen to answer instead, "Yes, as a matter of fact, I do. How about taking my sister?"

But mostly, I'd still give almost anything to have spent that Saturday night in December of 1968 heaving gutter balls and doing my best to dodge Leanne's malicious barbs. For half a lifetime later, this is how I see it: I once sacrificed and deeply wounded a true friend for the slim chance to have a fleeting adolescent romance with someone with whom I had never exchanged as much as two words, and with whom I never would.

⤸

Not all's well that ends well. But I'd like to imagine that Joanie sees it differently. When I chose The Snow Ball over her party, you see, she didn't know who Donny Goldman was. By what I assume is mere coincidence, however, they met and began dating the following year. Often, I'd see them holding hands in the hallway at school. They ended up being an item for months. Donny even took Joanie to his senior prom, but they broke up when he went off to college.

Although we never once spoke face to face, Donny surprised me by writing to me from his school in the Midwest a couple of months later. Judging from the way he began the letter, he was, in fact, the sweet, gentle boy I had imagined him to be from afar:

I was just sitting here and listening to tapes and wondering what I should do. Then this little voice in the back of my head said, "Why don't you write a letter?" So I said, "Hey, voice, who should I write to?" And then the little voice said, "Patty."

Sound ridiculous? Wait until you've spent 2 months in college – you would be hearing little voices too...

He went on to joke that my brother must have been jealous because he wasn't thin enough to be excused from the Vietnam War for being under-weight, as Donny had been. He concluded by saying that he'd see me over Thanksgiving break. But he never called.

We also managed to miss each other the following year, when I happened to visit his school on a college tour, only to discover that he had gone home for the weekend. This prompted another letter, in which he asked me to give a little notice the next time I decided to drop by. But I had no reason to ever revisit. And I never heard from him again.

After I graduated, I never saw Joanie again, either, but my parents kept me posted. She got married young, they told me, to a sports hero she had met at college. Within a few years, however, the marriage came to an end, and Joanie moved back home. It was there that she once again encountered Donny. He had returned to our hometown after college and had turned out to be a decent, dependable fellow, just as I had expected. They began dating again and eventually married. The last I heard, they had three kids.

Truth, as they say, is stranger than fiction, but I swear this is no tall tale. I can only hope that if I ever cross Joanie's mind and she takes my measure as a person, I no longer come up short.

On the Nose

_̮ᶜ᷈_

MY PRIDE IN BEING JEWISH is as plain as the nose on my face. The nose on my face, however, is not actually mine.

There, I've said it. I've come clean after over forty years. That's how long it's been since my nose was "done." Or should I say "done for"?

My mother, bless her misguided soul, would have said "done for your own good." Maybe she was sadly right. Who knows how different my life might have been if I'd lived it with my nose intact?

Occasionally, I wonder. I also shudder at the phoniness and self-loathing that I think plastic surgery often signifies. "I've got to be me!" crooned the late, great entertainer Sammy Davis Jr., who had the _chutzpah_ to choose the double whammy of being both black and Jewish in America. Thanks to rhinoplasty, I've got to be someone else. Nobody knows what I'd give to get my old nose back.

There were few pictures snapped of me during adolescence, so I'm not even sure what I'm missing. Judging from the few family photos that remain, at age 10, captured at my brother's bar mitzvah, I had a pert little knob of a nose, covered with a constellation of freckles. A year later, my parents separated when my father moved out for the first of many times. Right when I began to develop, our Kodak moments were over.

I still remember the day during the fall of eighth grade that I dragged my mother out to buy me my first training bra, only to discover that I was no longer in training. But while maturing nicely above the equator, I'd also developed a less welcome bulge further north. My nose had begun to enlarge, to far less popular approval. In my family, any unnatural growth, be it wart, mole, or major organ, was greeted by my father with the same merciless decree: "Have it off!"

By 15, I was fending off my parents' entreaties regularly. Why, they asked, should I live with such obvious and unappealing imperfection? They wanted me to have my nose "fixed."

Why fix it, I'd reply, if it wasn't broke? I could smell just fine.

And so I proceeded to hold my colossal nozzle high, until the "Ken" and "Christine" incident.

"Ken," as I'll call him, was a slightly older boy on whom I had a long-term crush. "Christine" was a "friend" of mine.

She was brainy, maybe even brilliant, but keenly lacking in the heart department. She didn't seem to have many deep feelings of her own, so she would appropriate mine. Whenever Christine detected that I had some interest in a boy, she'd vie for his affections. Unfortunately, she possessed two commodities that gave her a distinct edge in competing for the attention of any high school boy: blonde hair and blue eyes. One fetching smile from her flashed in his direction, and I could kiss my would-be Sir Galahad good-bye.

I naively let this happen to me time and time again. She deliberately stole away Dan Guthrie, a bright, sardonic boy with blonde Brillo-like curls who was nearly the love of my life until he moved away in ninth grade. She appropriated the affections of Tommy Fitzgibbon, a soft-spoken sophomore who got up the nerve to kiss me in the biology lab. But when Christine dared to make a play for Ken, it was more than I could bear.

Ken, a close friend of my brother's, was also a stellar student in our high school. With a fact-packed mind like an encyclopedia, his main claim to fame was having been the star contestant among the brainiacs that our high school sent to compete on the TV game show *It's Academic*, an adolescent precursor to *Who Wants to Be a Millionaire?*

In fact, years later, as an adult, his astonishing treasure trove of trivial knowledge would one day lead him to score heavily when he appeared as a contestant on *Jeopardy!* But at the time all of this happened, he was an awkward, studious, but good-natured nerd. In other words, just my type.

Ken had never demonstrated any perceptible interest in my existence until he chose to sit next to me on the school bus one spring afternoon and chat all the way home. Shy although I was, I couldn't mistake the way his eyes appeared to glisten, perhaps with budding passion. Foolishly, I later phoned some of my friends to confer about the incident in excruciating detail and confide my runaway excitement about it. Overnight, word reached Christine.

She sidled up to Ken the next day in study hall. By dismissal time, he had asked her out. The news sent me racing to my bedroom after school in a torrential flood of tears. Completely crushed, I sobbed for hours. Rather than try to console me, my parents pounced while I was down for the count.

Christine had won, they said, because she had something far more precious than straight blonde hair: a small, straight nose. My hideous hump was standing squarely (no, make that pendulously) between me and any hope of true love. Until I agreed to shed the shnoz, I was doomed to a lovelorn life.

At the tender age of 16, my sense of self-worth was on shaky enough ground. I had always been painfully aware that I was not particularly pretty. Caught in the throes of adolescent rejection – the ultimate in vulnerability – I believed every word that they said.

The surgery was performed almost immediately, during spring break. I didn't dare tell my friends until after I had woken up from the anesthesia. Had I divulged my plans in advance, they might easily have managed to dissuade me. By the time I phoned them to 'fess up, it was far too late.

I'm still amazed to recall that I chose to attend my good friend Karin's birthday party a few days later, boldly facing both boys and girls with the skin beneath my eyes noticeably black and blue from the surgery, and my swollen nose still swathed in bandages. Sick of solitary confinement, I was not only reluctant to miss the occasion but dying to see people my own age. Besides, I assumed that everyone would figure out what I had done soon enough anyway, when I returned to school mysteriously transformed.

By the time the bandages did come off, Christine had – no surprise – already tossed Ken aside. As irresistible as I found his charms, to her they were apparently not sufficient to outlast a single date. But I can't say that I truly blamed her. In light of everything that had happened, I'd abruptly recovered from my former infatuation myself. In its place I developed a deep-seated sense of resentment toward him that lingered for many years. Of course, I don't hold him morally responsible for considering another girl more attractive than he had found me. But neither could I help feeling that he had played a starring role, however unwittingly, in changing my face and my fate.

Although my appearance was subtly altered from that day forth, my social life underwent no instant change. But that's only human nature. After people are used to seeing you a certain way for years, I don't believe they're capable of changing their perception of you. I don't think you're capable of changing your perception of *yourself*, either. It's as if you might lose 50 pounds, but if you were on the chubby side when you were young, then the Goodyear Blimp is what you, and they, will still continue to see.

My love life did improve dramatically, though, as soon as I reached college. I couldn't understand it at first, and kept looking behind me to try to figure out at what or whom a boy was really staring. During freshman year alone, I dated, among others, a senior who was co-captain of the football team, a popular DJ on the campus radio station, and the photo editor of the school newspaper. But that probably had less to do with my newly tapered nose than other inversely proportional changes. By then, you see, I had developed two anatomical commodities of my own which made me difficult to compete with for the attention of almost any college boy.

Meanwhile, I've remained embarrassed about having had that surgery all my life. When I was in my 20s, my good friend Suzanne, who is infamous for her bluntness and candor, had the nerve to ask me repeatedly if I'd had a "nose job." Although I knew the answer was probably unmistakable, out of sheer shame I vigorously denied it. This query was asked and answered many times, always the same way.

Evidently, Pinocchio syndrome doesn't run in my family, for my repeated falsehoods failed to make my abbreviated nose grow back.

I'm still ashamed to this day, although no longer to the point of needing to lie. How sad it is to be surgically altered rather than learning to take pride in who you are or how you look. And how cruel it seems for anyone to tell a teenager, whose confidence hangs by a gossamer thread, that she can only become lovable with the aid of a cosmetic procedure.

I'm not saying this to punish my parents – to malign my late mother or father. They genuinely believed that they were acting in my best interests at the time. I can't imagine, though, that I will ever consider such extreme measures to be in the best interests of my daughter. Or anyone else's daughter. Or, for that matter, my son.

This leads me to an interesting question.

Next to my older brother's whopper of a snout, mine was a mere Whopper Junior. Why, I eventually asked my mother, wasn't his nose ever altered, too?

"No comment," she replied, with an uncomfortable laugh. Neither was she forthcoming on another perplexing area: Why, when my parents were harping incessantly about the need for me to marry a fellow Jew, did they need to make me look *less Jewish?*

For isn't that, in essence, what Jews having nose jobs is all about? (Or, as my above-mentioned, extremely direct friend Suzanne insists, isn't it about Jewish men lusting after Gentile women – fine-featured *shiksa* goddesses?)

This, though, is what I really want explained: I went on to marry a nice Jewish man. Meanwhile, my brother, with his muzzle intact, ended up marrying a Gentile. Ironic? Yes. Mere chance? Heaven nose.

Drive

~⌒~

WE HAD JUST DROPPED OFF the last of the crowd after a long night of bar-hopping in Binghamton. Several deposits had been made in the vicinity of the dorm complexes, but as Harpur was largely an off-campus-living college, we had spent the past hour traveling all the way to Vestal and half-way through Endicott. When we had first left the Honky-Tonk, the car had been crammed with mildly intoxicated teenagers layered giddily upon one another's laps. But now I sat sprawled across the passenger side of the front seat as my older brother Joel, a sophomore at this upstate branch of the State University of New York, drove the seven miles back to his modest apartment in Owego.

"Know what?" he began, interrupting a fantasy I was lost in featuring a bearded young man in a black leather jacket I had spied gulping beer straight from a pitcher. "It's funny, but I have this strange, uneasy feeling that everyone there was mad at me tonight."

I reached into my jean jacket pocket and fished out a crumpled tissue – slightly used, but still functional, I figured. I gave my nose a good blow.

"Not that anyone actually said anything," he continued. "It just seemed like each kid there was giving me these annoyed looks, for some reason or another. I don't get it. Even if they were all having a lousy time, I don't see why it was my fault."

"It wasn't," I assured him. I tucked the tissue back in place for future use, then shifted slightly in my seat to face his side of the car, although he was too absorbed in the double yellow line to look back at me. "It's probably just that everyone wanted to do something different, and you were the only one with a car, so it was basically up to you," I said. "They were all arguing over whether to go to the Oasis, or the Harpur Pub, or just grab a pizza somewhere, and in the meanwhile we kept sitting around for hours. Inert. Like cattle. If cattle craved beer."

He smiled vaguely and raked a few fingers through his thick, dark brown hair. "You didn't even want to go in the first place," he ventured. "Did you?"

Soon to be 17, and now a senior in high school, I tended to be shy around his college friends. Shy around almost everyone but my immediate family, for that matter. "Nope," I admitted. "Not really."

In fact, I would have been perfectly content sitting around his slovenly college quarters, watching TV with him and his prematurely crotchety room- mate from Queens, Jack Goldberg, on whom I harbored a secret and hopeless crush. Yet as a typical restless teenager and frequent houseguest, grateful to be welcomed by my only sibling for another desperately needed weekend away from home, I had readily gone along for the ride.

"And I've nearly resolved not to brutally murder you before the night is out," I added. "So I wouldn't worry about it."

"But – "

"Seriously," I interrupted. "Everyone was pissed at you for stupid, selfish reasons, all of which will be forgotten by tomorrow, or certainly the next time you all go out."

"Yeah, you're probably right," he said, and he fell silent, allowing me to slip back into my reverie about the bearded boy with the pitcher. I had some trouble reconstructing the hero's face, however, and by the time I had assem- bled a reasonable facsimile of his rugged features, my brother's voice intruded, shattering this provocative image again.

"I was just thinking," he began. "You know what would bother me more than anything?" He didn't turn to see me shake my head. He simply assumed I was interested. "Have you ever thought about what it would be like to find out that a close friend secretly disliked you?"

He paused briefly, giving me a moment to cringe inwardly at the awful vision he was trying to evoke.

"I'm not talking about people who just finding you annoying sometimes," he continued. "I mean, there are lots of habits I have which bother the hell out of people."

"Really?" I asked with genuine surprise. Inhibited to the point of being almost paralyzed in public by acute self-consciousness, I had always envied my brother's brazen air of self-assurance. "For instance?"

"For instance... " I could practically hear his brain groping for a good answer. "For instance, I know that everyone finds it annoying that I smell."

Had we been back at the bar, this would have caused me to spit out my ginger ale. (At 16, I was too young and actually too sensible to drink anything stronger.) "You do?" I asked, barely stifling a giggle. "Why the hell don't you shower a little more often, then? Why don't you wash your clothes?"

"Because," he replied with a shrug, "I don't really feel like it, and no one seems to care about it enough to stop being friends with me."

This was true. Back in high school, as editor-in-chief of the student newspaper, *The Oracle*, and also something of a rebel, he had been the kind of boy whom other kids listened to and liked. That was probably how he had ended up at a state university when my parents could easily have afforded to send him to a more prestigious private school.

His senior year had run from 1969 to 1970, the height of social upheaval in America and of student protests against the Vietnam War. After his first two issues of the student newspaper had come out rife with anti-war editorials, my brother had been put on notice that the next edition could not be printed until it was approved by the school administration. Rather than risking censorship, my defiant brother had persuaded the editor of a small, local paper, *The North Castle News*, to print the paper free of charge and circulate it throughout our town by inserting it inside hers. This woman had been nice enough to print 500 extra copies, which my brother and two similarly rebellious classmates had surreptitiously placed on desks throughout the school the next morning before classes convened.

My brother was immediately sent to the principal, who chastised him mightily. The enraged man began shouting that the incident would unquestionably go on my brother's permanent record. What's more, if the principal ended up losing his job over it, and his children ended up "eating ham instead of turkey next Thanksgiving," as he put it, then my brother would live to regret it, he warned. Indeed, the following spring, despite having stellar grades and SAT scores and being captain of the tennis team and editor of the school newspaper, my brother was rejected by every college to which he'd applied, with the sole exception of his "safety" school, for which he had been vastly overqualified. There was no way to know whether the principal actually had made good on his threats. Rather than wasting my parents' money on the safety school, though, he had arranged to be admitted to the significantly less costly State University of New York at Binghamton.

All this did little if anything to undermine my brother's nonconformist spirit. During his senior year of high school, one of his main extracurricular efforts and local claims to fame had been the creation of a holiday he called National Gorilla Week. During this rather unconventional mock-occasion, loosely modeled after the ecologically oriented Earth Day, he had exhorted people to get back to Nature by resisting social pressures to bathe, shave, or otherwise eradicate their own natural scents by engaging in routine acts of hygiene. The original event had initially fallen in mid-November. My basic instincts about my brother, however, along with my keen olfactory powers, indicated that in college he had chosen to follow this creed pretty much all year round.

"So you're saying you realize that you smell, and that it bothers people," I said.

"Sure," he replied. "But they accept the way I smell as part of the way I am."

Or maybe he thinks they *like* it, I thought. Kind of like dogs.

Perhaps it was a product of growing up male in a Jewish household in the 50's, but my brother was used to getting what he wanted, everyone else be damned. I'm not talking about getting material things. I don't mean he was spoiled. I'm the one, between the two of us, who got all the spoiling. He, meanwhile, got what I really wanted. He got the sense that he could make things happen. He got all the confidence and drive. I mostly faulted my parents, who were so permissive with him that they actually let him name me.

Seriously! When my mother learned that she was pregnant for the second time, she worried that my brother would resent having a new addition to the family. So she bought a Little Golden Book called *The New Baby*. In this 1948 classic, a baby is born into the family of a little boy named Mike. When he hears that his mother is pregnant, Mike asks endless questions about his future sibling, such as "Who will bring the baby?" and "Will it have red hair like Susie next door?" Ultimately, a little girl is born with blue eyes, and they name her Pat, after a great aunt. After reading this story for months to my brother, who was then 2, my mother asked him how he would feel about having a brother or sister of his own. This would be fine with him, he replied, provided that it turned out to be a girl with red hair and blue eyes like the one in the book, and that they named her Pat.

This alarmed my mother. She had light brown hair, and my father's was dark brown. Never had there been a redhead in the family. So when I was born with tufts of auburn hair and topaz-blue eyes, she viewed it as a miracle and felt that she had no choice but to comply with his demands.

"But that's not what I mean at all," my brother was saying now in the car. "I wasn't talking about trivial things like the way you dress or how you smell. What I meant was what if you found out that someone you were close to – someone you really trusted – wasn't just bothered by some stupid habit you had, but really, actually, disliked you?"

Interesting question. The kind that often kept me awake in the middle of the night. Accustomed to feeling on the edge of things – never quite at ease in any situation or social group – I'd always harbored suspicions that almost everyone hated me, or at least considered me peculiar. In high school, I'd managed to find myself a small entourage of friends. But judging from the way those friends talked to me about each other in private, I could only imagine what they said or secretly thought about me when I wasn't around.

"It wouldn't happen like that," I told him. "Good friends aren't that shallow. When they decide they hate you, or that they don't want to hang out with you anymore, it's usually for some better reason than that you don't bother to use deodorant."

"Probably," he agreed. "But wouldn't that be even worse?"

I didn't answer him.

Going around a curve, we passed a car traveling towards us with its brights on. The light was so intense that I couldn't help but squint.

"Hey," I began after a while, then paused to reconsider.

"What?" he asked.

"I was just going to say... nothing."

Damn the weather in upstate New York! It was only mid-November, more than a month to go till true winter, and I could already see my breath inside the car, with all the windows cranked shut. Next time, I'd have to remember to pack thick socks and boots. Why should I have cold feet?

"I was just thinking," I began again. "Remember when Mom first found out that Dad was carrying on – 'philandering,' she called it; that was practically her favorite word – and she kept asking you to talk to him and make him stop?"

"Of course," he said. "Was she nuts?" He snorted disgustedly, then shook his head. "No need to answer that. But seriously, was she crazy? I was only 13 at the time."

"Yup. Crazy. Always was. Always will be."

"Why do you ask?" he said.

"No reason," I replied. "Except that... well, I did it."

His eyes left the road for a long second, and his glance met mine head-on.

"But if I was 13, you couldn't have been more than 11," he noted.

"That's right," I said. "But it didn't happen right away. I didn't do it for awhile. This was last year, when I was 15."

"Sometime after I left."

"That's right," I said. "You were away at college. Mom was out somewhere that day. It was this bleak, depressing, overcast Sunday, and Dad and I were home alone."

He drove in silence, perhaps letting the scene fully sink in. "So what happened?" he asked at last.

"I don't know," I said. "He must have done something to tick me off. Maybe he was talking to his girlfriend on the phone, and I happened to pick up an extension."

This was a commonplace occurrence at home that I had learned not to mention. Almost nightly, whenever my father was home, the phone would ring once or twice during dinner, and when I got up to answer it, the caller would click off or just remain dead silent. "Must've been a wrong number," I would announce when I returned to the table, trying to sound nonchalant. But we all knew exactly who'd been on the other end.

"Anyway, he must have done something crummy enough to make me rant and rave for nearly an hour," I continued. "I started off calling him an immature bastard."

"You said that?" he asked.

"Yup," I said. "Why not? He was screwing around on Mom. What was he going to do, spank me for being disrespectful?"

He gave a quick snort in agreement.

"Then I confronted him pretty rationally for awhile, about all the responsibilities he wasn't fulfilling," I said. "I told him that if he'd had half a conscience, he would've divorced Mom while she was still young – or at least young enough to find a new husband who might be nice to her once in a while. But then I fell apart and started calling him all sorts of names that I don't feel much like repeating. Like – "

"That's all right," he cut me off. "I can pretty much imagine what you called him. Oh, jeez, I'll bet he loved that! Did he blast the hell out of you, or what?"

"He couldn't," I said. "I chose that particular moment to bring down my report card. Remember when I used to always get straight A's? Well, junior year, all that went straight to hell. My lousy grades were my proof that our whole family was falling apart. *Yell* at me? Actually, he cried."

"Oh, man."

"I know," I said. "Can you imagine?"

He didn't answer. Didn't even shake his head.

"I never told anyone," I continued. "But afterwards, I hated you for it."

"Hated *me?*"

"That's right," I said.

"And that was because I did what?"

"Nothing," I said. "You did… nothing."

More than two years my senior and nearly eight inches taller, he had long, literally, been my big brother. And I'd long gotten used to letting him play that role.

In early days, he'd often played it to his own benefit, taking shameless advantage of my relative weakness and youthful gullibility. Once, when I was only 4, he had forced me to play the piano and chant "dirty words" along with him about our least favorite baby-sitter, a tubby teenager named Beanie. Believing me to be a voluntary accessory to the crime, my mother had stormed in, yanked me into the bathroom, and proceeded to make good on her threat to wash my mouth out. (To this day, I can't use Ivory soap.)

Then there was the time, two or three years later, that my mischievous brother ceremoniously introduced me to "little pizzas" while we were ravenously awaiting our order at The Roma Café, a local Italian eatery. Pushing over the rotund, metal-capped glass shaker on the table that was filled with dried, multicolored hot pepper flakes, he announced that I was in for a special treat. All the white specks tasted like crust, he said, the red ones like tomato sauce, and the yellow ones just like cheese. The only way to get the full pizza effect, of course, was to gulp down a handful all at once – an act that I dutifully performed and then clutched my mouth and instantly began shrieking for water.

Even so, he could also use his brains and brawn to serve as my public defender. I may have functioned as his personal punching bag at home, but if any other kid in the neighborhood ever gave me grief, he or she almost certainly would have hell to pay.

And best of all, by far, were the countless hours we'd spent together as teenagers in our subterranean playroom, batting a Ping-Pong ball back and forth until we reached a thousand, while he gave me advice about boys, and we repeated lines of dialogue from *The Catcher in the Rye*, *The City Boy* by Herman Wouk, and other favorite books that we'd both read, while we briefly managed to escape the domestic war raging upstairs.

"Just think about it," I said. "You were the older one. You were the *guy*. You were the one who had all the confidence." I blew out a long puff of frosty, white sigh. "That's how it felt, anyway. Felt to me. I thought that you should have done it instead."

There was a distinct slackening in the car's pace. "Come on! He was our *dad*," he said. "We were just kids. Mom – she had no right to ask either one of us to do anything. It was none of our business, anyway."

I shook my head slowly. "Yes, she did," I said. "It was too our business. No one else knew what was going on. Besides, he never would've listened to anyone else."

At the time that we took this drive together, I still believed that whole-heartedly – believed that my father wouldn't have listened to anyone else. But that didn't necessarily mean that he would have listened to or heeded what either one of *us* said, either.

The truth was that, however much he had wept the day that I'd confronted him, my father hadn't curtailed his brutal conduct toward my mother, which was verbally and often physically abusive, in any perceptible way. He was self-absorbed enough to remain immune to what anyone might say, even his own teenage daughter. He was going to do what he wanted to do. More recent experience had reinforced something that I had long known in my heart – to stop him from doing anything would take more than words.

Late one night during the previous summer, when my parents had returned from an evening out, I'd heard the sounds of loud arguing emanating from the garage, followed by a cascade of swift footsteps as my mother ran into the house. I'd raced downstairs to see her face stained with dark rivulets of mascara descending from her eyes like the inky tentacles of a jellyfish, her clothing and hair wildly disheveled.

It was the summer of 1971, and in keeping with current fashion, she had taken to wearing a blonde "fall," a long hairpiece that she wore in a loose bun fastened atop her head. Given the many curled tendrils extending from the center of this creation, my brother and I had dubbed it "the octopus." My parents had begun to argue on their way home, and upon parking my father had lost all self-control and physically attacked her, seizing her by the hair with such brute force that this hairpiece had been ripped from her head. Seeing my mother dash up the stairs, my father in close pursuit, still grasping the mass of curls in his hand like Medusa's head, my brother hadn't stopped to ask what it was about or consider what he might say to protect her. He had simply run to the kitchen, seized our largest and most lethal-looking carving knife from the silverware drawer, then raised it toward my father menacingly, threatening to use it if he didn't "get the f--- out."

I ran upstairs and berated my father hysterically as he hastily packed a suitcase in their bedroom. My brother continued to stand guard downstairs, still brandishing the knife until my father, still enraged, left. I no longer recall how many weeks or months passed before he finally returned home. A few days later, I was sent to live in Israel for the rest of the summer, presumably to give things at home a chance to settle down.

The next time I'd spoken to my father had been in August. He phoned me on his birthday at the kibbutz where I was living, eager to hear me wish him a happy birthday. But the overseas connection was terrible. He kept asking me to talk louder because he couldn't hear me. I just listened to him sounding sad and far away. I refused to speak up.

When I returned home at the end of the summer, we didn't discuss the incident. In fact, no one in my family had ever mentioned it again. But my brother had every right to bring it up now. At least, I figured it was now his turn to throw *something* back at me. Whether I ended up with a mouth full of soap, or "little pizzas," or something far worse, I would have to take it and defend myself, however possible. Defend myself like a man.

Only a few years later, fresh out of law school, my brother would not only begin to bathe regularly, but would trade in his rumpled, plaid flannel shirts and frayed corduroy pants for pinstriped suits with somber ties. The used, ungainly black '65 Oldsmobile F-85 in which we were riding that night would eventually give way to a series of sleek, late-model Lexuses and Mercedes. And as one of the top criminal defense attorneys on Long Island, he would charge his clients astronomical hourly rates to represent them and, as menacing as a gorilla in court, win almost every case that he took.

But that night he was still a teenager and my only slightly older, wiser brother. Instead of conducting a thorough cross-examination, he chose to abandon any attempt at self-defense. Maybe he was tired. Maybe it was late. But he just let the prosecution rest.

And so we continued driving along for another few miles, each listening to our own private thoughts.

"I didn't realize you did it," he finally said. "And I never knew you hated me."

"You never knew a lot of things."

He turned to look at me, his eyes widened like headlights with the high beams on. "What else was there?"

"Never mind," I replied. "I think I'll save it for the next time I hate you."

We continued in silence for the rest of the trip, although there were many things we each might have said. Just as he turned the car into the driveway, I asked, "Well? Does that answer your question?"

He didn't answer. "I wonder if people always get over it," he replied, pulling up the emergency brake before he switched off the ignition.

P.S.: I Loved You

_6_

THERE I WAS ONE MORNING, eating my bowl of Multigrain Muesli ("six whole grains blended with juicy raisins and fruit!") when I had an irresistible impulse to write a letter – an impulse that was wholly against _my_ grain. The letter, you see, was to a famous humor columnist, someone I admired but had never actually met. Personally, I don't understand why most people crave fleeting contact with the rich and/or famous. I've never asked anyone for an autograph, and have absolutely no desire to chat live on-line with the likes of **Kim Kardashian** or **Iggy Azalea**. However (now that I've caught your attention by mentioning those famous names **in bold**), let me assure you that this humor columnist is no mere celebrity to me. Why, compared with my affinity for the two intellectually so-so sex kittens I just mentioned, he and I are practically _family_.

OK, perhaps any close relationship between us existed mostly in the mind of my mother, who used to mention him with almost religious fervor during our frequent phone conversations. The poor woman tried to bolster my self-image for years by insisting that I was a perfect cross between him, actress Jane Fonda (a redhead like me) and the late, great essayist Erma Bombeck. (I've steeled myself against trying to envision what such a triple-threat might look like, and I advise you to do the same.)

Her ardent preoccupation was only heightened when this humorist began intimating in his syndicated newspaper column that he had branched out from his Christian upbringing in order (if only by connubial association with his current wife) to embrace lox, bagels, and the Five Books of Moses.

Given the values in my household of origin (where most adults would be less interested in knowing why the chicken had crossed the road than what its last name was, so they could judge whether the chicken was Jewish), this last development made him almost as good as family. Why, it was nearly as much to his credit as his having won the Pulitzer Prize or penned dozens of books.

That may be more than the total lifetime output of Jane Fonda (including movies and exercise videos), Ms. Bombeck, and me put together.

Yet the connections between the good Humor Columnist and me are not as tenuous as you might imagine. Perhaps I should spell them out, if only to allay any suspicions that I have gleaned the intimate details of his life via the normal avenues: Internet research or stalking.

Like him, I grew up in the suburban, sitcom-like setting of Armonk, New York, a town 40 miles north of New York City, where his most adoring fan remained and would get all tingly every time he referred to some local landmark, like Harold C. Crittenden Junior High. We narrowly missed attending school together, since I entered the combined junior and senior high schools in our town the year that he left for college. His younger brother, "Paul," though, was one of my older brother's two best childhood friends.

Actually, to my mind, Paul was just as much my own personal partner in crime. I must confess that I fell in love with him at first sight during my freshman year of high school, when his blonde, bowl-cut mop of hair popped up in the window of the biology lab while I was in class one day, and he began making weird rabbit ears at me.

Those irresistibly romantic antics ruined my entire adolescence. From that day on, it didn't matter who asked me out on a date (which did happen on occasion, despite my having heavy metal on my teeth and far more interest in Franz Kafka than Frank Zappa). From that moment on, I only had sighs for him.

That may sound sweet now, but think of it this way: While all of the normal teenage girls in my school were busy acting fickle, I spent all four of those formative years remaining faithful in my heart to a boy who knew me well, saw me nearly every day, and never seemed to consider for a second that I was a real, live girl.

That, at least, is how it appeared to me at the time. I can't be sure if or when the object of my juvenile affections ever may have begun to reciprocate any of my feelings. After all, he wasted at least a year groping "Katie Callaway," a sweet, pretty, and impossibly skinny classmate of mine. (And to think that their lustful liaison got started on a church retreat!) But he managed to drive me home from school regularly in his mother's Plymouth Duster, then to hang around endlessly in our '50s split-level, playing the piano, listening to The Beatles' White Album, and writing subversive plays in rhyme.

Once a dedicated and promising musician myself, I had abandoned playing the piano at age 12, soon after my parents had first separated. But I could sit rapt for hours listening to Paul perform Beethoven's "Moonlight Sonata" and other selections, from classical to rock, in our living room. A musician of astonishing skill, he often composed music of his own and always performed with intense feeling. There seemed little doubt that he would grow up to be a professional musician and perhaps even famous someday.

His greatest gift, however, to my mind, was his zany, irreverent, and alarmingly manic sense of humor. In fact, having missed the chance to share the sweat-scented corridors of my high school with his famous sibling, I grew up convinced that Paul was the man most likely to become a humor columnist and the celebrated-sibling-to-be.

I'm not sure I can accurately represent even a semblance of his wittiness here. Too much of it depended more on his rapid-fire delivery than what he actually said. He just always seemed to be bursting into a room muttering some absurd, philosophical sort of mumbo-jumbo or a nonsensical non sequitur, like "Toadstools in July!"

Take the hand-written, eight-page letter that he sent to me the summer after he graduated high school, while I was attending an arts program at a college in Michigan. Written when he was 18, it began like this:

So, you old educational giant! I'll bet you're having a really dandy old time learning this, studying that, enjoying another thing! Yessirree Boberoony, I wish I was in your shoes, except I'd probably develop arteriosclerosis or some other sort of crippling disease which would yield me permanently unmitigated for life.

It proceeded to barrage me with news, both real and fictional, including that he had taken the liberty of signing me up for a matchmaking service so that I could have my "PERFECT DATE (!!!!!)" and that he had recently established "an entirely new organization, known as the 'Austrian Spanking Society,' or simply the ASS."

It concluded:

> *...I'll bet you're out there pretending to be learning and things like that, but (ho, ho) I know that really you're reading <u>Seventeen</u> and <u>Teen Idol</u> and <u>Black Beauty</u> and Nancy Drew mysteries and things like that! You don't fool me at all! No, not even one frog hair! You're as clear as a transparent oak tree!*
>
> *...Now, don't forget to jot down a note here, or a message there, to let me know just how things are coming along. Don't get rowdy, now. And don't become a head or freak or anything. And don't do this. Don't do that! Don't do ANYTHING! Just sit around and meditate! Remember, you've got your two fists — use them! Beat up the next ostrich you see!*

OK, so some of that humor, I'll admit, was pretty sophomoric. Then again, much of his famous older brother's brand of humor is totally sophomoric. You also must bear in mind that, back then, given my tender age (only 15) and my adoring disposition, I might not have been quite the most discriminating reader who ever lived. No wonder I thought the way Paul finished another letter may have been the best postscript of all time:

> *"P.S.: I have to go take a P.S."*

In truth, so reliable was his ability to crack me up on contact that my lingering, incurable case of love at first sight was largely just a chronic case of laugh at *every* sight. No doubt, part of his interest in spending so much time with me – his friend's little sister, who was two years behind him in school and nearly three years younger – was that I was such a receptive audience. How gratifying it must have been for him that, as melancholic a creature as I was at that time, he had the almost magical ability to make me giggle just by opening his mouth. Certainly, it was through no fault of his own that one of the worst fights I've ever had with anyone was provoked, or at least aided and abetted, by him.

Although my parents' relationship remained icy enough throughout my childhood to be endlessly on the rocks, not until I reached my mid-20s did they actually divorce. In the interim, for nearly 15 years, my father repeatedly moved in and out of our house to go live with his girlfriend, Elaine. He came and went at will. He would be home for a few weeks and then out for a few weeks, home for three days, then out for three months.

As unsettling as this setup may sound, his leaving was actually a welcome respite. Whenever he was gone, my mother was visibly miserable, and we lived with crippling uncertainty and overwhelming stress, but at least there was a lot less hitting and yelling.

During his periods of extended absence, he'd come to visit my brother and me. Since my parents' marital turbulence was considered a private matter, to which even my best friends could not be privy, I began to blame his frequent absences on business trips. "Oh, my dad's in Chicago again," I'd say, or, "He had to fly to the West Coast."

To make amends for not being home, or perhaps to assuage his guilt about it, my father often arrived for his visits home bearing gifts. Those fabricated excursions helped explain to my friends why I got presents that were unrelated to holidays or birthdays.

But sometimes there was no need to make excuses, because there were many gifts that I was not allowed to keep. When the items in question were apparel, in particular, my mother was invariably suspicious that my father's mistress had helped him pick them out.

Given the cheap, cheesy-looking nature of most of these garments, there was good reason to believe her suspicions. I wouldn't have had the desire or stomach to hang these skanky items in my closet, let alone wear them to school. So I rarely resisted when she would insist that I return them. One Saturday afternoon, though, things went differently. Paul had just popped over for an unexpected visit when my father arrived for his.

I don't remember what city I claimed my dad had just returned from that day. I don't know if I even bothered to make up a destination. I only recall that as soon as he arrived, even before he took off his coat, he handed me a large cardboard box. It was bound in colorful, flowery wrapping paper, but its contents proved to be even more vivid. I anxiously tore off the paper and pried open the box to find a bright velvet sports jacket. It was printed in squares of assorted lively patterns, from paisleys and posies to squiggly abstract designs, all mixed together in a random manner in the style of a patchwork quilt.

"That's so cool," Paul said.

My father urged me to try it on. I slid my arms into the narrow sleeves, and then smoothed down the sleek lapels with the palms of my hands, nimbly fastening the buttons at my waist. It was, miraculously, almost a perfect fit. The jacket was tailored like a traditional blazer, but the whimsical mix of patterns in a riot of reds, oranges and assorted jewel tones made it look anything but old-fashioned.

"Totally cool," Paul declared.

"Yeah," I agreed shyly, "it is. And for the first time since my father had first left, I felt two distinct emotions. I realized that I adored him, despite everything that he'd done. And I knew that nothing could possibly convince me to give that blazer back.

I decided to keep it on. I even twirled before my audience of two to show it off.

A few minutes later, my mother opened her bedroom door, walked down the long hallway that overlooked the living room and paused at the top of the stairs.

She bid my father a subdued hello and warmly greeted Paul. Then she noticed me. "What's... *that*?" she asked.

"Just something Dad brought me," I said. Then I took it off and hung it on a chair.

She waited for hours, until both Paul and my dad had left, to have it out with me.

"Just who do you think picked that out?" she asked.

I shrugged defensively. "Who?"

She placed her hands on her hips, elbows akimbo, and snorted in exasperation. "You know perfectly well who."

I couldn't even look her in the eye as I said, "We don't know that. Not for sure."

It wasn't proper to wear anything that bright, she said. "Just look at it! Red velvet. It's too flashy."

"Actually, I think it's kind of cool."

"Oh, really."

I debated her. Argued with her. Pleaded. Begged. Although I was normally diffident, soft-spoken, and relatively mature for a 15-year-old, I eventually even cried.

Then, finally, I put the jacket back in the box and stored it in a corner of my room, ready to return it with some lame, concocted excuse the next time my father visited.

The fact is that it was just an article of clothing, and a rather ugly one at that. It was not something worth hurting my mother over. Her behavior may sound heartless, or at least a little cruel, but I decided to accept it back then and, in retrospect, can understand it even better now. Maybe she should have considered that I was still only a girl and given me a break for once. Yet the truth was that it was horrific enough for her to have to relinquish her husband of twenty years, her own case of love at first sight, to some other woman. Why should she have had to endure seeing material evidence of that woman, and her hideously gaudy taste, on her own daughter's body or hanging inside her own house?

Besides, the sorry truth was that no mere jacket in any pattern imaginable, or even *every* pattern imaginable, was going to convince Paul to love me as much as I loved him. No mere jacket was going to guarantee that he would notice me. His admiring outburst had just been the first overt sign that, in some small way, he might admire me a little, too.

⟶

The only other evidence that he was fond of me, aside from the extensive time we spent together, came in the countless letters that he wrote to me over the years to come.

During summers, he sent reams of wacky missives when I went away to camp. Then began the steady stream of dispatches he sent after he left for college.

Most of the later letters were typewritten, but his typing was anything but neat. On the contrary, most of them were riddled with accidental or deliberate typographical errors that often created touches of unintentional humor.

Take the letter that he wrote to me during his freshman year, containing this rather colorful anecdote:

I conducted a scientific experiment in here a little while ago. I took a peice rather a piece of rye bread and soaked it and left it out so that molds would grow all over it, in a biological manner of speaking. Finally, when molds grew on it, it looked like (and probably was) puss, and besides it had red things starting to grow all over it. When I looked at it with a microscope, I saw little living beings buzzing around, building a great city. Then, when the smell became unbearable, I threw it all away. I looked just like vomit. I mean IT looked just like vomit.

That letter also included a short note of thanks:

Never did I respond to your cookies, which were good, and here I thank you belatedly, for whatever that is worth. However, I thought that I would wait, because you wrote "letter to follow" and I didn't know if you meant a letter from me to you or from you to me. OH, THESE MIXUPS!

Another letter, from the end of that term, began with gratitude for baked goods, too: "Well! Got your cookies!!!!! Thanks a bundle! Loads of luck!!" So did yet a third, sent in April of 1973, three days after his twenty-first birthday. (Again with the cookies? Who did I think I was, Betty Crocker? I mean, could I have been any more *obvious?*)

Your cookies were a big hit with my taste buds. Your package was a big hit with everybody in the dorm. Freddy ("El Freako") Guadalupe wants your phone #.

Most of these letters were single-spaced, and went on for several silly pages. Some arrived accompanied by a small collection of random objects, such as a movie ticket stub, a baseball card, and a physician's report authorizing him (at a healthy and trim 5 foot 8¾ and 145 pounds) to participate in school athletics. Obviously, I was thrilled to receive it all. Yet when I combed this correspondence for any romantic content, as I invariably did, I was invariably disappointed.

The lengthy letter that he sent to me at art school provided the one rare exception. It showed uncharacteristic honesty (or was it just more characteristic nuttiness?) with its concluding sentiment: "LUV (that says Luv because I'm too embarrassed to say LOVE)." But more typical was the two-page letter that ended with the affectionate salutation, "Alright, Goddamnit, Paul."

Yet what more should I have expected? Throughout those years, our relationship had always remained consistently close, invariably pleasant... and perpetually platonic.

Then came the summer that I was 17, right after I graduated from high school.

For the three previous summer vacations, I'd spent a month at home working and a month away. That year, I chose to stay home all three months and work for my father. Knowing that I was about to leave for good, I was no longer in such a hurry to escape. Plus, I was afraid to leave my mother alone with my testy father, who was living at home again and had recently purchased a handgun after being attacked by a neighbor's dog.

Despite his presence, we were back down to only three in the house. My brother had decided to take a long trip and was off driving cross-country and back with a friend.

His absence left my family with an extra ticket for our annual excursion to the American Shakespeare Festival in Stratford, Connecticut. Reluctant to let it go to waste, my mother suggested that I bring a friend along. I got up my nerve and asked Paul.

Those theatrical interludes still rank high among my few fond memories of childhood. The Shakespeare theater always had troupes of minstrels in period costume strolling the grounds before performances, and we'd always cart along the same fancy picnic supper: jumbo shrimp with tangy cocktail sauce, my mother's own Southern-fried chicken, and rich, homemade chocolate cake with fudgy icing for dessert.

I don't remember what play we saw that night. But what followed when we got back home was strictly Romeo and Juliet... minus the murder and the double suicide.

It began soon after *The Tonight Show*, starring Johnny Carson, signed off the air. Paul and I had been sitting in our wood-paneled downstairs playroom for at least an hour, watching and chatting, chatting and watching. I assumed that he would leave before long. But he just kept sitting there, watching and chatting, chatting and watching. Sitting right beside me, nattering on about almost nothing.

Then he turned to me and said it.

"Do you think it would be OK if I, uh, kissed you?"

I almost choked at this outburst. A muffled "OK, sure!" was all I could get out before we tumbled in a heap on the couch. He kissed me. I kissed him. It was more than OK. And he was still there at 6 a.m.

He told me that night that he had always been attracted to me. I said I didn't believe him, but that it didn't really matter, as long as he felt that way now.

From then on, Paul and I developed a nightly routine. He would come over to my house after dinner and sit downstairs with my family, chattering and watching television. Soon after the unsuspecting adults finally went upstairs to turn in, he would call goodnight to them loudly, but never actually leave. Instead, we'd curl up together on the playroom couch, talking softly and "making out" for hours.

I still wonder if my parents knew what was happening, and simply turned a deaf ear to his car revving up in the driveway at dawn. I couldn't tell at the time. But just in case they decided to come downstairs, we didn't ever dare do too much on that couch. Besides, we were waiting until two weeks after that first night. That's when my folks would depart for our family's annual trip to a rustic fishing camp in Maine. They had agreed (dunderheads that most parents were in 1972) to let me stay behind, all alone.

Well, not quite all alone. The night after they left, Paul and I could not believe our good fortune. Instead of arriving after dinner, he came over *for* it and I cooked for him, as though we were an old married couple. We decided to catch a scary movie (perfect for a date, since it gave you a good excuse to clutch each other tight). Then we returned to an empty house and giddily repaired to my bedroom, where we finally got to sleep together. And I do mean SLEEP!

For one thing, we were absolutely exhausted from all those all-nighters.

For another, why rush things? We had a whole week of solitude ahead of us.

Or so we thought.

The following morning, I was stunned to be awakened early by the sound of the door leading from the attached garage to the house creaking open and slamming shut. Could it be a burglar? Even worse, had my parents for some reason returned so soon? Frantically, we pulled on scattered clothing and crept downstairs. The intruder turned out to be neither of the above, but something, or someone, almost as bad. My brother had decided to surprise me by returning home a full week early from his trip to Los Angeles.

The real surprise for me, though, came from Paul. He instantly reverted to his old ways. Actually, worse. Previously, we'd been good friends. Now he acted as if I were invisible. Clearly, he didn't want people to know that we'd become a quote-unquote item.

I soon realized that he had been concealing our involvement not just from my parents, but from all of his friends and family as well. When the three of us stopped by his parents' house that day, Paul's mother expressed amazement that my brother had been away on a trip. She had assumed that Paul had been at our house all those nights visiting *him*. (And I'd thought that earlier in the week, when she'd insisted on giving me a sweater of hers that she said she never wore – a vivid number in orange, pink and yellow that would have been too bright for my father's girlfriend to wear, even in psychedelic 1972 – it was because we really *were* almost family.)

In retrospect, I have no trouble understanding his desire for complete discretion. What teenage boy wants his parents privy to his romantic escapades, or has the nerve to tell his best friend, "I'm messing around with your little sister"? But then things got even worse. When my brother grew bored at home and convinced Paul and me to join him for a weekend visit to some former classmates in Boston, the awful charade continued. Paul didn't touch me, speak to me, or even look directly at me the whole time we were away. Clearly, I was again just his friend's little sister, or so he wanted everyone to believe.

The thing is that – despite my utter lack of self-esteem – a lifelong passion for books, theater, and old Hollywood movies had led me to develop fairly high expectations about love. I'd grown up with the quaint notion that when I finally found the man of my dreams, and he finally recognized that I was the woman of his, he would want everyone to know about it. He'd be proud, or maybe even inspired to sing, or write, or shout about his feelings to the world. So even if my overall sense of worthlessness, or unworthiness, made unrequited love something I could accept – or at least endure, for years on end – realizing that the love of my life actually was ashamed of his feelings for me was not.

That's when I finally made myself face the facts. I decided that I had wasted the so-called best years of my life being hopelessly infatuated with a talented genius who was clever, sweet, and quirky, but who was either too embarrassed or too much of a total boogerhead, as his brother might say, to admit to anyone else that he liked me back.

Maybe it was just as well. High school was over. Summer was over. And a week or two later I got to enter college emotionally open to all the heartaches, heartbreaks, and drunken escapades that commonly passed for passion at fraternity house sangria parties.

Paul and I still continued to exchange letters. And yes, although I shudder to admit it, I continued to send him cookies. But by then I had permanently recovered from my crush, and we never made the slightest attempt to rekindle our summer flame again.

Paul was neither the first nor the last man on whom I maintained a hopeless crush. Yet not until many years later, long after I was married and had children of my own, did it occur to me how strange and possibly even disturbed my devotion to him had been.

I was talking to my teenage son about a girl he knew. She'd been pursuing him relentlessly for more than a year, even though he had made it quite clear that he regarded her as a good friend, but any romance between them was outside the realm of possibility.

"I just don't get it," he grumbled. "If I meet someone I'm attracted to, and she doesn't seem to respond, after about two weeks I give up and go find somebody else."

At first, I couldn't believe that anyone, let alone someone who had been raised by me, could have such a sound, sensible attitude toward love. Then it occurred to me: That was probably the way most people behaved. My son was simply healthy and normal.

And I, clearly, was not.

Wondering if my behavior was some sort of syndrome with an actual clinical diagnosis, I looked up the problem on Google. Within seconds, three words popped up:

Obsessive Love Disorder.

"Obsessions are a true anxiety disorder created in response to a very stressful, overwhelming and painful situation," stated a Web site called PsychotherapyHELP.

If you ask me, adolescence was a very stressful, overwhelming and painful situation. Actually, you might easily say that about every other phase of my life.

"A crazy family, school or work environment," it continued, "may cause an over-anxious or emotionally injured person to escape these painful realities by retreating to a safer, although sometimes uncomfortable, world of fantasy and obsessions."

Crazy family? When it came to my family, "crazy" didn't begin to cover it.

Instability in the parental relationship could exacerbate the symptoms, it said. So might having a father who seemed highly evaluative, authoritative, critical and detached.

Evaluative? Authoritative? Critical and detached? Weren't most fathers like that? Or was it only mine?

Continuous disapproval from such a father could leave a child feeling criticized and inadequate. The end result? "The young child grows into adulthood arrested at an earlier stage, continually failing to establish normal, healthy, bonded love relationships. S/he becomes attracted to and fixated on unavailable and emotionally inaccessible partners, many of which do not feel the same way about him/her."

I couldn't believe I was reading this. At the same time, I felt a sense of relief. After all those years, I realized that I might not be the only person who acted this way. And that when I did it, perhaps it wasn't my fault.

Who knows? While growing up, I became fixated on many young men. My feelings for Paul were merely the most prolonged of these and most intense. But maybe they were perfectly normal, and just a natural result of his having been bright, delightful, adorable, unattainable, and infinitely more appealing to me than any boy my own age.

Or maybe I didn't fall for him simply because he was clever, sweet and off-beat. Maybe I remained stuck on him not despite but *because* he didn't share my feelings. Perhaps he was my refuge from a relentlessly chaotic childhood, an escape route into silliness and a safer world where every sentence ended with an exclamation point... or three.

After all, the joy of just being around him felt like visiting a lush, tropical oasis in the desert of my lonely young life. It also allowed me to feel attached to someone without taking the risk of having him love me, then leave me, like my dad had left my mom.

And until I could actually escape from my family and my troubled world, by starting college and ultimately a new life of my own, he actually, probably had been my "PERFECT DATE."

After college, I never lived at home again. But my mother periodically passed on greetings from Paul. He briefly supported himself as a piano teacher and tuner after graduating from college, and he regularly attended to our Acrosonic upright, the one on which he'd once played Beethoven so beautifully in our living room. After I was married and my husband and I bought our first house, my mother sent that piano to us as a house-warming present, and I found Paul's name and a tuning date scrawled inside the lid.

I didn't mean to lead you on a saccharine trip down Memory Lane, however. What I wanted to explain was about the morning that I decided to write a letter to Paul's famous brother. There I was, innocently eating my bowl of Multigrain Muesli, when my mother called to read me his latest column, then began blabbering about him again. (Now, there's your stalker!)

"I'm not as obsessed with him as you are," I observed, trying to shut her up. I expected her to get defensive. After all, in her warped mind, he was nearly *mishpocheh*. OK, I can't spell at all in Yiddish, but that means "family." Yet she didn't get defensive. Not one bit.

"I'm *very* obsessed with him," she agreed. "Did you know that Mensa [her other obsession] has a group devoted to him that faxes his columns back and forth? He's sooo bright! You know how Erma Bombeck is regarded? Well, he's moreso... if it could be."

Maybe she was right. But I couldn't help thinking about this column he once wrote, entitled "How to Be a Professional Writer or Just Look Like One." In it, he explained the secrets of how he gets all his work done at home. Mostly, it was a heap of references to sitting around clipping his toenails, which seemed kind of self-indulgent.

As a professional work-at-home writer-slash-mom, I spent most of my time clipping *other* people's toenails. I never seemed to get anywhere near my own, let alone my computer. And then there were all those other distractions. How were you supposed to resist the urge to vacuum or help your dog scratch all of those hard-to-reach places? How does anyone resist leafing through boxes of old letters?

I really wanted to know. And so, to surprise my mother for an upcoming birthday, I wrote Paul's brother a letter. I explained what a fan of his my mother was. So that he wouldn't think I was just another fawning reader, I also filled him in on our common history, juicy parts and all, and included photocopies of a few old letters from Paul. Then I enclosed a birthday card for her, which I entreated him to sign and return to me a.s.a.p.

Amazingly, he did sign the card and return it just in time for the big occasion. It was difficult at first to make my mother believe that the signature and brief remarks inside the card were his. When I finally convinced her that they were authentic, she shrieked. Then she placed the card lovingly on her mantle, where it remained for the rest of her life.

I must admit that I also held onto the short note that came enclosed with it, which was addressed to me and signed by him, my first and only actual celebrity autograph. It didn't say all that much, but like most of Paul's wit, it was not really about what it said. Just thinking about it puts me in a good mood.

Meanwhile, I also held onto something else, something even more precious.

Soon after Mr. Good Humor Columnist returned my mother's birthday card, he forwarded everything else that I had sent him to Paul. A few days after the card arrived, I received a letter from my old friend, the first one I'd gotten in more than 25 years.

Once again, it was single-spaced and long, although, with the aid of a computer, his typing had drastically improved. Enclosed were several photographs, picturing Paul, his wife, and their three lovely young daughters.

Although Paul had aged, I would have known him instantly had we met on the street. He looked much the same. Only his blond hair had thinned and turned mostly gray. His once-whimsical writing style also sounded older and seemed to have sobered up.

"I have made up my mind that I will write this letter like I had to write all those typewritten letters," he began. "I won't backspace. Life doesn't afford us the opportunity, so I have to learn to write, and speak, as if my life depended on it."

And so I began to get a picture of the man he had become since we'd last met.

He gave a brief synopsis of everything that had happened to him in the interim; the jobs he'd held, how he'd met his wife, the deaths of his parents, the births of his girls.

I was more than a little disappointed to hear that he had forsaken his musical ambitions long ago. Instead, after taking his mother's persistent advice ("Get a good job! You're so smart! You could make a lot of money!"), he had earned a degree in computers and was now working for a large corporation. Yet he betrayed no regrets and seemed focused on other priorities: "doing my best to be a good husband and father, and all that."

He'd been married for 16 years to a woman he'd met when he'd tuned her piano. "She is, fittingly enough, tone-deaf." But I was elated to get the sense that they were happy. He described his wife as "an angel," without a hint of sarcasm or silliness.

I must admit that I was also thrilled to hear him confess that he'd been jealous following our long-ago fling when he had sensed that my feelings toward him had cooled and that I had grown interested in one of my brother's other friends instead.

Yet most moving of all was what he said about our years of friendship.

"You are a special girl," he wrote, "the kind who dumb-ass guys overlook, but intelligent men treasure. And now that you are all grown up and I am all grown up, I have to say that I am truly sorry for having been, or having appeared, insensitive or unkind."

He went on to explain the hard times he had gone through himself, both during and after college, including that fateful summer during which we had gotten involved.

> *But I've never forgotten the past, and it lives with me every day. It fills me with sadness when I realize that like the typewriter, we cannot backspace...*
>
> *I wish that I could be 20 again and tell you that you were the best girl I ever had the privilege to go out with when I was young; so you were. And although I was not very mature, God gives us diamonds along the way, and you were one.*

No more nuttiness, exclamation points or excuses. Just the sincere sentiments that I had so long ago longed to hear.

His words were so kind and comforting that I almost didn't care if they were true. By the time I'd finished reading the final sentences, tears were streaming down my face.

So in the end, maybe I didn't waste the supposed best years of my life infatuated with the wrong fellow. Maybe, even though I was a fool for love, I wasn't a fool at all. Maybe if life were more like a computer than a typewriter, and I could backspace at will – even go back several decades – I would leave the past pretty much as is.

OK, so I wouldn't have sent quite so many cookies. And I wouldn't have given up on Paul so readily when he faltered in front of my older brother. But otherwise, I wouldn't change this! I wouldn't change that! I don't think I would change A THING!!!

And knowing that definitely puts me in a good humor. Or moreso... if it could be.

Miss Taken Identity

THOSE WHO FORGET THE PAST are destined to repeat it, or so, at least, it's said. Those ten words have always filled me with dread. After all, the past is something I strive daily to escape, yet my memories are more pocked with holes than a slab of Swiss cheese or the surface of the moon.

I tell myself that memory gaps are often a defense mechanism triggered to help overcome experiences best forgotten. If that's the case, though, then why do I recall so many heartbreaking events and recollect so few that were good? Surely, in a childhood sullied by neither illness nor poverty, there must have been a few bright moments.

To reconstruct the past, I must turn to family members or photographs, but there I usually am stumped again. Many relatives, such as *Bubbeh, Zaydeh*, and feisty Aunt Lily, have long since departed. Then there was Grandma Mary, once sharper than a tack, who by the time she'd reached her mid-nineties couldn't remember what she'd just eaten for breakfast. As for photo albums, mine are chockfull of their own vast chasms. After all, when things aren't happy at home, no one thinks of running for the camera.

The odd thing is that the few photographs I do possess are full of missing pieces themselves. It isn't a matter of poor preservation. Family members have edited my past by intentionally tearing people out.

Take the snapshot from 1965, the only remnant I have of my only sibling's bar mitzvah. In it, my older brother looks plump with a rodent-like overbite, like almost any 13-year-old Jewish boy before braces and a teenage growth spurt work their magic and charm. My father, resembling an adolescent himself, sports a buzz cut reminiscent of early astronauts. As for me, at an awkward and gangly 10, I look wan and waif-like in a pale pink gingham dress, a flourish of white eyelet lace cascading from the throat to the hem. Yet worst of all is what you don't see: my mother. Ashamed of the hideously dated, shiny olive green dress she chose for the occasion, she tore herself out a few years ago, soon after she noticed the cherished yet unframed photo propped up on my mantle.

I don't know why she felt entitled to mutilate a snapshot that belonged to me, but I suspect that this inclination to revise history is genetic. At least it runs in her family. Years ago, in my early 20s, I gave my maternal grandparents what I considered to be a rare, flattering image of myself taken on a vacation in Haiti. The next time I visited, I noticed that Grandma had admired the shot enough to display it in a corner of her bedroom mirror, but only after snipping it in half. It may have been a matter of trying to save limited space, or wanting to see only me. But I suspected that she simply disapproved of my having posed with my arm around our tour guide, a young Haitian man who happened to be black. Perhaps she feared that other people would assume he was my boyfriend.

Sure, some family photos have simply grown tattered over the years accidentally. But far more common in my life have been these deliberate acts of photographic vandalism.

Do you think that's too strong a word? I don't. Even if the pictures in question often include my mother, they belong to me. I loved her dearly – of course I did – but I have little sympathy for the fact that, in her own peculiar way, she was just trying to save face. As nasty as the past may be, you can't undo it by destroying the records. Besides, in trying to salvage her own identity, she obliterated much of mine.

Another prime example is the photo that was taken on my first day of college. My father drove me to school alone. My mother, a longtime teacher and school administrator, had already begun school herself. I suppose that my father and I must have chatted during the four-hour drive up the New York Thruway, although I can't remember a word. I only recall the solemn lecture that he delivered to me the night before. He spoke so obliquely and circuitously that only later did I grasp the basic gist: *Be careful in college, but if you screw up and "get in trouble," don't worry. Have an abortion. I'll pay.*

Once there, he must have helped transport my bags and boxes into the dorm. But the only thing I remember clearly now is how I looked, because my roommate's father chose to capture the occasion on film.

The snapshot he took showed my roommate, her mother, my father and me posed in front of a modern cinderblock dormitory. In it, I appear uneasy and underfed, dressed in a madras top and cut-off jeans that I insanely believed made me look fat. I treasured this photo and displayed it proudly for many years on my bulletin board – until my mother got her hands on it one day. It occurred to her that people might mistake my roommate's mother for her. Although similarly blond and exceedingly sweet, this lovely woman did not quite match her aesthetic self-image. *Schweeeep!* She seized the offending print and, with one swift motion, removed the other mother.

Still, it's one thing to have someone surgically remove herself from your photo collection, and quite another to have a close friend cut him or herself out of your life.

Out of your life, as though you'd never met.

For no apparent reason.

That has happened to my husband and me in several instances over the years. Once, some close friends for more than a decade abruptly and mysteriously dropped us. We'd met as young couples and instantly bonded. Later, with similarly aged children, our two families appeared perfectly matched. Then, one day, they inexplicably withdrew. They began spurning our invitations with flimsy excuses. Once our constant companions, they now constantly had other plans.

Had we done anything obvious to offend them, we gladly would have apologized. But since nothing in particular had happened, we didn't have the nerve to ask what was wrong. What kind of excuse could there possibly be? Maybe they had made new friends, or had just decided to move on.

Of course, almost everyone has instances in which once-close friends gradually drift away. Fortunately, the ever-shifting circumstances of life introduce others to take their place. There are half a dozen women I alternately refer to as "my best friend" – and that doesn't count the vast cast of supporting characters who email me regularly, are Facebook "friends," or often call me to chat. No wonder I can hardly keep up with the laundry, let alone finish most books I begin to read or write.

Yet like doomed King David of Biblical times, who could have had almost any woman he wanted except for the one he chose, I foolishly set my sights during sleepless nights on companions who are no longer mine. I pine for the dear friends whose changing fortunes lured them halfway across the country. I yearn for the garrulous group of coworkers I lost the day that I left my last job. But most troubling of all is the friend who I probably sacrificed more to my own stupidity than the stampeding pace of modern life: my first college roommate, "Beth."

The last time I recall laying eyes on her was at my wedding, three decades ago. What did I do? Or what *didn't* I do? To this day, I have no clue.

At times, I would give almost anything to be able to call her up, just to see how she's doing or to reminisce about old times. I hear something – an old song, a bit of gossip – that only she could truly appreciate, and I have no one with whom to share it. Yet, to be honest, what I want almost as much as her company is to know why I can't have it – to learn why she chose consistently to ignore my letters and refuse my calls.

The lengthy lapse has given me plenty of time to mull over the possible reasons for our rift. I've pretty much narrowed them down to two.

One is petty, yet all-too-human, the kind of resentment that surfaces in newspaper advice columns almost every day. The second is much more likely, but also much darker. It stems from a terrible lie I told her over 40 years ago.

It was a whopper of a lie, as untruths go, and I knew at the time that it might be a moral miscalculation and come back to bite me in the tush. What I didn't anticipate was that she probably was destined to learn the truth anyway. Neither could I have foreseen that this one fabrication would unravel our friendship and potentially ruin her life.

⸺ ᥫ

An online service designed to help former classmates reunite allows subscribers to compose their own personal profiles by taking a multiple-choice quiz.

"What's the first thing that pops into your head when you think of college?" it asks, then proceeds to suggest several alternatives:

a) Dating
b) Partying
c) Graduating
d) Sleeping
e) Studying
f) Did I go to college? It's a little hazy.

Although I never was one to party hearty, or to get anywhere close to a full night's sleep, at varying moments I might easily choose almost any one of the above. But for another such question, only one potential answer will do.

"What best describes your first roommate?" the questionnaire asks. The responses offered range from "The Hippy" and "The Jock" to "The Recluse" and "The Party Animal." But only one option fits perfectly for the party in question: "My Best Friend."

Considering how superficial my first school's roommate-matching survey was (I don't believe it asked much beyond whether I was an early bird or night owl and a neatnik or a slob), and considering how few close friends I made among the other girls on campus (none), the extent to which Beth and I got along was nothing short of a miracle.

It's even more amazing if you consider how little we appeared to have in common. Beth had gone to an all-girl's Catholic high school. I was a coed public-school-educated Jew. She favored classic, tailored clothing. My eclectic personal style might have been described as "hippie goes to Bloomingdale's." Her overriding passion was political science. I lived to read and write.

But despite all our basic differences, we were basically variations on the same theme. We were both almost precisely the same height and weight. We were both soft-spoken and shy to the point of being awkward and almost speechless in social settings. We'd both grown up in the shadow of an outspoken, domineering, slightly older sibling.

And we both were destined to lose our virginity to the exact same boy.

—❦—

I still have the letter that she sent to me the summer before we met.

I guess you've figured out by now that I'm going to be your roommate. Hi! I know these kinds of letters are unendurably boring, so I'll keep it short.

I live on Long Island in suburbia. I went to a very small, private girls' high school in the next town. I'm interested in government and history, and I'm planning on going to law school...

I have a feeling that I'm bringing a pile of unnecessary junk up with me. So if you write me back maybe we can decide on who will bring what & we can share stuff like phones. I hate to say it but I'm bordering on being an incurable SLOB.

I just thought maybe you might be interested in what I look like. I have long black hair, blue eyes and freckles. I'm 5'5 and usually skinny...

Well, I've bored you enough for awhile. Please write & tell me about yourself.

See ya,

Beth

A few weeks later, we converged in a small double room in a large, modern suite at Kirkland College in upstate New York. This private women's college, a spanking-new, ultra-progressive, artsy institution, was destined to virtually disappear within a decade, eaten alive by Hamilton, its much older, more traditional brother school across the street.

Its eventual demise was something that anyone there who was half paying attention could easily have predicted. By contrast, the instant friendship that sprang up between Beth and me seemed solid and destined to endure. Similarly self-deprecating and riddled with self-doubt, we were not just roommates, but a complex mutual support system. United by a common enemy – the odd-ness and other-ness of everyone else – we lived together, laughed together, and invariably studied together, sharing three meals a day and one minuscule, chronically messy room without a single moment of resentment or the slight-est inkling of rivalry.

The last facet of that all-for-one-and-one-for-all scenario changed abruptly the first night of sophomore year. After settling into our new two-room suite, we decided to repair to the official college hangout, The Pub.

This boisterous grotto, filled with deafening chatter as students strug-gled to be heard over the din of pinball machines and rock tunes blaring from the jukebox, was where everyone on campus wound up most nights to see who was there and be seen. What Beth and I were hoping to see was any one of the many male upperclassmen with whom we had grown secretly infatuated the year before. So it was no great thrill to be promptly approached by three unfamiliar boys who turned out to be from our own class. Even to girls who are sophomores in college, sophomore boys seem, well, sophomoric.

Or so I believed.

"God, wasn't he cute?" Beth gushed to me after these three stooges had finally departed, as we navigated our way back to our dormitory in the dark-ness and pre-autumn chill.

"Who?" I asked, genuinely mystified.

"You know," she said. "Tom. The guy with the red hair."

"Oh, right. Sure," I replied. But until then I hadn't noticed.

Tom, though, it turned out, had noticed *me*. The following day, he asked me out.

My heart sank at the invitation. I didn't know what to say. I'd felt no instant spark ignite in his presence, and evidently Beth had. Yet all she had expressed was initial attraction, not undying devotion. And although he wasn't necessarily my type, he seemed too nice to insult by refusing outright. So somewhat hesitantly, and guiltily, I said yes.

Beth, it turned out, was right. Tom, by most standards, was major-league cute. With deep auburn hair, hip wire-rimmed glasses, and a taut, muscular build, he offered a rare, alluring amalgamation of hunky pecs and intellect. He also proved to be reasonably clever and was a devoted English major, like me.

Yet I found myself almost sleepwalking through our first date, and continued to feel my thoughts and gaze wandering every time we met. I should like him, I thought. Any girl would. He's handsome and witty, sexy and smart. But given my mindset that September, my heart wouldn't have missed a beat even for a movie star or modern-day Adonis.

⤶

Evolution, I've noticed, has a mysterious way of speeding some things way up and slowing others down.

For example, everyone talks about how much more sophisticated kids are these days than we were. And compared to my generation, my parents and grandparents didn't have a clue.

On the other hand, by the time my great grandmother turned 19 — the age I was approaching — she had been married for three years and was the proud mother of two. My grandmother, at 19, was married and had given birth to my mother's older sister. Even my mother, as a college sophomore, was already engaged to my dad. As for me? Let's just say I was in no hurry to get tied down, let alone procreate. But shedding my innocence was a whole 'nother issue, one that had long been on my mind.

For as far back as I can remember — and I can remember pretty far back — I was always interested in boys. It all began with Mark Eckstein, a neighbor whom my older brother dubbed "The Nickel Kid" because in first grade I once offered him a nickel I had left over from my lunch money to admit that he liked me. (He sheepishly accepted this modest stipend, but said that he would have professed his feelings for me free of charge. Labor costs: 5 cents. Lifelong memory: priceless.)

By the time I reached high school, I was always actively interested in *someone*. And there always seemed to be someone who was somewhat interested in me. But my rate of getting involved in actual relationships was another matter entirely. For one thing, the object of my interest and the interested party were rarely one and the same. For another, on the two rare occasions that these two phenomena miraculously managed to coincide, the boy in question and his family, for totally unrelated reasons, abruptly moved away.

The only thing that kept me relatively sane through these lovelorn years was a small circle of friends, other girls who found themselves in a similar predicament. You can't get away with feeling too sorry for yourself for being chronically dateless when your best buddies are dateless, too. And yet by senior year, instead of striving valiantly to bolster one another's spirits, we ended up mostly wallowing in a communal sense of abject gloom. Academically, we all had applied ourselves conscientiously enough to rack up stellar grade point averages. But socially, not for a single day had any of us made the grade. On the contrary, we all felt supremely uncool and universally rejected.

After all, we were convinced that we might be the last five virgins left in the entire school.

At this point, we were so resigned to our local identities as social outcasts, though, that there seemed to be no prospect of improving our status while we remained at home. Our only hope lay in the futures that loomed ahead of us once we left town. And so, with great bravado, we hit upon a sort of collective group pact. Maidenhood, once considered mandatory for proper young ladies, felt to us like a terrible disease, and among our main objectives in going away to college was to be cured of it a.s.a.p.

I don't know what happened to the rest of them in this regard, but by several odd twists of fate, my entire freshman year flew by without my finding a remedy for this affliction.

Although I became romantically involved with a boy within weeks of my arrival, we never consummated the relationship. For one thing, this nice Jewish boy had been raised the old-fashioned way and claimed to be opposed to premarital sex. For another, even though college students (like all humans) are prone to throw such moral principles to the wind in the heat of passion, my moments of passion with him were prematurely curtailed. After months of paying more attention to me than to his studies, he flunked out at the end of my first semester and went home for the holidays for good.

Although I had countless other crushes and dalliances for the duration of that year, nothing all that serious (or all that sexual) ever evolved.

And so I found myself entering the summer before my sophomore year stuck back home again with no romantic prospects in sight and my virtue insufferably intact.

Like all four summers during my high school years, this one promised to follow a predictable pattern. I'd spend the first month or so employed at the only job I could find – working as a secretary for my father, who owned his own business in New York City – and the last month making up for this drudgery by taking a trip of my own choice.

The destination for that year's excursion emerged when my father read in the newspaper about an archaeological dig in Southern Illinois seeking student volunteers. Affiliated with Northwestern University in Chicago, this program not only promised the romance of excavating ancient Native American relics, but also offered college credit.

Yet before departing for the Midwest, there was one urgent piece of business to which I needed to attend.

I had managed the improbable, by surviving a full year of college with my chastity unchallenged, but my mother had no faith that I could accomplish the impossible and actually get through another. So she whisked me off to her gynecologist to have me put on The Pill.

I still chortle inwardly when I recall the scene in the doctor's office that day. Although prescribing birth control for teenagers – particularly those of college age – has since become commonplace, in the early 1970s this practice was still relatively new. And enhancing her stuffy, middle-aged doctor's discomfort was the fact that he happened to have a daughter about my age who, by pure coincidence, happened to attend the very same college that I did.

No wonder, upon my entering his office, a rather awkward dialogue ensued.

Doctor: So, I understand you're here to obtain a prescription for birth control. Tell me, just how long have you been dating your boyfriend?

Me: Excuse me? Well, actually, I don't have a boyfriend.

Doctor: You don't? (Mysterious coughing spell, followed by extensive clearing of his throat.) Oh. Well, then, let's see. For how long would you say you've been having, uh, relations?

Me: Relations? You mean sex? Umm, actually, I've never had sex.

Doctor: I don't understand. You don't have a boyfriend. You don't have sex. Why then, in God's name, do you want to go on The Pill?

When I told him I was doing this purely at my mother's instigation and insistence, he asked his nurse to summon her from the waiting room at once. She not only backed up my story, but somehow persuaded him that her point of view made perfect sense. Twenty minutes later, I left his office with my first and last prescription for birth control pills.

It was my last because its assorted side effects on my body were so unwelcome and so perverse that for the rest of my life, I never again wanted to take anything like it.

I've heard that such medications have since been changed to contain significantly lower dosages. And for the sake of the women who take them, I can only hope that's true. For these insipid little tablets had three highly deleterious effects on me: They made me so nervous that I felt like my whole body was buzzing. They made me so edgy that I could hardly sleep. And they increased the size of my breasts so substantially that my already ample bra cup size leapt up a letter grade or two.

In this distressing condition, I ended up flying halfway across the country to an archaeological site in Kampsville, Illinois, armed and looking extremely dangerous. Given the relentless heat of the summer sun, my fellow volunteers and I spent most days excavating mounds of dirt dressed in only the briefest of shorts and tank tops. Given the physically demanding nature of this work, we built up enormous appetites. And given the thrifty nature of this non-profit venture, we were fed a low-budget but calorie-sky-high diet consisting mainly of peanut-butter-and-jelly sandwiches and cookies.

Between my new medication, the carb-laden food, and the long hours of muscle-building labor (the operative word in this experience turned out indeed to be "dig"), the work wardrobe with which I had come equipped soon became rather snug. No wonder the Indiana Jones wannabe at the helm often brought potential investors over to meet me, the 18-year-old redhead in clingy tops.

Far more gratifying was that I eventually attracted the attention of "Steve," a nice, subdued graduate student employed in the local library. Every evening after dinner, I'd sit across the room from him, patiently reading until he got off work. At closing time, he'd shut the doors and turn off the lights. Then we'd settle down on the carpet in a darkened corner of the reference room to kiss.

One night we walked to a nearby lake and curled up together on its sandy banks. Despite an onslaught of mosquitoes feasting on my bare arms and legs, it was the single most romantic evening of my life up until then. But the next night, after the library closed, he told me things needed to change.

He knew that I was sexually inexperienced. Being slightly older, in his early 20s, he was not. He was convinced, however, that letting me sacrifice my honor to him would be dishonorable for him and a serious mistake for me. We barely knew each other, and before long I'd be returning East, probably never to see him again. My first taste of passion should be with someone who really loved me, he said. And as much as he really *liked* me – and liked kissing me – it was unrealistic to expect our relationship to emotionally ever get past first base. Remaining at first base physically was, for him, becoming unbearable torture. There was no point in continually starting something up that we had resolved never to finish. Thus, it was time to break things off.

I found it difficult to argue with this logic, even though the incredible decency of his attitude made me like (and lust after) him even more. And so I found myself, more than halfway through my six-week sojourn in Southern Illinois, all alone once more.

Yet I had little time to sulk. A big cookout was scheduled for the following night. And soon after arriving, I found myself face to face with "Jack," another grad student I had met before but never given a moment of thought.

Jack had orangy-red hair, even redder than mine, and gray eyes the color of dusk. He also had a mind as sharp as the pointy metal trowels we used to chip away at the dirt. There may have been 100 other people gathered there that night, but I barely took note of anyone else, or realized when the last of them had left. We spent the whole evening locked in private conversation, pouring out our most private thoughts, our deepest fears and fondest dreams. So guarded did I act under normal circumstances that never before had I managed to connect so instantly or completely with anyone. I felt like I knew what he would say before he said it, because I was thinking the same thing myself.

The barbecue had been held a long walk away from the rustic barracks in which the students were housed, and Jack had driven over. It must have been nearly 11 when he offered me a lift home. We climbed into his cluttered compact, but he didn't turn it on. For a short while, we continued to chat, staring out the windshield at the darkened sky. Finally, when I turned to meet his gaze, he leaned over slowly and let his lips meet mine.

"Don't let me do anything you don't want me to," he murmured into my hair.

To be honest, there wasn't much at that moment that I didn't want him to do. Yet after we had kissed for a good, long while, and I'd let his hands wander anywhere he wished them to go, he abruptly pulled away. Retreating into his own seat, he folded his arms over the steering wheel and hunched forward to bury his head.

"There's something I have to tell you," he began. "Something awful. Something that I really regret."

I braced myself, feeling as though we'd been speeding down a highway with the top down and my hair flying, and then he had suddenly stopped short.

"I can't believe that this happened," he finally groaned. "It isn't what I expected to do. And honestly, I've never done anything like it before."

"Just say it," I prodded. "Whatever it is, I'll understand."

"No," he replied. "Why should you understand when I don't understand myself? I can't believe that I met someone like you. And I can't believe that I kissed you. Because, you see... well, I'm married."

"Oh," was all I could say. "Oh, God!"

Although only 25, he had already been married for several years. Most likely this had happened as a matter of necessity; he and his wife already had a 5-year-old daughter. Now working toward his doctorate in anthropology, he had left them back home for the summer while he helped run the dig. But I would have little time to adjust to this alarming news. His wife and child were due to arrive for a visit the following day.

"You'd better take me home now," I told him, when I could find my voice again. I was hoping the shocked numbness would last until I could smother my sobs in a pillow.

I called my parents the following morning. They booked me out on a flight the next day. I spent the afternoon packing and pouring my heart out to a sweet girl named Robin, my best friend there and the only one to whom I'd grown close enough to tell why I was leaving. Later that day, walking through town, I had the sickening misfortune to spy Jack and his family strolling by across the street. His little girl was tiny, blonde and adorable. His wife was also blonde, but coarse looking and still apparently carrying a considerable amount of baby weight.

Another young woman might have shrugged it off, or at least had the fortitude to finish out her remaining weeks of work. That woman would not be me. All through my adolescence, my father had been cheating on my mother, and I had known about it. Adultery, to me, was almost as bad as murder. Adultery had killed my childhood. It was an act I considered unforgivable, and I had sworn I would never commit it myself. And now, albeit unwittingly, I had almost become an accessory to the crime.

It may sound excessive, even insane, that I reacted so acutely to a single night. Keep in mind, though, that I was only 18, and a highly vulnerable 18-year-old at that. Ravenous for love, and so recently rejected by my library beau, I had allowed myself to dive into a deep, churning sea of desire, but not yet learned to take a deep breath first. Still, I knew that the magnitude of my feelings and the intensity of my reaction were too strong to make much sense. So when I related all the grim details to my family, and later to Beth when I returned to school, I told them all a low-grade lie. I claimed to have been seeing Jack for several days before he'd confessed. This may have made him seem more deceitful, but I figured that it was the only way to justify how completely I had fallen apart.

$$\smile$$

Back at college in September, I was still so overwrought that I had to begin making conscientious efforts to get Jack out of my system. I told myself that I could start to recover if I could go for a full minute without having him enter my mind. At first, this seemed like too lofty a goal. Then, one day, after a particularly lively lecture class, I realized that I hadn't thought of him once for nearly an hour. I guess I'll live, I thought.

Allowing myself to dare to care about someone else was another matter, though. My nerve endings weren't close to being repaired enough to consider taking the risk. No wonder poor Tom, the sophomore (and another redhead, no less), couldn't make any headway in my heart.

Even so, I decided it was foolish to spurn him. It was better to have someone to hang out with than to remain solitary, and in my emotionally shattered state there was no one I preferred.

One Friday night in late September, Beth and I were sitting in The Pub with Tom and Mike, one of the other three stooges, when Tom offered to drive us all to The Horseshoe Lounge, a nearby dive. I'd heard of "The Shoe," as it was known, but never been there. We were sick of being interminably stuck at school. He didn't need to ask twice.

The campus pub only served beer, and rarely would I down more than one. The Shoe, however, sold hard liquor. Catering to both students and local working folk, it offered libations that were reasonably cheap and remarkably potent. After a few rounds of pool and a few mixed drinks, we were in unusually high spirits. So instead of turning in for the night, Beth and I consented to prolong the evening by repairing to Tom's room.

Popping an Allman Brothers' album onto his stereo, Tom motioned for me to sit on the floor beside him. Beth and Mike, who had no discernible chemistry between them, settled on opposite sides of the room. The lights were low and the music deafeningly loud. So when Beth eventually announced that it was time to leave, I assumed she couldn't hear it when Tom began to stroke my back and whispered to me plaintively, "Stay."

I don't know if it was the effects of all the alcohol, or the intoxicating urgency of his touch and his voice, but I told Beth to go ahead, promising that I'd return home soon. Mike gallantly offered to escort her back to our dorm. Moments later, we were alone.

Tom, at this point, settled on the edge of his bed and pulled me down beside him. Although startled at first by the acrid scent of liquor on his breath, I felt giddy and submitted to his probing tongue. With one swift motion he peeled my pullover sweater off my back and over my head. I made a brief, lame effort to resist. But when I felt his fingers fiddling with the zipper of my corduroy jeans, I knew there was no turning back.

In the few movies I'd seen that portrayed graphic sex, the women always kept their eyelids blissfully closed, their lips parted as they moaned with breathless rapture. Now, instead, I found my eyes shooting open in unanticipated horror, my face contorted in excruciating pain as he rose and fell above me, vigorously pursuing his own delight. So unexpected and acute was my keen discomfort that it sobered me up in seconds.

"Stop! Please, stop!" I howled, pushing him off firmly as I drew myself away.

"Huh? What's wrong?" he murmured, sounding more perplexed than concerned.

I told him that, due to my previously chaste state (something of which he had been fully aware), his efforts were far too agonizing for me to bear and he needed to cease at once. I expected him to understand, perhaps even to feel remorse. Fat chance. Maybe it was merely the liquor in him talking, but his attitude was that I had to be kidding. One way or another, I was going to have to help him to achieve his desired end – and no, it wouldn't suffice to simply, uh, lend him a hand.

Someday soon thereafter, I would develop enough self-assurance to know that I could simply say no to anyone at any time, and that feeling reluctant to do something was reason enough not to do it. Given my total naiveté at that time, though, I felt embarrassed and obliged to cooperate. After all, I had lingered in his room alone until well past midnight and had led him to believe that I was ready and willing. I didn't want to seem like a tease.

Most of all, though, given the stark, bleak landscape of my current mindset, I'd grown to believe that nothing really mattered, anyway.

So I gritted my teeth and managed to submit until, in due time, he was done.

Striding across the campus to my dorm moments afterward, still aching sharply between my legs, I kept repeating in a whisper to myself, "I'm still the same girl I was yesterday. I'm still the same girl I was yesterday." But I knew that I was no longer a girl. And that the words I was whispering weren't true.

The next time I saw Tom, he acted as though everything was fine between us, and so, therefore, did I. But on the following weekend, I did what I should have done from the very start. I made a date with him for Saturday night, and told him to pick me up at 7. Then at 6:45 I went to the campus library, leaving Beth behind in our suite. When I returned, a few hours later, they were both still there. And they were together from that night on.

—◌—

As hard as it sometimes seems to believe, one woman's toad can turn out to be another's Prince Charming. Despite the sheer callousness Tom had shown to me that night in his room, for Beth he turned out to be a sweet and surprisingly attentive boyfriend. There was only one issue they ever fought about, or so she divulged to me in due time.

Beth, like me, had managed to sail through both high school and freshman year of college with her virtue unsoiled. Tom, on the contrary, having enjoyed copious female companionship, was a comparative man of the world. And like my temporary boyfriend from the library, he found getting aroused to no avail to be a frustration that he couldn't bear. After several weeks, he'd begun pressuring her relentlessly to succumb to his desires.

I thought about how things had ended with my library makeout buddy. That, at least, had made sense. We'd had no viable future together. Beth and Tom did, though.

"Why, exactly, are you so reluctant?" I asked. "Have you considered giving in?"

"Are you kidding? she demanded huffily. "Whose side are you on?"

"Huh? Yours, of course," I said with a reassuring laugh. "Seriously, though, think about it. Sure, it's obnoxious for him to be so pushy. But if you hold out for too long, you just might lose him. Once guys start having sex, I think they expect to keep having sex."

"I never thought about it that way," she said. "Who knows? You might be right."

What, then, was her objection? I'd gathered from assorted late-night chats that she had no ironclad scruples or expectations about saving herself for marriage. I also knew that she was totally smitten with the guy. "But you aren't ready to sleep with him," I said. "Why not?"

"I guess I'm just holding out, like you," she said. "I mean, you're still a virgin."

"No," I said, "I'm not."

Her eyes widened to the size of walnuts. "*What?* What are you talking about? You never told me!" she cried.

The fact is, I hadn't told her because I was too embarrassed at the time, ashamed of myself for having slept with a boy I didn't love and whom I suspected she did. But as difficult as it might have been to admit it back then, telling her now was impossible. Beth and Tom had been dating for months. How could I say I'd slept with her boyfriend?

I had blurted out my revelation impulsively and didn't have much time to think. So before she could grow suspicious, I furnished the best alternative that came to mind.

"It was Jack, last summer," I said. "The guy in Illinois."

"The *married* guy?" she asked in a hushed tone, unable to disguise her disdain.

"Yes. Before I knew that, obviously," I said. "Even so, I was afraid to tell you."

She nodded, understanding totally, then shook her head. "So, what was it like?" she asked.

I wanted to prepare her, but not to scare her. "I'm sure the first time must be different for everybody," I replied. "But I wouldn't hesitate to speak up if it hurts."

Whatever happened between them next is their business. I never heard any audible sounds emanating from the next room. All I know is that they continued going out through their remaining years of college. I soon transferred to another school, and we were a little lax about staying in touch.

"Tom & I got engaged on the steps of the Metropolitan Museum of Art last Thursday," announced a picture postcard that I received from Beth three or four years later. The following summer, I had the honor of serving as a bridesmaid at their wedding.

The newlyweds decided to live way out on Long Island. I, meanwhile, moved to Manhattan. Occasionally, I took a train out to visit my old chums. Less often, they ventured into the city to see me. But they were now old married folk. I was a single woman, driven to date.

When I finally met my own husband-to-be and got married – a good half-decade after Beth and Tom had tied the knot – I hadn't seen them in several years. I invited them to the wedding, of course, and was thrilled that they could come. But I neglected to reciprocate by asking Beth to be one of my bridesmaids. And there were so many other guests at the reception that we barely had time to talk.

Life, as we all know, gets awfully busy. Weeks, then months, flew by. When I gave birth to my first child, after two years, I felt mortified that I hadn't even told Beth I'd been pregnant. I called their house the night after I returned home from the hospital. Tom answered the phone and said Beth was upstairs with a bad back, but that he'd tell her the good news and was sure she would return the call. She never bothered to, though.

Even so, I mailed them a birth announcement for my son, then another when my daughter was born three years later. I also sent them annual holiday cards featuring photos of my kids. Not once did they ever respond. Eventually,

I wrote Beth a letter begging forgiveness for whatever egregious thing I might have done to antagonize her. When it, too, remained unanswered, I decided it was time to give up.

I did dare to call Beth's parents' house a few years later, though, when I heard that Beth and Tom had divorced, and that Beth had moved back home. Her mother answered and said that Beth wasn't home. She was sure that she'd be thrilled to hear from me, though, and was certain that she would call me back. But she never did.

Over the years, I convinced myself that she might just be reacting to a trivial slight. Yet I also concluded that, if so, she probably had every right. How foolish I had been not to reciprocate her gesture by including her in my wedding party. No doubt she had been insulted to discover that I had not one but two maids of honor, along with six bridesmaids. What difference should it have made to me that we essentially had lost touch by then? Beth was still and would always be one of the best friends I'd ever had.

I'd arrived at the theory that she felt offended because, as far as I could recall, I hadn't heard a word from her since my wedding. Then one day, foraging in the attic, I came across a postcard that had been mailed during someone's summer vacation in Europe. It thanked us for the incredible time that its senders had recently enjoyed at our wedding. And it was signed with love from Beth and Tom.

I don't know how I had forgotten receiving it originally, but I was sickened to recover it now. If she harbored no resentment for my nuptial snub, then what other inexcusable act had I possibly committed? What conduct was so unforgivable that she would refuse to acknowledge the arrival of my children and shun all attempts at contact?

Only one answer came to mind.

Over the years, I had always hoped that Tom would have the decency to keep our drunken rendezvous under wraps. Surely, he had nothing to gain from revealing it. And since Beth had never once mentioned it to me, I'd always assumed that she didn't know. But having been married now for years myself, I know how few secrets people manage to keep from their spouses. I also know how dark revelations have a way of coming to light.

Perhaps he hadn't told her for years. Then, sometime after I was married, he had. Maybe he'd mentioned it casually, assuming that she already knew. Or perhaps he'd thrown it in her face during a heated argument. Maybe, discovering my deception, she even suspected that we had been intimate together while she and Tom were involved.

And even if my suspicions were wrong – dead wrong – the staggering guilt I felt imagining what she must think of my behavior deterred me from ever calling her again.

As I've said, in the many years since I last saw Beth, I've had plenty of time to make new friends. Yet I often think about something my son said to me the day that he graduated from high school. Instead of feeling euphoric about having reached this major milestone, he grew unmistakably melancholic. All of his long-time friends would soon be dispersing to different colleges, he observed. Even if they got together occasionally during school breaks, he could foresee that their relationships would never be the same.

"Don't worry, honey," I said, trying to console him. "Once you get to college, you'll make plenty of new friends."

"I know that," he replied solemnly. "But new friends don't replace old friends."

And, of course, he was right.

I've also begun to wonder if, in choosing to tell that lie to Beth, I was wrong.

At a book lecture I once attended, the speaker, a rabbi's wife, discussed how lying is regarded in the Jewish religion. There are three justifications for being untruthful, she said. You can lie to maintain your privacy. (If someone says she heard that you're getting divorced, and you feel it's none of her business, you can deny it even if it's true.)

You can also lie to maintain modesty. (If someone congratulated you for having run a successful fundraiser for the Jewish Federation single-handedly, you could insist that countless others had helped, even if you actually did almost all the work yourself.)

Plus, you are actually obliged to lie in order to spare someone else's feelings. ("Does this dress make me look fat?" is a question to which there is only one possible answer.)

I'd like to think my fabrication to Beth fits somewhere within that final category. I'd also like to propose a fourth justification, a new loophole in the official laws of lying: Lying for someone else's own good.

Maybe then I can finally let myself off the hook.

Throughout this tale, for all these years, I have blamed myself for every blunder. It never occurred to me way back then to fault poor, unhappily married Jack for deceiving me into falling hopelessly in love with him. I only longed shamefully to be with him still, and felt desperately sorry for him, so young and yet already stuck in a loveless marriage from which he was tempted to stray.

Nor did it occur to me to blame Tom for prolonging our painful sexual encounter. I thought he was simply being 19, and being a guy, and that I should have known better.

It also never dawned on me to resent Beth in any way. But just think about it. What sort of person cuts a close friend off, even if she's done something fairly dreadful, without giving that person a chance to explain? And did I truly do anything that terrible? Even if my behavior somehow backfired in the end, I obviously meant well at the time.

Yet I still feel miserable now.

We all have certain things we consider non-negotiable in order to feel good about ourselves. Some people need to achieve financial success. Others need to win at sports. Many, mostly women, have to be thin, or beautiful, or to have the most beautiful, smart, talented, or otherwise impressive kids. All those things can help make us feel better. But in tallying my score at the game of life, I'm far more focused on personal relationships.

I'm the first to admit that I have major deficiencies when it comes to being a wife. But with only minor and totally justifiable exceptions, I was a relentlessly dutiful daughter to both my parents. And, with all due humility, I defy anyone to find a more devoted mother than me.

But I also like to view myself as a true and faithful friend. I value my friendships above almost all else and am always ready to put myself out to offer whatever one of my friends may need, be it a sympathetic ear or moral support. ("No, that dress doesn't make you look fat!").

In not allowing me to be her friend, Beth makes me question that. She makes me question who I am. In her case, I am no friend at all. I've utterly failed at our friendship.

Or has she failed me?

It's hard to tell. I only know that in ruthlessly removing herself from the picture, she has stolen a chunk of who I am.

It's like my mutilated photo collection, but in this case, I feel like a major part of my self-image has been torn out by someone else, and I have no way of getting it back.

That's what's wrong with this picture. And why I'm not just destined to repeat the past, but I remain stuck in it.

Whatever I did, or didn't do, I wish that we could be friends again.

I wish that Beth could forgive me. Or that I could forgive myself.

Because in the photo album that is my mind, there are only a few nice, old shots. And those are my pictures – *my* pictures – and I want those pictures back.

The Catch

∽

I WAS YOUNG, WIDE-EYED, AMBITIOUS, but shy. I was living my dream life in New York City... and all I could do was cry.

Newly graduated from a college near Boston, I had hastened to Manhattan to start my adult life and launch a career in publishing. What else was an English major to do? But taking precedence over all other concerns was my eagerness to rejoin my college boyfriend, who had graduated a semester before me. Together we had leased a modest L-shaped studio in a dingy downtown high-rise on the corner of Thirtieth Street and Third Avenue. A distinctly non-doorman building, it was charmless and deflatingly nondescript, yet the best on our combined starting salaries that we could possibly afford.

"Tell me, why are you young people always stacking up?" my grandmother in Florida had demanded to know when I'd called to announce my change of address.

"The term is '*shacking* up,' Grandma," I'd said, rolling my eyes (a totally futile gesture, since we were on the phone). Had I bothered to offer a more illuminating response, either to her or myself, I would have admitted to ulterior motives. Namely: No matter how whole-heartedly I embraced the then-prevailing feminist ethics of economic and emotional independence, a small part of my soul was still stuck firmly in the '50s. And that part was passionately in love, afraid to be alone in the city, and convinced that in due and not too distant course, this boy and I would be happily joined in marriage.

My matrimonial ambitions were wholeheartedly endorsed by my parents, who vocally frowned upon my living arrangements, but managed to act accommodatingly modern and look the other way.

Unfortunately, my roommate – like most young men who enjoy domestic benefits like free laundry services, gourmet cooking, and carnal knowledge without commitment – had a distinctly different agenda. So did his father, a prominent and rather controlling furniture designer who happened to be his boss. Convinced that, at 22, his son was far too young to form such a serious romantic attachment, my prospective father-in-law offered his son a big fat raise and a promotion. More money, and much more responsibility.

There was a catch, of course: Accepting it required moving to Providence, Rhode Island, which was at that time a far less alluring and somewhat seedy city several hours away. My boyfriend, nothing if not a dutiful son, vacillated. I encouraged him to take the bait, though, assuming that I'd outsmart good old Dad and accompany him. Relocating, even to then-provincial Providence, might be good for us. At least, I figured, it would whisk us away for awhile from the meddlesome scrutiny of both his family and mine.

I figured wrong. Perhaps his father was right in suspecting that I had too much influence on his son, but he had even more. My boyfriend reluctantly accepted the post, then suddenly announced that, by his father's decree, he was leaving me behind.

We briefly tried to maintain the relationship long-distance, but when several weekend visits proved disastrous, I accepted a blind date arranged by my brother with one of his friends, a nice Jewish lawyer. I also dared to divulge these plans to my boyfriend when he announced unexpectedly that he intended to be in town that weekend. Big mistake! The date was a flop – my brother's friend clearly wasn't interested in me – and I returned home to find my apartment nearly emptied of furnishings, most of which had been designed by my boyfriend's father and supplied by him. Evidently, my boyfriend, who still had a key to our flat, had chosen to pay a visit in my absence with a large truck and clean the place out. Only the mattress and box spring, our one joint purchase, remained. My clothing, underwear and all, sat scattered on the floor in forlorn, sagging piles, like puddles of fabric, where the chest of drawers had once been.

So there I was weeks later, living by myself in an L-shaped, nearly unfurnished studio, which suddenly seemed unbearably roomy and desolate, as though the "L" in L-shaped stood for "Lonely." Or maybe "Left," as in "He left me for dead." It was little consolation that I'd recently received a promotion of my own. The publishing conglomerate at which I'd landed an entry-level job upon graduation had offered me my first professional magazine post: editorial assistant in the offices of *Field & Stream*.

Make no mistake. This stodgy men's periodical, a glossy tribute to the pleasures of hunting, fishing, and the Great Outdoors, only looks like it originates in some folksy, frontier milieu. Most of its contents are generated by contributors who presumably live in backwoods cabins, favor plaid flannel shirts, and speak with a pronounced Midwestern twang. But the actual magazine is assembled in a modern Manhattan skyscraper by well-educated editors wearing natty business attire. Or at least it was back then.

It was there, beginning in the spring of 1978, that I spent my days. Along with answering phones and performing other servile tasks, I learned how to proofread using professional notation. I also got to edit three monthly columns, on cooking (involving rare delicacies like freshly killed squirrel), humor (homespun hunting and fishing yarns about assorted critters and "the one that got away"), and motor vehicles (mainly pick-up trucks and other rugged vehicles that inelegantly predated the SUV). All the while, I was taught to exercise literary restraint. If a writer stated in a story that he had "done shot a bar" in the woods, then the reader needed to hear it just that way and would know darn well that the speaker hadn't fired his rifle at a rural watering hole.

Altogether, despite my college degree and a complacent, know-it-all attitude, I still had plenty of marketable skills left to master, from trying to raise my pitiful typing speed to learning to get to work punctually. Yet I still managed to find the time, sitting at my desk covered with unsolicited manuscripts, to mourn for my decimated love life.

As unprofessional as that may seem, the magazine's small staff was so close-knit that I didn't need to hide my misery. Everyone there feared and avoided Jack, the editor, a crotchety, aging patrician who no doubt displayed a menagerie of menacing-looking beast heads in his house to prove his once-keen marksmanship. Everyone wished they could get out into the actual field or stream more often, to get their fingernails dirty practicing the earthy pleasures we were preaching instead of making a dull, antiseptic living dispensing advise about them. (Everyone, that is, except Aggie, the ultra-efficient office manager, and Andi, a young, newly engaged assistant editor, who apparently lived to shop.) And everyone (except tyrannical Jack) knew about my misfortunes in romance.

David, the managing editor, was particularly supportive. A true sportsman and good-humored *mensch*, he corrected me gently whenever my inexperience in the field, stream or journalistic matters glared through. He covered for me when I made egregious clerical errors, such as neglecting to file another editor's expense report for weeks, prompting him to demand I be fired. And he overlooked it when I took extended lunch breaks to catch a breath of fresh air (or what passed for fresh in Manhattan).

On one such excursion in early June, I set out in search of a Father's Day gift. My dad was a successful businessman who lived and labored in Manhattan. Like my co-workers, however, his passions put him far afield of this concrete jungle. An avid sport fisherman, he had dragged our family nearly every summer of my childhood up to a charmingly rustic fishing lodge in northern Maine. His luxury Midtown apartment was filled with paintings of fish and other wildlife to create the illusion that he could look out his window onto a tranquil lake. In short, he was the ideal reader of *Field & Stream*, and my landing a job there was among the only things I ever did that truly impressed him.

Never mind that he rarely had the time to venture outside Manhattan. To help bolster Dad's self-image as Davy Crockett, my brother and I had concluded that the ultimate present for the upcoming occasion was a top-notch fishing reel. So, armed with advice from several editors, I had set out for Herman's World of Sports, then Midtown's most popular purveyor of equipment for the outdoorsman.

When I entered the fishing department, though, I found that both the stock and the staff left much to be desired. The racks lay in noticeable disarray, the cash register deserted. The only other person visible among the rods and reels was another customer.

Searching in vain for any item on my suggested list, I didn't pay much attention to this fellow until we ended up facing each other across a narrow aisle.

"They call this the top sporting-goods store in the city?" he grumbled aloud. "It's pathetic. There's hardly a Penn in the place."

Dressed in a nicely tailored, light gray suit, he looked to be in his late 20s. He was also quite tall and exceedingly thin, with a fairly prominent nose. Yet altogether – I now noted for the first time – he fit decidedly within the realm of attractive.

"Nope, barely one to be had in the whole joint," I concurred. "Then again, if you're willing to drop that kind of dough on a reel, why not go for the good stuff?"

"And that would be?" he asked, arching one brow.

"Garcia Mitchell," I said, "obviously."

"Oh, right," he concurred. "Of course."

"Daiwa also makes decent tackle," I said, "if you don't mind buying Japanese."

At this point, the meager merchandise had lost all appeal. I had his full attention.

"Huh! Most good-looking women I meet don't know much about fishing gear," he said. "No offense, but you don't exactly look like Nature Girl."

"No offense taken," I said. I was too busy trying not to blush at the compliment. "Actually, I've done my share of fishing over the years," I confided when I could find my voice again. "Now I just help other people have all the fun. I work at *Field & Stream*."

"You're kidding!" he exclaimed. "That's amazing! I read that all the time."

I was used to this kind of gushing from men, but taken by surprise at his next line.

"In fact, I happen to be in the process of starting a new sports magazine myself."

Now it was my turn to gush. "You are?" I asked. "Seriously? *That's* amazing. What is it? When will it hit the stands?"

"What?" he replied. "Let's just say we're not quite at the 'hit the stands' stage yet. I'm still busy getting the funding together."

"Oh, I see," I said. "That still makes you a rival. A spy from the enemy camp. And here I am, giving away insider information." I held an index finger up to my lips. "I'd better start watching what I say."

"Indeed you had," he said, whipping a ballpoint pen and small pad out of a pocket and pretending to jot down notes.

"Actually, my magazine won't be in direct competition," he said. "It isn't specifically about hunting and fishing. We plan to focus mostly on professional sports."

"Oh, phew!" I said, wiping my brow in feigned relief. "But I guess that means the crew over at *Sports Illustrated* had better watch out."

"For sure," he said. "But, as you see, I have my own personal affinity for fishing. In fact, I wouldn't mind picking your brain about that."

"Pick away," I said. "I'll tell you everything I know. Fortunately, that won't take long. I need to get back from lunch."

"That's OK," he said, "Maybe I can call you at the magazine sometime."

"Oh," I said. "Sure. If you'd like."

"Or," he ventured, "if you're not busy, we could have dinner tomorrow night."

There came that blush again.

I wavered. I wasn't accustomed to going out with complete strangers, especially in New York City. Let's face it: These days, I wasn't accustomed to going out, period. But maybe a new romance was just what I needed. And he seemed refined... and so nice.

"Actually, tomorrow night would be fine."

"Excellent," he replied. "So, how do I reach you?"

Out came his pen and little pad again. He promised to call the next day.

—❦—

I was so excited walking back to the office that I forgot to slip in surreptitiously. No matter. The minute I had relayed news of my encounter to Andi, the assistant editor, she sounded the general alarm.

"Hey, everyone! Guess who's got a new boyfriend!"

Surrounded, I told my tale, then I braced myself for a lecture about the dangers of getting involved with strangers. It never came. Instead, Glenn, an affable, prematurely balding editor, hurried into his office and returned, waving the latest issue of *New York*.

"I think I just read about that new magazine," he said, flipping to its gossip-oriented "Intelligencer" column. "Just look. Is this the guy you met?"

Indeed. The names matched.

"Honey, you hit pay dirt," Glenn announced, patting me glibly on the shoulder.

"You sure did," Andi piped up. "That guy has got to be loaded."

I shrugged and laughed shyly. "Could be," I said. "I don't really care about that." I returned the magazine, sat back in my chair and picked up a manuscript to edit.

Around me, I could sense everyone exchanging glances. I tried to tune them out, yet wasn't absorbing a single word on the page. "But that doesn't mean I won't go out with him," I added, not daring to look up. "He's actually pretty cute... for an editor."

———⟡———

The call came as promised the following morning. We arranged to eat dinner in my neighborhood. He'd meet me at my apartment building around 7, he said. Then we would decide where to go.

I cringe now to think of the dress I chose to wear that hot June night: a sleeveless, royal blue polyester shift with a multicolored floral print and self-belt that tied in back. Accented with a pair of shiny black patent-leather flats, it made me look sweet and innocent. I cringe even more, though, to think of how sweet and innocent I *was*.

My hair was wet from the shower, but I didn't dare turn on a blow-dryer for fear I wouldn't hear him arrive. I expected him to buzz me from downstairs in the front lobby, so I was a little startled, shortly past 7, to get a knock right on my apartment door.

"One of your neighbors was coming in just as I arrived," he explained, after I had spied him through the peephole and unlatched the door. "So I decided to do the gentlemanly thing and come up and get you."

"How nice," I said as he strode past me, although it felt a bit invasive to have him barge right in. I watched as he glanced right and left, taking in the modest furnishings, which I'd done my best to replace. "I assume you had no trouble getting here."

He had shed his business suit for a button-down dress shirt and neatly pressed slacks. But his brow looked moist, his cheeks pink from the city's summer sizzle.

"None, other than that I couldn't find a cab, and the subway was the usual inferno," he said, brushing a few strands of damp, dark hair back from his forehead. "I'm about ready to pass out from the heat. Could I trouble you for something to drink?"

"Oh, sure," I said. I led him into the narrow, cabinet-lined alcove that passed for a kitchen in New York City. "Water OK? Or should I see what else I have?"

He watched as I bent down and peered into the fridge. Like most single, young Manhattanites at the time, I tended to eat out almost daily. The shelves were nearly bare. "Water's just fine," he said. I closed the door and reached into the cupboard for a glass. "Then again, that bottle of wine in there looked awfully nice."

I had never been much of a drinker, nor, on my meager salary, much of a spender, either. The bottle to which he referred was a then-popular yet unequivocally lowbrow Almaden Chardonnay. But in the summer heat, I had to admit, it did look inviting. I pulled it out carefully, feeling the film of moist condensation cool against my fingers. Then I exchanged the tumbler I'd taken down for a narrow glass goblet. There was no need for a corkscrew. This little vintage was so unpretentious that the top screwed off.

"Aren't you going to join me?" he asked with a low voice, once I had filled his glass and begun to replace the cap.

I hesitated, then glanced at the golden liquid glistening in his glass as he raised it to me enticingly. "Well, all right," I answered. "Might as well, since we're opening it."

I took down a second goblet. He performed the pouring honors for me, then wandered into the living room, cupping both glasses gingerly in one hand, the bottle grasped firmly by the neck in the other.

Before joining him, I found a couple of wedges of cheese and arranged them neatly on a plate with some crackers. My mother had brought me up to be a good hostess. Besides, I always made it a strict policy not to drink on an empty stomach.

By the time we had traded all the introductory basics, we had managed to drain our glasses and polish off a generous second round. The cheese was also disappearing rapidly, I noticed. For a skinny guy, he sure could eat.

The natural light filtering through my window was also beginning to dissipate as dusk swiftly enveloped the city, its shadow falling like a giant net dropping onto a live, writhing animal. Watching him chat, silhouetted against the darkening skyline, I decided that his distinctly WASPy features looked remarkably handsome, prominent nose and all. He appeared to be growing noticeably fond of me, too. At least whenever I spoke, he stared intently into my eyes. And when I reached out to flick on a nearby lamp, he caught my hand and stopped me gently, then slipped an arm hastily around my shoulder.

"For a tough-talking Nature Girl, you're awfully sweet," he said, lifting my chin firmly to his until our lips drew together like magnets clicking together, north to south. His mouth tasted of sour grapes and Jarlsberg. So, I suppose, did mine.

It had been a while since I had been kissed, and several years since I had kissed anyone other than my recently departed paramour. Feeling his arms tighten around me, I realized for the first time just how much I had missed all that. How much I had missed being touched. Normally, my better judgment would have told me that I had no business doing quite so much touching with a man I had met only the day before. My better judgment, however, had just finished downing two glasses of Chardonnay.

When I felt him fiddling with the zipper at the back of my dress, though, I knew that things had gone far enough. "Don't," I murmured, freezing and trying to pull away.

"Don't what?" he asked playfully, easing the metal tab halfway down my back.

"Do that," I said. Pushing him away more forcefully, I managed to extricate myself from his insistent grasp. "Seriously. Cut it out. I'm not taking anything off."

"Nothing?" he asked coyly, either misjudging my resolve or deciding to ignore it.

"No." Standing and stepping back, I reached behind and slid my zipper up again. "In fact, it's getting late," I said. "Shouldn't we go to dinner?"

Raking his fingers through his hair, he stood and walked languidly toward me. "OK, we'll go, if you insist," he said. Then he cradled my chin and raised it again. "Soon."

If you've ever been inside a studio apartment, you know how cozy they can be. Everything you need for everyday living is all there, combined in one room. These nifty, streamlined spaces are also known as "efficiencies." The question is, efficient for whom? Under normal circumstances, I would never have let a man I'd just met into my bedroom. Problem was, I already had. My bed, in plain sight of the couch, was just a few feet away.

Within minutes, somehow he was stretched across it, and inexplicably, so was I. Out of sheer modesty (I remain, after all these years, a shy and proper girl at heart), as well as lingering, acute humiliation, I will spare you the unsavory details of the lengthy tussle that followed. After all these years, I'm still trying to sort them out myself.

The problem was not just that, at the tender age of 23, I was monumentally naïve (not to mention, lame defense though it may be, much the worse for wine). I was also, at this point, physically turned on and emotionally torn. And despite some decidedly ungentlemanly behavior, my gentleman caller still appeared to be an appealing prospect. Articulate, well-educated, and presumably poised to soon make his mark in my chosen field of endeavor, he was not someone I wanted to risk alienating just yet.

Years later, I still wonder if I could have controlled the situation, maintaining my purity, dignity, and future romantic options with him by using a firm yet clever retort. Instead, the only shred of dignity I can claim is that he never did manage to remove my little dress. Then again, he didn't need to. The night was too hot to have worn pantyhose. My light cotton panties must have slid right off.

Sometime in more recent years, the expression "date rape" was coined. It even became a common practice for women to accuse men with whom they had agreed to go out of sexually assaulting them. Perhaps this term is a bit too strong to use under the circumstances. In any case, I would have had slim chances of pressing charges. I was so young and foolish that, afterwards, I tried to act like I didn't mind what had happened.

I did mind, though – so much so that, along with my sense of dignity, I had lost my appetite and begun to feel ill. When he announced that it had grown too late to go out for dinner, after all, I readily agreed, and greeted this news inwardly with great relief.

It was late enough, in fact, that after he left, I climbed right into bed. I didn't fall asleep for hours, though. Going over every detail in my mind, I couldn't stop wondering. Why had I let him? How had I managed to let things get so out of hand? And almost worst of all, what was I going to tell my coworkers about my evening the next day?

As often happens during a restless night, I eventually drifted off to a fitful sleep, then accidentally overslept. I had hoped to slip into the office unobtrusively, but by the time I arrived, I faced a full, captive audience.

"Finally, here she is!" Andi cried as I peeled off my cardigan sweater, arranging it neatly on the back of my chair.

Hearing her call, Glenn bounded out of his office like a puppy eager to play. "So, how was it?" he asked, planting himself cross-legged against a corner of my desk.

"Oh, that's right. Tell us all about your big night!" agreed Aggie, rolling toward us from across the room, still seated in her office chair.

Even David wandered out of his office, hands in his pockets, to join the crowd. They all looked so hopeful that it was hard to look back. "It was fine," I said.

"Fine?" asked Glenn, mocking me. "You go out on a hot date with some studly guy who's about to start his own magazine, and all you can say is 'fine'?"

I shrugged, and managed the hint of a smile. "It was *mighty* fine?" I said.

"Come on, give us all the gory details," urged Aggie. "Where did he take you? What did you eat?"

I hadn't actually bothered to plan out a single word. But I felt like I had no choice. So I took a deep breath, let it out, and began to describe the date that should have been.

"OK, he rang me from my lobby right at 7," I began. "I was all ready to go and ran right down."

"What were you wearing?" interrupted Andi. "Something reasonably stylish, let's hope." This was a girl whom I'd once heard have a shrieking meltdown at her boyfriend over the phone for canceling a dinner date, sobbing that she had worn a special new outfit that day – as if she ever wore anything else. Raggedy Andi, she was not.

"I wore pants," I answered decisively. "Nice, long black ones, and a white silk top with a zillion buttons. He had on a striped oxford shirt and khakis. Very Brooks Brothers. He looked good."

"Sounds great," said Glenn. "So, where did you and Mr. Brooks Brothers go?"

"Oh, you know," I said. "He hadn't made any reservations, so we just wandered around my neighborhood, checking out menus. Finally, we settled on Café Mimosa."

"Oh, I love that place!" piped up Andi. "And I just adore those mimosa drinks! But you know me. I love anything with Champagne."

"Me too," I agreed. "But he wanted wine, so we split a bottle of the house white." Why not, just for fun, throw in a smattering of truth?

"Nice," Glenn said. "And what did you eat?"

"Let's see," I answered, stalling. "He ordered the seafood crepes, stuffed with scallops and shrimp. I prefer to eat light when it's hot. I went for the salad Nicoise."

"French! That sounds yummy," said Aggie. "And romantic. What about dessert?"

"Oh, by then I was completely stuffed," I said. "He ordered the chocolate mousse. I just had some decaf. Then he walked me home."

"And then?" ventured Glenn.

"Then, what?" I asked.

He leaned toward me and lowered his voice. "Did he kiss you goodnight?"

"Oh, come on," protested Andi. "Isn't the girl entitled to a little privacy?" She shifted her perfect Barbie Doll body to face mine. "So, did he kiss you goodnight?"

"Never mind that," said David. "The real question is, are you going to see him again?"

Not if I can help it, a small voice inside my head squealed.

"Oh, I don't know," I said calmly instead. "I'm not sure he's exactly my type."

"Are you kidding? He'd be my type," said Andi, fluttering her gleaming ring finger, "if I wasn't already taken."

"You're probably right, he would," I said. "I know he sounds like quite the catch. "The thing is… Let's just say, he comes on a little bit strong."

"Strong?" asked Aggie. "What do you mean?"

At that moment, Jack sauntered in, in his usual stony-faced fashion. "Morning," he grunted, to no one in particular, and disappeared into his office.

Never before had I been so happy to see the humorless old coot.

"OK, people," said Aggie, "party's over."

There were groans all around. I closed my eyes and let out an inaudible sigh as my audience scattered.

Despite my lack of sleep and inner turbulence, I had my work cut out for me. I spent the next hour writing captions for a story about cooking possum. I kid you not. As if I weren't already feeling queasy enough. Then, just after 10, my phone extension rang.

The woman on the other end asked for me. I told her that she already had me.

"I'm sorry to bother you at work," she began. "But it's the only number I had." She paused, then mentioned the man I'd been out with the previous night and asked if I knew him.

My still-empty stomach tightened with dread. "Know him?" I asked, not entirely sure I wanted to answer the question. "Not well, really. But yes, I guess I know him. Why?"

"Because I live with him," the woman said. "I'm his fiancée."

"His...? Oh, my God." That was all that I could manage.

"That's right," the woman said. "I suppose he didn't happen to mention me."

"Mention you? No," I said, "he definitely did not."

"I can't say I'm surprised," she said. "And obviously, I see that you are."

I was what? Surprised? Surprise is supposed to be something happy. You get to be surprised by a birthday party or an unexpected gift. You're surprised when things turn out for the better. My only surprise in this case was that the situation could get any worse.

"Stunned would be more like it," I said. I could hardly hold onto the phone. "How, if you don't mind my asking, did you happen to get my name and number?"

"Yes, you must be curious about that," she said. "I guess I might as well tell you. I found them in his sport coat last night after he got home."

"You mean you searched his pockets," I said.

"Yes," she said. "I have to admit it. I did. I'm sorry if that sounds pathetic to you. But there's something that you need to understand."

"Understand?" I asked. "What do you mean?"

"Just this," she said. "Don't think you're the first girl he's ever done this with. Don't imagine that you're special. He does it all the time."

"Does what?" I asked.

"Whatever you did," she said.

"We didn't do anything," I said. "We just went out to dinner."

"Dinner," she repeated with a sharp, bitter laugh.

"Yes," I said. "We did."

"Oh, come on," she said, sounding tired. "I find that hard to believe."

"Why?" I asked, becoming more insistent. "It's true."

"That you went out to dinner?" she asked. "That's impossible."

"Why?" I asked.

"I'll tell you why," she said. "You couldn't have gone out to dinner because he's broke. I mean totally broke! He doesn't have a penny to his name."

Why was she saying this? How could it be true? He looked so polished, like the perfect country-club member or prep school grad. "What about the magazine?" I asked.

"The magazine," she snorted. "Oh, yes. He's been working on that for years. Working on getting it started, I should say. He hasn't done any real work – the kind where you actually get paid for it – since I can remember. I pay all the bills," she said. "That's why he lives with me."

"Oh, boy," I said. "That must be awful."

"Yes," she said. "It is. It's awful. It's also why I don't believe you went out to dinner last night. He doesn't have the money to go out to dinner. If he did take you out, I'll kill him," she said. "He hasn't taken *me* out in five years."

OK, I could easily imagine her frustration. Still, how's this for the annals of believe it or not? This woman seemed far more incensed at the thought that her fiancé had taken another woman out to dinner than by the prospect that we might have had sex.

"I'm really sorry to hear that," I said. "But let me assure you that we did have dinner together last night. He didn't pay for it, though. I did."

"You?" she asked.

"Yes," I said.

"Oh, come on," she said. "Why would you take him out for dinner?"

That was an interesting question. So was this: Why didn't I just open up and tell her the truth? Why lie to someone I had never met about someone whom I hardly knew?

I don't think I was trying to protect him. It was more about trying to save face. The truth seemed too humiliating to admit.

In fact, it was too humiliating to admit even to a stranger who possessed so little pride herself. Think about it. Sure, it must have required a lot of nerve to phone me. Still, this girl was engaged to a man who sponged off her habitually, cheated on her regularly, and lied to her shamelessly about it. How much self-respect could she possibly have left?

The other reason I didn't come clean was that once you begin to lie to people, it's really hard to stop. In order to tell the truth at that point, you have to admit that you were lying in the first place, and that's just way too embarrassing. So, instead, you have to keep the fibs flying, like a street juggler keeping brightly colored balls looping in the air, lie upon lie upon lie.

"I don't know why I took him for dinner," I said. "Why do you pay all the bills?"

"Because I love him," she said. "As pathetic as that may sound. But what about you?" she asked. "Why would you pay for his dinner? You hardly even know the guy."

She had me there.

"You're right," I said. "But he seemed so nice. I did feel a little weird paying for him, but he said that he'd accidentally forgotten his wallet, and he promised to pay me back."

"Pay you back?" she scoffed. "Oh, yeah, right. Don't count on it, honey. He's been promising me that for years."

"I see that," I said.

"The question is, what happens now?" she asked. "You might as well know, I confronted him after he came home last night. I told him that I'd found your number."

So they'd already discussed this. Talked about me. "What did he say?" I asked.

"Oh, he denied everything," she said. "He made up some ridiculous story about how your meeting had something to do with his magazine, but I knew that he was lying. What I'd like to know is what you plan to do next. Are you going to see him again?"

As his fiancé, and his sole financial supporter, I guess she had a total right to ask.

"See him?" I asked. "Let's see. He deceived me, he's chronically unemployed, and he's engaged to be married to another woman. Why would I want to see him again?"

"I don't know," she said. "Maybe because, as you said, he seems nice."

I wasn't about to tell her that without her help, I had already managed to discern otherwise.

"Let me assure you," I said, "if I hear from him again, you have nothing to fear." Not from me, anyway. "If you still want him, don't worry. He's all yours."

Throughout the call, I had been careful to keep my voice low enough to prevent anyone around me from catching anything of substance. Still, the color of my face, or sudden lack thereof, must have betrayed me.

"Who was *that*?" demanded Andi the moment I hung up. "You were starting to get so worked up there, I thought it might be your date."

"Actually, you're close," I said. "That was his fiancé."

This was more than enough to make her sound the general alarm. Over the next twenty minutes, I had to repeat the story at least three times, with certain details omitted, of course. I didn't want to raise the issue of who had paid for the dinner, lest it come to light that this was a dinner no one had ever actually eaten.

David was most decent about it, managing to disregard the fact that my love life was beginning to imperil that month's production schedule. "If you need to get a breath of air," he offered gently, "feel free to take an early lunch."

"Thanks," I said, "but if it's all the same to you, I think I'll just stay at my desk."

Even if I longed to escape the pitying glances of my cohorts, the outside world seemed far too treacherous. I'd also had more than enough of getting caught unawares. I needed time to compose myself and prepare something to say, just in case my date called.

—⟲—

As it happened, time is what I got. By the time that he phoned me again, eighteen months had passed.

In the interim, I had briefly reunited with my old college flame again. Can you blame me for seeking refuge in the safety of a familiar face and someone closer to my age, despite his antics with the moving van? But at 23, he was still far too young to even speculate about our long-term prospects together, and we finally broke up for good.

Meanwhile, I also moved on from *Field & Stream*, which similarly offered a safe haven, but little promise of a future career. A childhood of fishing vacations in Maine would never be enough to let me rival Jack, let alone rise above perky Andi in its ranks.

In fact, my working days there turned out to be numbered. I was mystified when David stated that I'd learned enough to seek my fortunes elsewhere, then began allowing me time to write letters seeking employment to other magazines during the day. I realize now that, with my continued indifference toward my clerical duties, he must have been under pressure from the frustrated editors that I served, but not had the heart to fire me.

One of the many letters I sent landed at a popular urban magazine the day that an editorial assistant there happened to quit. I would soon learn that at a busy weekly, even if they tell you they'll keep your résumé on file, they never have time to look at any file. When a position opens up, they simply hire whomever turns up at that particular moment. On the day that someone quit that August, the first someone who turned up was me.

Two weeks later, I bid goodbye to possums and pickup trucks forever.

Once again, I soon discovered the truth behind a media façade, although here it occurred in reverse. The magazine's staff may have masqueraded as the ultimate arbiters of taste, yet one of the trendiest, slickest, and most condescending publications in New York City turned out to be produced mainly by a bunch of oddballs and social misfits who dressed indifferently and rarely ventured out for a fashionable night on the town.

I also discovered how little I'd realized that in some respects, at *Field & Stream* I'd actually had it good. Being a monthly publication, it only went to press every four weeks. The other three weeks, no one ever worked past 5. At the weekly, we were on constant deadline and under nonstop pressure. Most nights, I didn't leave before 9.

So when my former date called me out of the blue one morning and said that his sports magazine had finally reached the hiring stage, you can't necessarily blame me for exhibiting some interest. He had noticed my name on the masthead, he explained, and thought that he might have the perfect job for me. Was I free to meet him to discuss it?

Despite the way he had behaved, I was still too ambitious to simply walk away. But I was also no longer quite so naïve. I suggested that we have lunch instead of dinner.

Even so, the moment we hung up, I began to feel consumed with regret. Was I crazy to consider going to work for a man so lacking in integrity? Did he really have a job to offer, or was this just some strange, demonic ploy to take advantage of me again?

The night before we met, I slept fitfully once again and woke up with a sense of dread. I was so anxious that I could hardly manage to dress, let alone apply makeup. That, I'm convinced, is why it happened. Racing down the narrow steps from my new apartment, I caught my heel and tumbled down a whole flight of stairs. I ended up canceling our meeting from the emergency room at Roosevelt Hospital with a fractured metacarpal, a small bone in my right hand. Not a major injury, but a huge inconvenience. It kept me in a cast for weeks.

By the time our meeting had been rescheduled, nearly two months had passed.

The afternoon we met, a Wednesday in mid-March, fell on one of those early spring days when the sun is so dazzling and the air so mellow that it seems like a sin to stay indoors. So when he suggested that we forego finding some crowded lunchtime eatery in favor of taking sandwiches to a park near my office, I readily agreed.

Seated a safe distance apart on a cast-iron bench, we started off once again exchanging pleasantries. I didn't dare ask about his girlfriend, but noted that he wore no ring. Even so, my only interest at this point was in his magazine. I figured that he was waiting until we finished eating to get down to business, but somehow my turkey on rye dwindled down to the crust without his so much as mentioning the subject of a position. I was the one who finally had to bring it up.

And even then, his sales pitch seemed faltering and far from polished. He nattered on, sounding distracted and vague. Perplexed, I queried him about the publication's design and image. He apologized for neglecting to bring anything concrete to show me.

"I stupidly left the mock-ups in my apartment," he said. "Why don't you come up and let me show them to you? I live only a few blocks away from here. Come on, it's still early. We have plenty of time."

I looked at my wristwatch. I looked at him.

Do you really think I'm that stupid? I wanted to howl.

Was I that stupid? I thought.

Slowly, I gathered the debris from my eaten lunch and stood to face him. "Please, just tell me now," I said. "Is there really a magazine? Do you really have a job for me?"

I could see the blood rising in his cheeks. "What are you talking about?" he asked. "Of course there is. Come up now, and I'll show you."

I raised a hand to my brow to block the sun, which was nearly blinding. I wanted to look him right in the eye. Then I looked away. "No, actually, I don't think I will."

"Are you sure?" he asked. He stared up at me coldly and slowly shook his head. "I guess you just don't want the job that much."

The fact is I didn't want *anything* that much. And years later, I still wish that was precisely what I'd said. Instead, I kept it short and not too sweet. "Nope. Guess I'll pass."

When I returned to my desk, it wasn't even one o'clock yet, and the office was still nearly deserted. But even as my colleagues began trickling in, no one stopped by to grill me about how my lunch had gone. No one even knew where I'd been.

So I settled back down to work, realizing that nothing much had changed. I still didn't have a boyfriend. I didn't have an exciting new job, or any prospect of getting one. At least I had regained something missing from my life, a small measure of self-respect. And maybe, just maybe, I had a future in that.

Husband Material

⎯⎯⤸⎯⎯

It's one of the most highly esteemed magazines on the planet. Brilliant articles. Irreverent and urbane cartoons. Yet every time I read a movie review in it, I'm tempted to throw back my head and howl. It's not that I rarely agree with its appraisals of the current cinema. Neither was I ever irked by one of its former film critic's flourishes of linguistic frippery, such as when he once criticized a movie for its prevailing "mood of self-pitying haplessness." On the contrary, I usually agreed with him, and often preferred his verbal musings to the marvels of celluloid mediocrity about which he wrote. The thing that unnerved me was that I happened to know this film critic. He and I once had a history together. Or, to be precise, a potential history. It was aborted before it could lead to a lengthy and satisfying future. Aborted deliberately. By me.

At the time, I was simply too young and shallow to perceive or pursue such a sound future. All's well that ends well, but what about the things that never even begin? Contemplating my foolishness at the time, my utter lack of moral values and foresight, how can I possibly help but wallow in a mood of self-pitying haplessness?

This man and I met more than thirty-five years ago, when I began working at a similarly prominent, though less high-brow publication. Although he was only a few years past 30, and noticeably nerdy, he was already making a name for himself writing film critiques. Quotes from his reviews found themselves reprinted frequently enough in newspaper advertisements to make his byline almost a household word.

To attract someone of his stature – although unprepossessing in height, he loomed far above me on the magazine's masthead – there were only three notable attributes of which I could conceivably boast: a) a sardonic sense of humor and b) and c) a noticeably ample bust. I can't say which of these qualities piqued his interest, but he paid inordinate amounts of attention to me and, within a few weeks of my arrival, summoned the nerve to ask me out.

I told him I was flattered. I told him he was sweet. But, I told him, it was against my better judgment to date anyone on staff.

My remarks were sensible, and the prudent wisdom they conveyed was sincere. In fact, I would be tempted to reach back in time and pat myself on the back if I didn't know that the last of those statements was categorically untrue. Instead, the only thing I have to be proud of in this scenario was that I already had sufficient feminine wiles and a firm enough grasp of office diplomacy to concoct such a credible excuse.

To be fair, I did hope to remain working at the publication long-term and dreaded the prospect of prolonged daily contact with a man I didn't expect to date indefinitely. But the sad fact was that I was too young to notice that he was a prime specimen of a rare, precious commodity that I would one day promote regularly to my own daughter. Something I call "husband material." Intelligent, hardworking, dependable, and Jewish – with a promising future, no less—he was a good catch and a potential good match.

Yet when you're only 23, as I was then, being dependable is the kiss of death. Fresh out of an erratic and rebellious adolescence, I didn't have the slightest interest in linking up with anyone on a permanent basis, let alone with a respectable young man guaranteed to be nice to me and to win my parents' unequivocal approval.

I wanted danger. I wanted thrills.

I wanted to date "Coulter James."

Coulter, as I'll call him, was also on staff at the same magazine, yet that wasn't about to discourage me. An ace reporter with a keen ear for cadence, he was also brilliant and eminently employed, but everything else about him exuded "rogue." Tall and brawny, with a mop of café-au-lait-colored curls, Coulter had virile, angular features and smoldering eyes the shade of the

Guinness stout they kept on tap in his favorite local pub. His hard-drinking nature and preppy-sounding moniker – actually his middle name – accentuated my certainty that we were from two different worlds. But this foreignness only enhanced his irresistible appeal. Whether he might ever reciprocate my affections seemed irrelevant. Juxtaposed against the perilous aura of this dissolute Adonis, all visions of romance with the steady, bookish film critic instantly faded to black.

Unfortunately for my virtue and my volatile imagination, Coulter did more than enough to encourage me. Openly flexing his flirting muscles with me, both inside the office and on after-hours excursions with other members of the staff, he gave me the impression that almost anything was possible. In fact, judging from the lascivious way he sized me up at times, there were only two things that prevented our public verbal jousts from progressing into intimate relations in private: his female roommate and mine.

Yes, word around the office was that Coulter had a live-in girlfriend. But it was rumored that this relationship had recently fizzled and that he was looking to move out.

⤳

My living situation was going through some interesting transitions of its own.

Working at a trendy magazine had its advantages: glamour, sophistication, and occasional entrée into what was then the world's most exclusive dance club, Studio 54. Yet sufficient pay to sustain a decent lifestyle, let alone my taste in clothes, was not one of them. Unattached and underpaid, I had quickly concluded that the only way to afford city life was to find someone willing to split the rent. And so, like many another single, young Manhattanite, I had resorted to hiring a professional roommate-matching service.

When I went to visit the first option on my list, I thought that I'd won the lottery. The door was opened by a statuesque, 6-foot beauty who turned out to be just my age.

"Dominika" was an artistic young woman of Russian descent who went by her first name only. She told me that her modeling career required her to travel abroad for at least half of every month. When home, she said she was busy working on a book and would welcome my help with editing. Despite her building's rather shabby exterior, the apartment was well-lit and spacious, boasting six rooms, two of which would be mine. All mine.

Gabbing with her for nearly an hour convinced me that we'd become fast friends. Days later, I moved in, only to encounter the sorry truth behind these many myths.

Dominika was not the affable, chatty girl she had seemed to be. She had run away from home at age 14 and lived a hard life. Far from being out of town for two weeks a month, she rarely if ever left the apartment, let alone changed out of her bathrobe. Although she had enjoyed some success as a fashion model, these assignments appeared to have mostly dried up. The one true statement she'd made, apparently, was that she was writing a book. It was an autobiographical work about how she really supported herself, by working as a high-priced call girl who flew overseas every few weeks to have sex with wealthy Arab men. Her agent was urging her to consider the title "My Arabian Nights."

As for the six rooms, although I was paying half the rent, only one became designated as my exclusive territory. This was just a glorified closet, barely large enough to hold a double mattress, and separated from the living room only by a thin, sliding door. Upon arriving home each night, I would quickly sequester myself in this refuge, hoping to avoid another confrontation with my strident suite mate. Yet rarely did my solitude last for more than a few moments before she would swoop out from her bedroom and begin banging at my doorway, determined to pick a fight or demand some domestic servitude.

One Saturday morning, rather than waiting for me to awaken so she could verbally accost me, she chose to post a large, scribbled notice on the refrigerator door. "I expect you to scrub the kitchen and bathroom fully – toilet, sinks, mirrors, floors – rather than trying to shirk your duties like you did last weekend!" (Who was I, Cinderella?) Another time, she had a minor-league meltdown and insisted that I move out at once. She couldn't continue to share her quarters, she said, with someone who would purchase pink toilet paper. It wasn't a color I usually favored myself, but I'd happened to find it on sale.

I tried to believe these affronts were nothing personal. After all, Dominika detested the rest of humanity, too. The only person able to escape her wrath was an older British woman who lived across the hall. As much as she loathed me, Dominika appreciated almost everything about this dry-witted Brit, except for her paunchy, middle-aged husband, whom she overtly held in contempt. No wonder she grew even more irascible than usual when this woman returned to London temporarily to attend to her ailing mother. So imagine my astonishment when I came home one Saturday night to find Dominika and her dear friend's husband huddled in our kitchen, kissing fervently.

Never mind husband material. This was hussy material for another sordid book.

My embarrassment about witnessing this encounter and feeble attempt to escape it lasted only a few minutes, until they had finished necking and he left. Then, pounding furiously on my cardboard-thin door, Dominika barged in and related her latest dilemma.

Why worry about a silly little thing like adultery when the world might be coming to an end? The date was March 31, 1979, and the whole country was in a panic. An accident at the Three Mile Island power plant in Middletown, Pennsylvania, the worst ever experienced in U.S. history to date, was threatening to unleash a nuclear meltdown. The governor of that state had advised many residents to evacuate the surrounding area, but as conditions at the plant remained unstable, the sense of peril extended much further. As far away as New York City, people had begun fearing for their lives, terrified that an explosion might release massive quantities of radioactive material into the atmosphere.

Dominika had no intention of sticking around to find out what might happen next. She wanted to flee the country immediately. I'm not sure whether she planned to seek refuge with her Arabian paramours, or perhaps to have a showdown in person with her absent British neighbor over the errant husband's affections (although what any one of the three members of this cheesy love triangle saw in any other was truly beyond me).

The way that I entered into the equation was this: Dominika didn't have enough money on hand for a plane ticket out. She proposed that I fork over the coming month's rent, and the following month's as well. This wasn't phrased as a polite suggestion. If I didn't do it right away, she intended to take my television and drop it out the window.

The TV in question was a nice Sony Trinitron that had been a gift from my father. Our apartment stood three floors up. So I was inclined to cooperate fully. The problem was that this tale predated the ATM – the automated teller machine – by several years.

There was no way I could get my hands on that kind of cash until the bank opened on Monday morning. But it took quite a lot of pleading to convince Dominika of that. Somehow, both the Sony and I managed to survive. By Sunday evening, things were back under control at Three Mile Island, but still ready to explode inside our apartment. A day or two later, I moved out.

With the aid of the roommate-matching service, which readily waived any added fees under the circumstances, I left Dominika's despotic domain on the Upper East Side. My new roommate appeared to pose no potential threats to my property or me. A bubbly, nice Jewish girl like me, and only a year or two my junior, Carol was only 4-foot-10, a petite aspiring opera singer with a gargantuan soprano voice.

Our apartment, in a brownstone on the newly gentrified Upper West Side, was much smaller than the cavernous accommodations I had shared with the Russian Amazon. Yet it was far better situated and infinitely more appealing, both inside and out. A cozy duplex of which I would occupy the downstairs half, it was femininely furnished with faded chintz chairs and other castoffs from Carol's parents' house in the suburbs. Here, for the next six months, I would take the place of her friend Nanette, a redheaded young actress who'd landed a role in the road show of some musical theater production.

The only problem with my new quarters was that Carol's upstairs bedroom was connected to mine by means of a winding metal staircase. This stairway looked stylish, but had been fashioned without a door on either end. The lack of privacy discouraged me from entertaining male company at home. It also obliged me to listen to the never-ending strains of Carol's voluble vocalizations. As lovely as her voice may have been, the frequency with which she practiced her craft would have tried the patience of even the most avid opera lover.

Even more disconcerting was the fact that this gave me a ringside seat from which to take in the impassioned sound effects that emanated from Carol and her own boyfriend during intimate moments. As sweet-natured as she was, she apparently did not share my penchant for privacy. And as with her highly audible crooning, whenever she had a feeling deep within her soul to express, she let it sing right out.

This lack of inhibitions, extending well beyond her bedroom borders, earned Carol a large flock of friends, into which she was more than willing to welcome me. Chief among these cohorts was her cute cousin Bobby. Until recently, he had been the adoring boyfriend of No-No Nanette, but upon my arrival he summarily decided to date me during her absence. Evidently, he came with the furniture. Or maybe that was me.

Together, we often went to watch Carol demonstrate her talents during open mike night at a local bar. As opera is not exactly favored in venues favored by young folk, she'd been obliged to expand her repertoire. Most celebrated was her rousing rendition of "Feelings," a schmaltzy tune made popular by singer Debby Boone in the late 70s. It never failed to bring down the house.

As talented as she was, I often wondered how so diminutive a diva was ever going to achieve any real stature as a professional opera singer. Would she be sought out to play romantic roles opposite some pint-sized Pavarotti? Would she be obliged to perform "Carmen" or "La Boheme" standing on an egg crate or perched precariously upon stilts? She herself seemed surprisingly undaunted by this issue. Yet to support herself during years of training, she had fortunately developed some alternative professional skills. Her father was an executive at a prominent company, and although Carol held no steady job, she often assisted him at trade shows.

In late October, toward the end of my residence there, one such commitment, a convention out in California, was scheduled to keep her out of town for an entire week. I hadn't had a full night of privacy in nearly six months and meant to take full advantage.

That brings me back to my pursuit of the elusive, compellingly handsome Coulter James.

I had mentioned to him in passing how excited I was that she was going away. The morning after she left, I sat down beside him in the office and got right to the point. "Well," I announced, "she's on the West Coast, so the coast is clear."

He apparently knew what I was talking about and didn't need much prodding. "Cool!" he exclaimed. "We should have a party. Help you celebrate. What do you say Philip and I pop over at around 11 for champagne?"

"Sure," I said nonchalantly, doing my best to disguise that I was both elated at this overture and perplexed that he wanted to include an extra guest and to schedule our meeting for so late at night. "Who's bringing the champagne?"

"You," he said with a wry smile. "I like it dry." Then he relayed the news to our co-worker Philip. Being married, Philip begged off, saying he was otherwise engaged.

"But you two go right ahead," he added, flashing us a naughty wink.

Working in the offices of a major weekly may be glamorous, but it's no picnic. With assorted sections of the magazine going to press in staggered stages, three different nights of the week, we were almost always staring down the throat of a looming deadline. The rest of that day proved typically hectic, with little time for chitchat. So I was surprised to see Coulter waving me over at around 6 when I passed his desk on the run.

"Hey, really," he queried offhandedly, "should I come over tonight, or what?"

"Oh, sure," I replied, trying to sound just as casual, even though I was floored. "Why not?"

He said that he had a dinner meeting, but would try to stop over at around 10:30, unless his dinner ran late.

I couldn't help wondering if his dinner "meeting" was actually a date.

I had a date for dinner myself that night, but I managed to extricate myself early and rush home, stopping by a local package store to pick up a split of Great Western.

Ten-thirty came and went with no sign of Coulter. I was beginning to figure he wouldn't show.

Then, a little before 11, the door buzzed.

We made ourselves comfortable on the living room sofa. It felt awfully strange to have him with me in Carol's quaintly furnished apartment. I couldn't quite believe he was sitting there, and I naively blurted that out in the course of conversation.

"What do you mean?" he asked, deftly uncorking the undersized bottle.

"I don't know," I lied. "Something to do with different worlds colliding."

Years later, "worlds colliding" would serve as the theme for several episodes of the sitcom *Seinfeld*, in which Jerry and his nebbishy pal George grow disconcerted that characters from different spheres of their lives are straying into other spheres. In one classic segment, Jerry becomes unnerved to meet the pool guy from his health club at a movie theater, and his former girlfriend Elaine, realizing that she has no female friends, alarms George by inviting his fiancée, Susan, to join her at a historical clothing exhibit.

In this instance, the phrase merely served as a perfect conversational conduit for us to begin discussing the hazards of two people from the same office having an affair.

In this regard, we both confessed to an almost obsessive predilection for privacy. Coulter expressed his urgent faith that I would have the self-restraint to remain discreet. I nodded, all the while thinking, "Discreet? Discreet about what? Nothing's happened yet." And maybe nothing ever would, since moments later he unleashed a histrionic diatribe.

Before anything further could transpire, he demanded to know what my feelings were for him. These were his toward me: He was interested in me, and attracted to me. Yet he was not about to fall in love with me, or expecting under any circumstances for us to become seriously involved.

"Don't think I'm all excited about this," he declared, the candor spewing from his mouth like crushed cubes shooting out of an ice machine. "I'm seeing lots of other women at the moment, including one I have a date with next week who I *am* excited about. I want to be sure you understand. I'm not going to think about you after this, or call you all the time." He raked his fingers through his hair, taming a stray curl cascading down his forehead. "We might 'get close' tonight and then never do it again. So don't expect anything."

"I won't," I said, glad for once that my voice had always been deep for a girl's.

Still, he eyed me gravely and folded his arms, surprised but not quite convinced.

"If you don't think you can handle it, we can just finish off the bottle and talk, and then I'll leave. Otherwise – "

"Don't worry, I can take care of myself," I asserted, cutting him off in mid-sentence. I didn't want to hear another word. At the same time, I wondered, "Can I?"

Despite my tremulous inner voice, the reassuring words I had uttered aloud should have been enough to quash his misgivings. But maybe he wasn't quite the rogue I took him for, because instead they merely provoked yet another tirade. He proceeded to rant and rave about how women were always claiming that they could take things casually, then ended up getting hurt and bitter and calling him up crying in the middle of the night. So he needed to make sure that the rules between us were clear from the start. He didn't want to feel any responsibility toward me, and he didn't want to lead me on.

Listening to this, I found myself feeling a bit sorry that I had changed apartments. It might have been nice to invite him back another night and unleash Dominika on him. Whether as a sadistic adversary or sexual partner, she would have been his perfect match.

This, mind you, was decades before the advent of hook-up dating Web sites like Tinder or that chillingly non-romantic term someone would coin, "friends with benefits."

There was something vaguely admirable about the brutal honesty of his bravado. It would have been refreshing had he not betrayed himself to be so profoundly cocky and vain. Instead, almost any woman with a lick of sense or self-respect would have quickly shown him the door. But I had just spent much of the previous few months hopelessly infatuated with him. Short of his revealing himself to be a rapist, racist, or anti-Semite, no mere speech would have been sufficiently repellent to instantaneously break the spell.

"Listen," I said frostily, summoning every ounce of pugnacity I had developed during three years of New York City life. "I can take responsibility for my own actions. Whatever happens between us, or doesn't happen between us, consider yourself absolved. I just think I'd better warn you, though, that you may have some misconceptions about me. The fact is that I'm seeing a lot of other people too these days. So don't expect too much from *me*. If you want to see me again, I suggest you call two weeks in advance."

It was as if we were two medieval warriors. We had each thrown down a gauntlet. Now it was time for the duel.

"Well, if that's the way it is," he said, then he reached up and flicked off the light.

And, in a flash, overcome by pent-up passion and rage, I felt myself surrender.

Surrender to the utter bliss and tenderness of his kiss, his tongue, his touch.

Oh, how could any creature with such harsh instincts have such a gentle touch?

God, he was good. I remember a close friend once trying to describe her first night with an incredibly adept and caring lover. "You know how some guys are mostly good at all the, uh, advance work," she had asked, "while others excel at the main event?" I had smiled and nodded knowingly, all too familiar with this classic case of either-or. But Coulter turned out to be a different species entirely. He was a true master of it all.

In fact, for our rookie time together, we seemed to make a remarkably good team. He apparently thought so, too, and by the time he had left, later that night, he was singing a vastly different tune. Any semblance of pleasure I could derive from this denouement, though, was decisively undercut by the reason that he had felt obliged to leave. Matters with his former girlfriend turned out to be slightly different from what I had understood. He was continuing to live with her only until he could find a place of his own, he insisted. But he also admitted reluctantly when I asked that their apartment had only one bedroom.

—◦—

Anyone who saw us at work the following day might have assumed that we had never even met. I wanted to prove that he could take me at my word. I was no clinging vine or needy wimp. I *could* take care of myself. I was so determined to outdo him in the total detachment department, in fact, that I continued to avoid him all week. The sorry truth remained, though, that I had a clock ticking on my time alone. Carol was due back on Sunday afternoon. So I eventually caved in and summoned the nerve to mention this. Initially, he shrugged at the news. But he came over to visit again on Saturday night.

Once more, we dropped our combative social armor, and I surrendered reluctantly to the fleeting miracle of ecstasy in motion. But immediately afterwards, he slipped out of my bedroom again while rebuckling his trousers, obliged to be home long before dawn.

___6

Carol returned on schedule, and once again my sentence to nightly solitude resumed. But my allotted interval in her apartment and her life was drawing swiftly to a close. Although my sojourn there had proven to be immeasurably more melodious than my previous arrangement, I now had reached my tolerance level for rooming with virtual strangers. My twenty-fourth birthday was rapidly approaching, and I'd been sharing my living quarters with assorted non-relatives since entering college at age 17. Before long, I was bound to meet the right man, someone with whom I would be delighted to share not just the rent, but the rest of my life. Until then, like Greta Garbo, I "vanted" to be alone.

After checking the going rates for modest rentals near my current neighborhood, I had come to the conclusion that I could swing this on my current salary with just a bit of financial aid. My father, who could easily afford to help, readily agreed to spot me an extra hundred bucks a month until my monetary intake caught up with my needs. And so I found myself spending the majority of my free evenings and weekends house hunting.

Coulter also apparently was eager to find a place of his own. When I encountered him during office hours, we confined ourselves to the topic of our respective searches for new abodes. Then, late one night, after a dinner out to celebrate a co-worker's birthday, we found ourselves heading uptown at the same time and decided to share a cab. When we reached my place first, I tried to hand him my share of the fare. But he pulled a bill out of his own wallet, dismissing mine with a faint smile. "Feel like company?" he asked.

After fumbling with the key, I was relieved to find Carol out for the evening. With Coulter's consistent history of making fast getaways, I figured that he would be long gone by the time she returned, anyway. Little did I know how right I was.

This time, we made no pretense of settling onto the couch for a pregame makeout. Instead, he headed straight for the bed, and I followed. This being early December, the temperature outside had plummeted sharply, and the darkened room had a distinct chill. Within moments, we were both undressed and entangled beneath the covers.

I felt him stroke my hair softly with one hand while the other playfully traced the sloping line that dipped at the small of my back. Wrapping my arms around his neck, I chose not to think about what I was letting myself in for, but just to relax and succumb. But when I bowed my face to meet his in a kiss, he suddenly drew away and sat upright.

"What the hell am I doing?" he muttered aloud, more to himself than me.

Startled and shivering, I drew the covers around me. "What's going on?" I asked.

"Going on?" he asked. "Nothing's going on. It's just that… this isn't right."

What was this, the reigning king of noncommittal, casual sex, having actual pangs of conscience?

Hard to imagine. Couldn't be. But then who was this stranger in my bedroom?

His face remained turned away toward the opposite wall, making his next words sound slightly muffled. "I've been seeing this girl," he said. "This woman, I should say. The one I met last month."

She was the same woman he'd mentioned that first time he'd come over, the night on which we'd drunk the cheap champagne. At that point, they had just been introduced. But he had continued seeing her ever since. Seeing her a lot. And somehow, gradually, she had found a way not only to break through his emotional chain mail and the chip stuck squarely on his shoulder, but to slip right under his skin.

"I didn't realize it until now, but I think that I actually love her," he was saying. "Yes, that's it. I think I do. So what am I doing here?"

And with that he picked up his clothes, pulled them on abruptly, and left.

Coulter, it turned out, was husband material too, but not husband material for me. All it had taken was the right woman – a delicate beauty who probably acted like she could take him or leave him – to turn a callous, pompous cad into a reliable, lovesick sop.

Of course, I felt hurt and humiliated at first. But before long, I took it in stride. With a new apartment on West 88th Street to decorate, the very first I could call my own, and no one within easy earshot to impede my social life, I had plenty to keep me busy.

The ironic thing was that now that I was no longer interested in Coulter James as a romantic prospect, I had no reason to go out of my way to pretend I wasn't interested. Even better, I had no possible reason to act around him like anything other than myself. In light of our few intimate episodes together, I felt comfortable enough to let down my guard around him. Gradually, I got to really know him and to really like him, and we became true friends. We grew so close, in fact, that when he and his girlfriend were married the following October, I was among the few co-workers invited to the reception. One day, he even burst out with an apology for the appalling way he had once treated me. And when I eventually left the magazine for a better job, we continued to stay in touch.

Carol's Cousin Bobby, meanwhile, who had once seemed perfectly content to "love the one you're with," in the inimitable words of Crosby, Stills and Nash, quickly forgot all about me and married the lovely, newly returned Nanette. I've never known what became of Carol herself, although for years, every time I saw an opera production advertised, I would check the cast for her name. Neither do I know if Dominika ever published that manifesto about her wild Arabian nightlife. I never saw her again.

Eventually, Coulter and I lost touch, as well. Many years, even decades flew by. Then, suddenly, I noticed his byline cropping up regularly in a newspaper where I live. After a few months of seeing it, I could wait no longer, and I gave the paper a call.

How surprised and pleased he sounded to hear my voice. He was still married to the same lovely woman. They'd been together for nearly 25 years. A few months earlier, they had relocated to my state to be closer to one of their children, who attended private school there. Coulter was working out of a distant bureau of the newspaper and lived more than an hour away from me. But he often traveled to the main office, not too far from my home. The next time he was in town, we would have to get together, he said. Maybe we could have lunch.

We exchanged sporadic emails over the coming weeks. Once, we even picked a tentative date for our lunch together, only to have it postponed by his work obligations.

The day after that plan to reconnoiter was scrapped, I went for a walk with my good friend Stacey. Far from my professionally arranged housing liaisons from earlier days, all strained and strange friendships of mere convenience, ours was the real thing. We had met at a local Jewish book festival years earlier and hit it off instantaneously. Along with speaking often to exchange the mundane details of our daily lives, we regularly trudged four miles around a nearby reservoir to stay fit while exchanging ideas, airing our innermost sources of anxiety and making personally incriminating confessions. Stacey knew all about my affairs with Coulter, past and present, and she had made it no secret that she regarded our intention to reconnect with unadulterated suspicion.

A former lawyer who was married to a judge, she arrived for this exercise session armed with almost incontrovertible evidence that she had reason to distrust Coulter's motives. As I'd mentioned, he had recently published a lengthy personal memoir. Leafing through the previous Sunday's paper, she had stumbled upon a review.

The critic had found plenty to admire in this lively work, which was filled with fond recollections of my old friend's formative years as a journalist. "Not since Forrest Gump – or perhaps Johnny Wadd – has there been a hero like [Coulter James]," it began.

I had never heard of Johnny Wadd before, and had no way of knowing that this was a reference to a character in a series of porno films made in the '70s and '80s about a lecherous private eye. The remainder of the review, however, made this abundantly clear.

It went on to praise the book's "vivid and sometimes comic depictions," and to pronounce its author "a graceful writer who can really give wing to a story." Neither was there any shortage of personal insights or exhilarating scenes through which the author traced his gutsy entrée into a challenging and provocative career.

Yet the manner in which my old chum had wended his way from complete obscurity to Page One status was evidently the least "provocative" of the subject matter. The review went on to state that, as proficient as the writing might be, "sadly, this compelling tale of [James's] quest to practice journalism with a capital J is often blown astray by an ill wind of sexual braggadocio. Besides far too many steamy pages, there's an entire chapter devoted to an account of the author's first coupling with one of his many paramours."

Evidently, his litany of anecdotes detailing his rise as a reporter had managed to be overshadowed by even more explicit sequences documenting his exploits in the sack. What's more, these prurient passages appeared to be totally gratuitous, rather than integrally woven into the journalistic theme. "Despite the author's claim that the soft porn episodes portray character development," the review said, "they seem more like a cheesy attempt to liven up the manuscript and shore up the author's credentials as a Casanova."

Most alarming to the feminist sensibilities of the male reviewer, however – and far more personally, to me – were "the offensive descriptions of his many,

many women, most of whom are no more than archetypal clichés of their religious or cultural heritage."

Thus there are "Smith College Goddesses," "Australian Beach Babes," a "Porcelain Protestant Beauty" and a handful of "Jewish American Princesses." [He] spends more time than a horse trader discussing the superlative breeding lines of his bed mates, so maybe it's no surprise that his "fillys" have "pony shivers" when [James] drops by.

All the colorful details were apparently far from restricted to cultural references. Whatever Coulter had applied to ethnicity, he had far surpassed when it came to anatomy. "Who knew there were so many ways to describe breasts?" the bemused reviewer noted. Within these pages, there were more variations in the shapes, sizes, and underlying personalities of mammary glands than there were ice cream flavors at Baskin-Robbins. "He's careful, for example, to distinguish between the 'muscular, smart-aleck' variety and the 'perky, smart-aleck' type," he said.

My first impulse was to run to the nearest bookstore and fetch a copy right away. But on further consideration, I realized that digesting the gory details of these sensual reminiscences second-hand was already almost more than I could stand.

Was it possible that our brief relationship all those years ago had found its way to become one more bit of sensationalist fodder for his book? Had I been one of the many "Jewish American Princesses" in his stable of sex partners, or just some run-of-the-mill "filly" to whom his caresses had given "pony shivers"? Had he found my breasts to be the "smart-aleck" type, and if so, had they ranked as "muscular" or "perky"?

Yes, I'll admit that I dared to think that I might have rated a part in his memoirs. And honestly, who among us would not be flattered to figure as a protagonist in an old friend's novel, or just to be considered memorable enough to play a colorful cameo role?

Then again, it's one thing to have commanded center stage in the sum total of someone's early life, and another entirely to realize that you were merely an extra, a walk-on role among a cast of thousands, in a salacious kiss and kiss and kiss and tell.

To be honest, I had never doubted that, had Coulter James been an action figure, he would have been Super Ladies Man, able to mount tall women in a single bound. Never had I imagined, from the moment I'd laid eyes in that magazine's newsroom on his winsome face, his tousled hair, and the long, thin, artistic-looking fingers on his hands, that I was anywhere close to the first foolish woman to fall prey to his seductive allure. Yet not until I read the book review in the paper that day had I recognized him to be quite such a sexual over-achiever or latter-day Lothario.

Had I perceived this way back then, I would like to believe that I never would have wasted my precious time pursuing him or submitting to his charms. Like everyone else, I like to think of myself as someone special in many ways, a woman who would be admired by men of discriminating taste, not indiscriminate lust. My only small comfort, assuming that he remained a man of integrity after his epiphany in my bedroom that final night, was that I may have played a pivotal role in his hyperactive romantic life, after all. Next to his wife, I might have been the very last in his very long line of lovers.

If I didn't have the heart to do research into this by reading the book, my dear friend Stacey was more than happy to do the honors (or dishonors, as it might be) for me. It was hardly a matter of literary self-sacrifice. She was still hell-bent on proving her point and unearthing fresh evidence to help her snatch me from the jaws of potential marital infidelity.

Within a week, she reported back. To my surprise, and immense relief, my reputation was safe. "The book only goes as far as the very first newspaper that he worked at," she said. Not to mention the countless women he had met and mated with while on and off that job. "He wrote 416 pages," she said, "and didn't even get to you."

There was always the threat that this memoir was just the first in a long saga. Who knows how many more hundreds of pages he might add to it in the coming years? He might still get to me yet.

In the meanwhile, I could only wonder why someone I knew to be a hard-nosed journalist had found it necessary to juice up a serious book with such cheap thrills. But I wanted to try to give him the benefit of the doubt. Maybe his publisher, to make the weightier subject matter more saleable, had strongly encouraged him to lighten the tone by adding some steamy stuff. Maybe writing about his many past exploits was a form of antidote to the reduced capacities and pleasures of middle age. Along those lines, perhaps the best way to sublimate his wanderlust after 25 years of being (presumably) a faithful husband was to vividly reconstruct and wallow in the many glories of his past.

Whatever his motivation, it seemed that Coulter, in writing his book, had delved enough into the past for both of us. I suddenly lost all interest in rescheduling a reunion. Without any explanation, his online messages to me were also abruptly curtailed. And although his byline continued to land on my doorstep, I never heard from him again.

⸺ᦁ

Coincidentally, not long after he vanished from my life, the film critic reappeared. This is not to say he made actual contact. He also had written a book, a personal memoir. And although its contents were not nearly as racy, perhaps due to his status as a film critic at a prominent magazine, he began making all the customary media rounds. Between morning shows, late-night talk shows, and newspaper interviews, like a rock star promoting his latest hit record or clothing line, he kept cropping up everywhere.

I must confess that I elected not to read his book, either. But given the endless amount of press it received, I knew what it was about. I also knew from the endless interviews that the film critic was no longer married. After many years together, he and his wife had recently divorced.

And even though I was married myself, I looked at him on TV with a discerning eye, and this is what I saw: He was still intelligent, hardworking, dependable, and, yes, Jewish. His prospects, which had once appeared promising, had in fact given way to an eminently successful past and present. So he was still a good catch and a potentially good match. But he was also still extremely bookish, and was still not my type.

I guess when it comes down to it, my notion of "husband material" is a bit of a joke, a myth, a generalization, with no more substance or validity than "one size fits all." The steady, responsible film critic would probably make someone else a fine husband someday, but there was no conceivable way that that woman would ever be me, not to mention my diabolical old roommate Dominika.

Of course, no woman in her right mind truly wants to marry a man who is dishonest, deceitful, unsympathetic, or unreliable, or who can't seem to hold a steady job. Yet all those qualities I referred to as "husband material" are really more about what most parents hope to find in a son-in-law. There are men who are built to last for the long haul, and others who should be considered little more than short-term dates. There are also those men, I've now learned, whom you shouldn't even date short-term. But true husband or wife material? It's just an amalgamation of traits that are intangible and difficult to define. It's something slightly different for everyone. It's that combination of inner and outer attributes that makes a person content to awaken every morning, day after day, year after year, to the same face, the same voice... the same snore.

It is not something you're likely to find in a bar, or a book, or by watching TV, or for which you might come across replacement parts at Home Depot.

And although you might find it online, it is also not something you're likely to locate by having unlimited sexual escapades with Australian beach babes, a porcelain Protestant beauty, or a handful of Jewish American princes or princesses, although finding it for the first time just might send "pony shivers" racing up your spine.

I don't know what it is. I don't know where to find it. But I can easily understand why anyone forced to live without it would wallow in a mood of self-pitying haplessness.

Love, Love Me Do

⤜᧵

IN MY TWENTY-FIFTH YEAR ON earth, I decided to turn dating into an Olympic event. Nearly every night after work, I met a different man for dinner, sometimes followed by a movie or show. I did not run out of conversation. I did not put on weight. The only thing I really worried about was my reputation, which, despite a lifetime of listening to my mother's dire warnings, had always seemed to me like a hard-boiled egg – immaculately white and pure, solid to the core.

One Saturday morning, I awoke in bed with an old friend from college, rushed out to eat brunch with another man, and then spent the evening in the company of a third. The next day, a fellow I had recently met had invited me for brunch at his place, after which we toured a museum exhibit of modern architecture, filled with photographs showing sleek structures of glinting, reflective glass – black and white, steel and light. Later, the night remaining miraculously uncommitted, I went home to my tiny apartment, locked the door, removed the phone from its cradle and cried. Perhaps I was not quite ready for the structure of life in the 1980s. Or lack of it. The shape of things to come.

Or maybe that wasn't it at all. Maybe it was just 1979, and I was gearing myself up for what would prove to be America's most egocentric, self-indulgent decade to date.

Who knows? Let's talk about this, instead: The pursuit of something finite. *Endful* love. The complete evasion of risk in our everyday lives and loves. Prepaid one-way fare. Getting off next stop, please.

⤜᧵

And so it went, for quite some time. I spent the better part of my mid-twenties racing nonstop from one brief and meaningless encounter to the next. As if I were a FedEx man with a truckload of empty packages to deliver, I kept giving nothing of substance, and would get nothing much in return. I tried to convince myself that this was fun, yet I neither slept, nor read, nor thought nearly as much as any serious person should.

"Why on earth do you do it?" demanded my practical friend Russ one Sunday night as he watched me prepare to go out in the rain for the weekend's final assignation. "Why can't you just say 'No'?"

Ah, the power of cold objectivity. No, you see, is not the proper answer when you are sacrificing almost everything in the pursuit of popularity. And rather a high-schoolish mode of popularity it was. Now that I had overcome the former nerdiness of my youth enough to be able to get a date with someone, I wanted to date just about *everyone*.

Why any of them wanted to date me is another question altogether, one to which I can only speculate on the answers. I did not dazzle them with my boundless beauty. I was far from gregarious, let alone socially at ease. But I had long red hair and a trim physique. I projected an aura of innocence and vulnerability that hovered over me like an invisible halo no matter what I did or with whom I did it. I also had a pair of pert knockers sizable enough to arrive wherever I went about five seconds before I did.

The problem was that after months of frenetic socializing, I still had not managed to attain what I'd been seeking all along – a sense of self-worth and well-being, or more than just a glossy veneer of acceptance among others. There was, instead, a soul-gnawing conviction inside me that my acquaintance was limited to that of foolish men with a shared fatal flaw: the misapprehension that my company was worth paying for. And pay they did, although all most of them got in return was my company over dinner and some lively conversation. I ate well during those years.

⌥

Not all the men I met could afford to wine and dine me in style, but material matters were inconsequential to me. Brains, wit, and integrity were the only forms of currency my heart was willing to accept. I was so busy, though, between going to work and this nonstop socializing, that sometimes I forgot to do a character credit check – to consider whether the man of the moment had enough to offer in this last crucial category.

Take "Albert," for instance. I did, for as long as I could. I met him one day at an office party held at the magazine for which I worked. He told me that he had convinced an editor friend who worked there to arrange the festivities just so he could meet me. Then he invited me home for dinner.

"You're my girlfriend now," he said.

A little blunt. Presumptuous, too, wouldn't you say? Yes, that was Albert for you. But at least I knew where I stood.

English and eccentric, Albert was, like too many of the men I met, a free-lance writer by trade. He was not especially handsome, but his charming British accent and acerbic wit, as bone dry as a martini minus vermouth, lent him a cultured, sophisticated air. A full fourteen years older than I was (meaning more than half my 24 years), he was nearing 40, but had never married. Instead, he preferred to live alone in his remarkably cluttered apartment. Yet now he had me to visit often and be at his virtual beck and call.

This, I soon learned, also put me at the *beak* and call of one William J. Eckles.

Mr. Eckles, as I was told to call him, was a nasty, nippy parakeet or similar variety of tame, talking bird who had a fresh mouth and a free run (or should I say fly?) of Albert's unkempt residence. At dinnertime, he was permitted to land on people's plates, and woe to any visitor who dared to shoo him off. He ruled the roost to such an extent that his was the only name in the household that was listed in the phonebook. I would have taken this as a clever ploy to let Albert avoid being reached by irate readers and bill collectors (only close friends would know to contact him via his avian alter ego) had he not treated Mr. Eckles with far more affection or respect than he ever afforded me.

One day, soon after we met, Albert called me to pitch a story idea. It was early November 1979, and in the aftermath of several dozen Americans having been taken hostage at the U.S. Embassy in Tehran, he said he had learned that hundreds of calendars of Iranian design were being returned to the Metropolitan Museum of Art's gift shop. This tidbit sounded like a timely idea, maybe even a scoop, and I helped arrange for him to get a writing assignment for a section of the magazine featuring short, gossipy blurbs.

When he called me late that night to "chat me up," as he liked to say, though, it came out in the course of conversation that he had exaggerated the situation substantially. The "hundreds" of rejected calendars to which he had referred consisted of precisely 13 that one single woman had returned in a shopping bag.

That wasn't much of a story, I told him. I suggested that he call the museum to get more examples and verify that there was an actual trend. This made him extremely huffy. Facts, he said, were never that interesting, and it was up to journalists to make them so.

"As long as you don't make them *up*," I said, beginning to regret that I had let myself get involved with this sorry excuse for a story in the first place. Or Albert himself.

At 1:30 a.m., my phone rang again. I picked it up, still seven-eighths asleep.

"Whose side are you on, anyway?" demanded an inimitable British baritone.

"Side?" I asked. "Albert, what are you talking about? You just woke me up."

"Oh, really?" he asked, seeming incredulous. "Sorry." But he didn't sound sorry. "I was just sitting here wondering in what way you're going to interfere with my story."

"Interfere?" I asked. "I never said I was going to interfere. I only suggested – "

"Suggested, did you?" he interrupted curtly. "Why don't you just stay out of it? Do you hear me? JUST STAY OUT OF IT!"

That's when I got fed up and quickly hung up. I might not stay out of it, but I would surely stay away. Life with Albert, I suddenly realized, was strictly for the birds.

And so I moved on…and on… to Stuart, a lawyer, and Jim, a banker. Then came Jeff, an investigative reporter, who was a decade older, flat broke, and sometimes openly hostile to me, but still remained irresistible because he was a political activist who had once helped found the SDS, Students for a Democratic Society, during the Vietnam War. (There's something intrinsically seductive to women, or at least to me, about political insurgency; on some level, I think I fancied that he was my own private Che Guevara.)

In the meanwhile, I was beginning to lose faith in my own taste in men. For some reason, I realized, I never seemed to fall for anyone who wasn't eccentric, neurotic, peculiar, passive aggressive, if not overtly abusive, and almost impossible to live with.

⤚ᴄ

Certainly, my inner radar must have been malfunctioning when, sometime during this dark, blue period, I chose to pursue "Sky Gray." The best thing I can recall about our odd, three-month quasi-relationship is that I spent most of it refusing to see him.

Sky, as I'll call him, was then one of New York City's most eligible bachelors. With his ice-blue eyes, clean-cut, perfect features, and dark, soap opera–star perfect hair, he was a major heartthrob – a hot, young meteorologist whose stellar rise on local TV news had been nothing short of meteoric. Yet I was just as enamored of his warm and winsome personality as his glamorous persona. Quick with a quip, well educated, and renowned for his involvement in charitable causes, he was a nice Jewish boy all grown up. In my admiring eyes, he was the perfect male package: a total *mensch*, yet totally hot.

He was also totally inaccessible. Then again, with a little ingenuity and a lot of chutzpah, maybe not totally.

One of the most appealing aspects of my job as an assistant editor at the magazine was getting to call assorted celebrities periodically to ask them all the same trite question. I had long been under the mesmerizing spell of the charming and eminently telegenic Mr. Gray when I chose to parlay one such assignment into a legitimate excuse to contact him.

This particular article, called "My Secret Vice," required me to prevail upon three dozen or so prominent people to divulge their secret passions, "soft-core indulgences that make us feel wicked or foolish but never seem

140

sinful enough to abandon." Pop artist Andy Warhol admitted to having secret urges for frozen Reese's Peanut Butter Cups. Dick Cavett, perhaps the most intellectual talk-show host ever to take up residence on late-night TV, confessed to stealing extra shower caps from hotel maids' supply carts.

Author Isaac Asimov, one of the forefathers of American science fiction, owned up to working in his underwear and, if the doorbell rang, greeting his guests in his work clothes. And socialite-slash-fashion designer Diane von Furstenberg became probably the first famous personality ever to announce shamelessly and publicly that she enjoyed popping zits. "Sometimes in elevators," she gushed, "I'm tempted to say to people, 'Would you mind if I squeezed your pimple?'"

Although some answers rolled readily off these prominent people's tongues, I was obliged to keep many luminaries on the phone for quite some time until they hit upon a suitable and reasonably amusing reply. In the case of Sky Gray, he came up with an answer promptly, yet I managed to keep him on the phone anyway until he asked me out.

Well, maybe "asked me out" is a bit of an exaggeration. I kept him on the phone, showering him with as many coy, witty comments as I could muster, until he remarked that we seemed to have a great deal in common and really ought to meet sometime.

"Really?" I replied. "When?"

"Excuse me?" he asked.

"*When* do you think we should meet?"

"Oh," he answered. "Hmmm, let's see. How about tomorrow night, after the show?"

The minor vice to which he had confessed was a big weakness for Chinese food. He invited me to come to the television studio earlier, in time to watch him do the news, instead. To help him recognize me (or perhaps simply to guarantee that the encounter would be in some way worth his while), he suggested that I bring along some egg rolls.

I guess I passed muster on his initial inspection. The egg rolls merely served to whet his appetite, though, so after the show he took me out to eat. It turned out that we did have a surprising number of things in common.

Working schedules, however, were definitely not among them. With the late news ending nightly at 11:30 p.m., we didn't finish eating until nearly 1 a.m. Exhausted but loathe to let our encounter end so quickly, I agreed to accompany him back to his place.

Now, no matter what kind of impression that may give you – no doubt precisely the same impression that it clearly gave him – I had never been in the general habit of going home with men whom I had just met, especially this late or on the very first date. Yet try for a second to put yourself in my shoes (the wobbly, high-heeled pumps I had put on, hoping to make myself look sexy). I was out with one of the handsomest and most sought-after men in New York. I'd watched him with heart-thumping adoration from afar for years. I found him to be even cuter and more appealing in person than he was on TV. And he genuinely seemed to be drawn to me, too. Should I actually have called it a night?

Maybe if I had, I wouldn't have ended up on my deathbed someday, years hence, thinking, "I guess I had an OK life, but I wish I'd gone home with Sky Gray." Then again, they say it's the things that you *don't* do in life that you always end up regretting.

If that is the case, then let's just say that the remainder of that night left me very little to regret. Hoping to win his approval and possibly even his heart, I not only stayed with him all night but also acted like I imagined a typical celebrity's girlfriend might act. That is to say, I acted a good deal looser than I ever had behaved in my entire adult life. I also stayed up much, much later than I customarily ever did on weeknights. And I had absolutely no trouble keeping him up, too… if you get my drift.

Still, I must confess that, all these years later, only one truly memorable moment remains stuck in my brain: getting to sit in his bedroom the next morning watching him expertly blow-dry that flawless, Ken–doll, soap opera–star perfect hair.

"I'll call you," he promised solemnly as he kissed me goodbye early so I could race home and change my hopelessly wrinkled clothing and high, wobbly shoes before going to work.

Once again, I resorted to my new, gutsy edge. "You will?" I asked. "Really? When?"

"Later," he replied. "I promise. Don't worry, you'll see."

Like many a slick television star, no doubt, he was *almost* as good as his word. "Later" turned out to be two weeks later. I felt heartbroken at first waiting for his call. Yet by the time those two long weeks were up, I'd already begun seeing someone else.

So when he finally phoned to ask me out, I bluntly turned him down. He evidently found this hard to believe, and even seemed to think at first that I was kidding or just being a tease. But I held firm. And so did he. And so we soon fell into a regular routine.

Every night at around 11:31 p.m., right after the eleven o'clock news ended, my telephone would ring. The caller would invariably be Sky Gray, phoning to ask me out. He would coax me, try to coerce me, and sometimes even curse me. But I would always insist that I already had a boyfriend and resolutely refuse.

I never proposed that he stop calling because my boyfriend got a kick out of knowing that I turned Sky Gray down every night, saying that I preferred to be with him. I also must confess that I enjoyed talking to Sky, whom I continued to watch almost nightly, and not just because I needed the weather report to plan the next day's wardrobe.

I guess I got a pretty big kick out of being pursued by him, and unsuccessfully wooed by him, too. Also, after our months-long negotiation, I was no longer smitten with him the way you are with someone from afar. I had gotten to know him and to truly like him. Under his superficially glib facade, I had found that, far from being impressed with his own good looks and social cachet, he was self-deprecating and surprisingly insecure.

Eventually, after a few months of this game, I grew tired of my other boyfriend. Soon after, when Sky's nightly phone call came, I shocked him by actually saying yes.

Once again, I met him in the TV studio. And once again, we went out to eat. It was so late by the time that we ordered, though, and I felt so tense about finally seeing him again, that I didn't have the slightest appetite. Even so, I was made to eat almost every word I had said to him during those nightly calls, or at least to pay for them dearly.

Maybe, after all those months, I was less attractive than he had remembered. Maybe, after having his nightly overtures rebuffed so many times, he wanted revenge. Yet what self-respecting form of revenge would possibly be complete without a little makeup sex? And so, I must confess, we ended up spending that night together, too.

For years after that, one of my friends would often introduce me to people as "the girl who slept with Sky Gray." That, in fact, sadly enough, was essentially at the time my greatest claims to fame. (Perhaps even sadder for me is that he was unquestionably never introduced to anyone as the man who'd slept with me.) But after that second night together, other than continuing to spy him on TV, I never laid eyes on him again.

6

My willingness to settle for these unsuitable, unsatisfying and mostly superficial relationships did not stem from a lack of emotional depth on my part. If anything, it was simply a way of guarding against my usual tendencies to fall too often and feel too much.

It had been less than a year since my first long-term, live-in romance, with my college boyfriend, had ended for good, and although I might deny it, my spirit was still fragile. That relationship, despite the usual flare-ups and fluctuations, had kept me reasonably content for two years. Although there had been plenty of habits (his, mine) and unhealthy ways of interacting (ours) that could have used some major adjustments, none had been quite troublesome enough to ever tempt me to flee or even wish to be free.

Once things between us had fallen irreparably apart anyway, I'd gradually come to relish the intoxicating thrill of being young and single in a city of endless possibility. New York City, to me, was a round-the-clock romantic feast, a sort of all-you-can-eat buffet for the heart, where you might meet someone new and intriguing, if not several such prospects, every single day.

The problem was that everyone else there seemed to be well aware of this, too. That made them similarly hesitant to form serious attachments, on the grounds that the moment you became officially involved with someone, you might encounter someone even more compelling in the next singles bar, or subway car, or passing on the street.

Personally, I made it a strict policy to avoid bars of any kind. I also tried to limit both eye and bodily contact on the subway and the street. Yet I met enough interesting men through work and friends to make resorting to such measures unnecessary.

As plentiful as the romantic prospects might have been, though, I had come to the sobering conclusion that modern city life was no fairy tale. Although the murky East River might be as forbidding as any medieval mote, my fourth-floor walkup apartment was no castle. There was also no handsome prince galloping into my life on horseback as of yet, so I might as well kiss a whole lot of frogs, I figured, or at least let them take me to dinner and a movie.

Recent experience had also taught me that it was pointless and even potentially self-destructive to invest myself too much in any one of these temporary, in-the-meantime relationships. Why set myself up for almost inevitable heartbreak? Few people, I'd decided, unless they are genuinely in love, want to bear the emotional burden of anyone else's trust and devotion. Besides, the moment that you show bare, naked need for anyone, or let that person know that you expect something – that he or she "owes" it to you to behave in a certain way, regardless of his or her natural inclinations – that person will begin to feel confined, which is akin to trapped. And when people feel trapped, love is about the last thing on their minds. All they want to do is escape.

I hated to even imagine anyone wanting to escape from me. Neither did I want to feel that way about anyone myself. So, although I was perfectly receptive to all the tingling and tummy rumblings of a heart-rousing new romance, I wasn't quite ready to meet Mr. Right. At this point, I was just looking for Mr. Good Enough for Now.

Too many men measured up to this basic job description, however, so I realized that I would need to establish a few basic dating ground rules. Actually, just two.

The first rule was that going out simply meant going out, and did not necessarily mean *putting* out. That is, I could spend an infinite number of evenings out with an infinite number of men, as long as I always (well, almost always) spent the night alone.

There was only one dependable way to enforce this credo. That was rule No. 2.

Rule No. 2 was that I could accept any and all invitations for six nights a week.

The seventh night, however, was to be kept strictly reserved.

Saturday night was to be kept strictly reserved for one of two people. I'd go out that night with whomever I considered to be the leading man in my life at that moment. Or, if there was no one around to play the romantic lead, I would spend Saturday evening with my friend, Lisa. Unless, of course, there was currently a leading man in *her* life.

Usually, we both remained emotionally uncommitted. So usually I saw Lisa, a trim, pretty woman my age with wavy, honey-blonde hair so long that it grazed her butt.

Lisa and I had been best friends since we were 9. I have a Polaroid of us dressed in colorful, cotton sun-suits to prove it. Lisa and I had spent most of the fourth grade doing headstands in her bedroom after school, listening to the album "Meet the Beatles." Undergoing middle school, high school, then college, Lisa and I had matured quite a bit. Most of the men we tended to meet had not.

Most of the men we tended to meet were not interested in lengthy commitments. These men wanted one thing and one thing only. OK, *most* men want one thing and one thing only. But the men we met were rarely the ones we wanted to give that thing to. And rather than risk having to admit that to them outright, we came to a quick realization.

We realized that on most nights of the week, we could claim with a semblance of legitimacy that tomorrow was a "big day" and we needed to go home and get some sleep. On Friday nights, we could claim that we were beat from all the "big days" the previous week and we needed to go home and get some sleep.

Saturday nights were the one exception. They were the one night of the week on which crying "work" just wouldn't work. Everyone knew that you didn't have to work on Sunday. The only way to put off a man on a Saturday night was to be honest with him. And even if you weren't *brutally* honest with him, he'd still finally understand that, although you might truly value his friendship, you weren't interested in him *that way.*

Most men would take you out endlessly hoping that someday they would get that one thing they wanted. Yet once one of them recognized that someday was never going to come, you might continue to "value his friendship," but the dating game was over.

And so, for two years, Lisa and I spent most of our Saturday nights together. No matter. We thoroughly enjoyed each other's company, and we had one important thing in common. Like most men we tended to meet, we wanted one thing and one thing only. But that one thing was to date.

⎯⎯⟲⎯⎯

On the morning that I turned 26, my father called to wish me a happy birthday. He, however, wasn't happy.

"I'm worried," he said.

"What are you worried about?" I asked.

"I'm worried about my grandchildren," he said.

"You don't have any grandchildren," I reminded him.

"Exactly," he said.

Oh, so that's what he was up to. "Dad, you have nothing to worry about," I said. "In the past year, three men have asked me to marry them."

"In that case, I'm *really* worried," he said. "I'm worried because you said no."

That was my father for you. Always trying to get me to do something I wouldn't do or to be something I wouldn't or couldn't be. Little did he realize that he would have had far more to worry about if in any one of those three cases, I had said yes.

One of the men who had proposed to me was one of my first college boyfriends. He was a lovely guy, witty, bright, and close to my age. He also measured up when it came to the two most important factors to my father, being a) employed, and b) Jewish. But there was no way I would have married him. He had been right for me when I was a girl of 17. Dating him now made me feel like I was *still* 17 – not in a good way, but in a case-of-arrested-development way. A life with him would not have led to a happy future. He was the Ghost of Marriage Past.

The second man was someone my father had never met because he was someone I didn't dare mention. He was a truly lovely guy, witty and very bright. He also measured up when it came to the two most important factors to my father, being a) employed, and b) Jewish. The problem was that he also measured up to my father when it came to age. They had been born the very same year.

Older to me meant wiser and therefore far more interesting than any man my age. But older also meant that he came complete with alimony payments, assorted middle-aged ailments, and two not-so-young children from a previous marriage. I knew that when I turned 40 someday, I wouldn't want to be married to a man on Social Security. Bachelor No. 2 was far too old for me. He was the Ghost of Marriage Future.

Bachelor No. 3 was also a lovely guy. He was witty, bright, employed, Jewish, and perfectly age-appropriate. He had never been married. Had no children. No ailments. He was also crazy about me.

But you can't make yourself love someone just because that person loves you and seems perfect for you. Besides, when it came to "Ronny," "perfect" was a bit of a stretch. The only thing perfect about Ronny was that he thought I was perfect for *him*.

Ronny and I had met at a party thrown by one of my best friends from college, "Ray." Ronny was a former classmate of Ray's from law school. So, in fact, was their friend "Ricky." I met Ronny and Ricky at the same time, on the same Friday night, at my good friend Ray's party. Ronny decided right away to ask me out for the following night. He didn't want to ask me out right away, though, because he didn't want to do it in front of Ricky. He figured that he would wait and ask me out at the end of the party. But by the time he finally got around to asking me out, Ricky had already asked first.

Outraged, Ronny demanded to know where and when Ricky and I were going out. Only later did I realize that I should have declined to tell him, because when I showed up to meet Ricky at the designated time and restaurant, Ronny showed up, too.

Ronny joined Ricky and me for a drink at the bar while we waited for our table. When our table was finally ready, Ronny joined us for dinner, too. Ricky kept ordering his friend to leave us alone. But feeling flattered by the duel being enacted before me, and rapidly losing interest in the wimpy and increasingly whiney Ricky, I did little to back him up. By the end of the meal, Ricky was furious. He stormed out in a huff, and two hours and a few too many drinks later, it was Ronny who came home with me.

By the next morning, or very soon thereafter, I came to my senses. I realized that Ronny was a lovely guy, incredibly witty, exceedingly bright, eminently employed, 100 percent Jewish, and perfectly age-appropriate. But he was also a little annoying, neurotic, and temperamental, not to mention too skinny for my taste. He also had many other qualities too hard to define or plentiful to enumerate that made him not right for me.

I did, however, genuinely "value his friendship," so much so that he became for me, in effect, a male version of my friend Lisa. If I didn't have a date, and I didn't want to be alone, I could always count on Ronny for good company. He was the first person I called whenever I felt sick or sad. He, meanwhile, evidently needed no excuse to call me. He phoned almost daily, both at home and at work, often three or four times a day.

Sometimes it was to invite me out to dinner. Sometimes it was for no reason at all. But the conversation always began the same way.

"P?" Ronny would say. He called me P.

"Yes, Ronny?" I'd say.

"Have I shown you my new wallet, P?"

"Yes, Ronny," I'd say.

"Isn't it nice leather?" he'd ask.

"Yes, Ronny," I'd say.

"Will you marry me, P?" he'd ask.

"No, Ronny," I'd say.

Sometimes, we'd discuss the merits of the brand new brass cigarette lighter I'd bought for him instead. (He happened to be a smoker, another deal-breaker in my book.) But the end of the exchange was always the same, in both the way it was asked and the way it was answered. Mysteriously, this never discouraged him from asking once again.

That done, we'd quickly move on to discussing our plans for the evening. Sometimes, after we ate dinner out together, he'd come back to my apartment to watch TV. And some of those sometimes, if the weather was too inclement to get a cab, or if he was simply too tired to get up and leave, he'd end up spending the night. I never had the heart to banish him to the couch; after all, my queen-sized bed was more than roomy enough for two. Occasionally on those evenings, out of boredom, or loneliness, or maybe just plain horniness, we'd end up messing around. Just a little. As I said, there would eventually be a label for that: "friends with benefits." Ronny and I were best friends. With occasional benefits. But I didn't want to actually date Ronny.

And I certainly didn't want to marry him.

Even my father, who was dying for me to marry, didn't want me to marry Ronny. I often brought him to my father's apartment when I was invited there for dinner; it was a good way to avoid being cross-examined about the fact that I was 26 and had no husband or potential fiancé in sight. I even brought him as my date to the wedding reception when my father finally married Elaine. On all of these occasions, my father made no secret of the fact that he liked Ronny but didn't consider him to be husband material any more than I did. In fact, when my father called me, which was not nearly as often as Ronny called me, he'd often mention, apropos of nothing, "If you marry Ronny, you're out of the will." He said that because cutting me out of his will was the worst threat he could imagine. If he could have come up with a more threatening threat, he would have said that instead.

Not surprisingly, these threats had a counterproductive impact. They made me consider whether I should marry Ronny, despite everything, just so I could vex my father. Yes, I was old enough to feel slightly ashamed for having no suitable suitors in sight, yet young enough to consider cutting off my nose to spite my face or, preferably, my parents.

What was extremely surprising was that, slowly but surely, my father's campaign to marry me off began to make headway inside my head. Maybe some hidden, purely biological force — a conspiracy of hormones, chromosomes, and neurotransmitters — was starting to change the chemistry of my brain and transform my usual train of thought.

Maybe it was just that I was going out with so many different men at once that I could no longer enjoy it. Every time I started to tell someone an anecdote on a date, I'd find myself obsessing. Hadn't I told him this already? Or had I told it to somebody else? Was I being reasonably amusing, or just an insufferably repetitive bore?

Or maybe it was the fact that I not only kept a diary, but also, tucked inside that diary, I kept a little list. On it were listed the names of every man I had ever slept with, what month I'd slept with him, and approximately how many times we'd "slept." It had begun to worry me that there were already enough names that I needed a list to keep track of them. It had begun to worry me even more that, even if I only slept with one man at a time for months at a time, and even if I sometimes slept with no one for months at a time, after several years of being single in New York, that little list was no longer little.

All I know is that when my father made those pointed comments on my birthday, I laughed defensively, dismissed them derisively, and gave them little further thought.

Not long after that day, though, I felt something gradually begin to come over me. Something new and strange, in that it was unprecedented in my life and utterly sensible.

So soon after my father made his comments, something began coming over me. That something was The Plan.

A voice inside my head began warning me that it was high time to start figuring out my romantic future. I'd noticed that many unmarried women I met who were over 30 exhibited an excessive eagerness to attract men. That terrified me. Women, I concluded, had a relatively narrow window of opportunity within which to meet and marry the right man. At 26, my window remained wide open, but I wanted it shut before I turned 30.

It seemed rash to marry anyone I hadn't known for at least two years. That gave me less than two years, or 730 days, to locate my perfect match. I had little time to waste.

I had to start rejecting anyone who clearly wasn't marriage material. Yet, since it was always possible to misjudge a ruby in the rough, I couldn't be too hasty about this. I'd have to give any viable candidate some time. But not too much time.

Three months. That seemed like a reasonable amount of time.

If after dating someone for three months, I couldn't picture myself marrying him, then I'd break it off and find someone I *could* imagine marrying.

That, in effect, was The Plan.

In theory, it was a good plan.

The problem was that I couldn't find anyone worth dating for even three months. What if two years went by and I was still alone? I began to panic.

I hadn't planned on that.

When I began to panic, I became so determined to fall in love with someone that I started to fall in love with everyone. I hadn't planned on that, either.

—⁓—

One day in January, late for an early-morning job interview with a man I'd once had the misfortune to date, I lost my balance and fell down a whole flight of stairs. Foolishly trying to break my fall with my right hand, I found myself in unbearable pain. Clearly, I would have to forgo both the dreaded job interview and that day's work. The situation seemed like an unmitigated disaster... until I hastened to what was then called St. Luke's–Roosevelt Hospital Center and fell under the expert care and hypnotic spell of the nice Jewish surgeon of my dreams.

"Dr. Aaron Bronsky," as I'll call him, not only set the fractured metacarpal bone in my injured hand, but also set my heart aflutter. I could only wonder what it would be like to have him attend to my other physical needs. I also wondered whether it had been deliberate when he'd leaned across my body for leverage while adjusting my cast and had rested firmly against me, his chest pressed sensuously to mine for one erotic minute.

I tried to remind myself that this magic spell had taken hold of me inside the operating room, under pain, local anesthesia, extremely bright lights and mental duress. But by later that night, all of these various potent influences had completely worn off, and my intense magnetic attraction to him had not. I kept trying to talk myself out of it. After all, I barely knew him. I knew very little about his personality or personal interests. I could barely remember what he looked like. I didn't even know whether he was married or not, or was involved with a serious girlfriend. (I had little doubt that he liked women.) It was all to no avail, though. I was smitten, or even worse. OK, worse. I was obsessed.

Having met him so serendipitously felt to me like a matter of *bashert*, the Yiddish term we Jews use when we think something is fated, or "meant to be." Before leaving the hospital, I had been scheduled to return so that the good doctor could remove my cast three weeks later. The thought of not seeing him again for three whole weeks appeared far more ominous than the prospect of having half my arm encased in plaster for months.

I probably should have kept such a sudden infatuation to myself, in the event that my friends might ridicule me. Instead, I dared to divulge my desires to a select few. One of them, my former college roommate, Hallie, was a doctor in the city herself. She said that she didn't know Dr. Bronsky personally, but thought that she knew *of* him. His father was a surgeon as well, she believed, one so renowned that there was a medical procedure that bore his name. She encouraged me to go for it. So did Lisa. Ronny, however, did not. He was – no surprise – positively irate.

One evening after work, I got up my nerve and called the doctor at the hospital. In truth, I was having a problem with my cast and thought that it might not be allowing my hand to heal properly. But there's no use denying that I was also anxious to hear his voice. I had to wait on hold almost interminably for him to come to the phone, but once he finally did, he was not only reassuring but also exceedingly warm and friendly.

I was elated until Ronny called moments later. He complained that he'd been trying me forever, but my line had been busy. I told him I'd been talking to the doctor.

"You were *what?*" he asked. He sounded exasperated. He said that I was a clown.

"Doctors can't go out with their patients!" he cried. It was clearly against medical ethics.

Oh, boy. Woops! I hadn't thought of that. Still, I wouldn't be his patient forever.

Finally, the day of my appointment came around. February 19. Casting off day. I had turned myself inside out for the previous three weeks over a man I had met only once, briefly. It was hard to imagine finally seeing him after such an agonizing absence.

I spent the entire day beforehand deliberating about what to wear and imagining what we would say to each other. Although I had fantasized throughout those weeks about plenty of imaginary, mildly suggestive conversations, I resolved not to prepare any speeches or attempts at clever repartee. Didn't spontaneity beat everything in the end?

Getting ready that morning, I felt homelier than I ever had in my entire life. The skin on my face had broken out as if I were still an adolescent, from nerves, no doubt. I was obliged to slather on makeup, hoping he wouldn't notice and that it would all be OK. As eager as I was to arrive, I spent so much time primping that I reached the hospital late.

They took me anyway. It was startling to be ushered into a cubicle cordoned off from the rest of the room by white curtains, and to sit facing the doctor's back across the way while he attended to another patient. I buried my face in a magazine that I'd found in the waiting room and tried my damnedest to relax. My heart was palpitating, though, like a big bass drum being pummeled inside my chest. I didn't register one word that I read.

I happened to glance up at the exact moment that he turned around and saw me. The drum in my chest went "ba-BOOM!" His eyes and voice betrayed an unmistakable excitement at seeing me. Or so it seemed. Alas, I perceived in an instant that he was not as devastatingly handsome as I had remembered. Slightly pudgy, particularly around the middle, he looked like he had a hard time passing up pasta or dessert. His compact frame was also short enough that, at a shade under 5-foot-6 myself, I might have towered over him in high heels. The skin on his face was pale and doughy, from spending too much time in the hospital, no doubt. His light brown hair was coarse, like wads of beige Brillo.

Still, my attraction to him had been based less on appearance than an impression I'd gotten of his character. So I was excited to be gazing into his warm brown eyes and sitting before him again. His touch was just as I had remembered it, gentle, comforting and yet arousing. It felt affectionate, which translated in my mind as potentially sexual. Nonetheless, I couldn't help noticing that he maintained a slightly detached air, friendly yet suitably professional.

That is not to say it was all strictly business. He playfully inquired if I had taken any exciting "trips" since last we'd met, and expressed relief that when going downstairs, I had evidently resigned myself to using them. Although I joked with him as well, I didn't dare say anything remotely direct about my feelings. And in no time it was over again, much too soon. Although it was a relief to have the cast removed, and it was encouraging to have a follow-up visit scheduled for a few weeks later, my heart sank as soon as I left.

I might as well give up now, I thought wistfully, riding in a taxi back to the office. He wasn't interested in me, after all. Maybe I was no longer that taken with him, either. Over those three interminable weeks, while I'd waited breathlessly to see him again, I had managed to blow both his virtues and our romantic prospects way out of proportion.

But such mind-saturating fixations don't fade away quite so easily. I had fallen so much into the habit of daydreaming about him that I was now overwhelmed by the agony of dashed dreams. By evening, I wanted him more than ever, or at least someone to fill the void that relinquishing my yen for him had left. It was lucky that I was about to leave town for my annual trip to Florida. Ever since my maternal grandparents had migrated south in the mid-1960s, I had spent Presidents' Week down there every single winter.

———

With my beloved Grandpa Charlie having died little more than a year earlier, I was more determined than ever to make my customary trek south to see Grandma Mary. After flying to Fort Lauderdale, I rented a car and zipped down I-95 to Galahad North, her high-rise apartment complex in Hollywood.

I pulled up to the green-and-white striped awning out front and greeted Irv, the building's scrawny, young head parking attendant, who'd always struck me as a bit too young and a bit too sharp to be a parking attendant. He recognized me right away.

"So, we're back to see Granny again, I see," he said, cheerily applying the royal "we." "How long will you be staying? Do you need any help with your bags?"

"Oh, thanks," I began, "but I only have this – "

"Because if so," he continued, "my brother would be more than happy to help. He's down here for the winter, helping me out while he, uh, sorts things out. Here he comes. Ever met my brother, Steve?"

Just then, a car pulled up, the driver's door swung open, and out stepped a lean, muscular young man with skin as tan as maple syrup who looked to me like a rock star.

And suddenly, "our" canvas duffel bag seemed awfully cumbersome, after all.

Big brother Steve not only helped me up to Grandma's apartment, but also took me out the following night. We didn't have dinner together because, as usual, I had already dined with Grandma at 5. We simply went for a drive in his beat-up old van. Afterwards, I listened to him play his guitar for awhile, then we took a walk on the beach.

I have to say I was a little surprised that Grandma let me go. When Grandpa had been alive, they'd been so overprotective that I'd rarely been allowed out of their sight. Once, soon after graduating from college, I'd insisted on going out for Cuban food with my old classmate Russ, then, figuring they were asleep anyway, I'd had the audacity to stay out half the night. I arrived home at 3 a.m. to find them frantically waiting up for me and to learn that Grandpa had already said *Kaddish*, the Jewish prayer for the dead, for me. It wasn't clear if this was because he feared that I'd been in a car accident or because he considered me to be dead to him, since no granddaughter of his would stay out so late with a man to whom she wasn't married. After that, they were *really* overprotective.

Now that Grandpa was gone, though, and I was a bit older, Grandma no longer seemed to challenge my right to a grownup social life; she only questioned my taste. She allowed that Steve was handsome enough, even if he was in need of a haircut. She only wondered how I could bear to listen to him talk. Even for a Southerner, he spoke at such a languid, halting pace that you wondered if his brain was running in slow motion.

The greater mystery, to my mind, was what he could possibly have seen in *me*. The only assets I had to offer him were that I melted in his presence and that I was younger than the rest of the building's female occupants by a good sixty years.

Switching my allegiance from an articulate New York surgeon to a slow-talking, Southern-born carhop may sound like going from the sublime to the ridiculous, but it wasn't all that hard to grasp. Throughout high school, I'd been sequestered with all the so-called geeks in the honors classes. In college, I'd been a consistent sucker for brainy, bespectacled, distinctly non-athletic types. Never once before in my life had I gotten close enough to a muscle-bound Greek-statue-come-to-life to even have a conversation.

Not that verbal exchange was in any respect central to our brief but torrid affair. Knowing that I would probably never see him again after that week – not to mention that I had left all of my birth-control paraphernalia safely behind in New York – I refrained from letting our physical relationship progress beyond a certain point. It hardly mattered. By the end of that week, he had managed to gain total control over my consciousness. Being with Steve was my reason for being. I was convinced that I had fallen in love.

All that I could think about was the way he looked standing on the sand at sunset. Tall and lean and glittering with energy and strength, his body was a dazzling vision, his arms and exquisitely sculpted chin so strong that I wanted to sit before him and just gaze up with awe and delight. I wanted to watch him move, and I wanted him to stand still so I could reach out and touch him, the way you're tempted to touch a sculpture in a museum. I wanted to feel the heat of his skin and to rest my head on his shoulder. I wanted to be all alone with him, and I wanted to be out in the world together so everyone could see. Just being near him filled me with such desire that I feared the sand beneath us would ignite.

Instead, I had to watch Irv fetch "our" car while Grandma hugged me goodbye.

The night I flew back to La Guardia, still **pining** for his touch, I had half a notion to jet right back. I could quit my job, live with Grandma for awhile... Then what? Why kid myself? It was just an impulse, a mad fantasy. Even as I spun the dream, I knew in my soul that I was not really in love with Steve. I was in love with love itself.

Re-entering New York on the verge of spring, and having just returned from a relaxing, tropical respite, I was crazy, almost drunk, with the notion of love. No doubt I would unleash my impassioned inclinations on the next available male who happened by. I could only hope that he would be too decent and honorable to take advantage of my heightened receptiveness and vulnerability. It was frightening to be wallowing in such an impassioned state, which I realized was beginning to stink of emotional promiscuity.

Yes, that's what I was. An emotional slut! It was actually worse in some respects than being promiscuous in the sexual sense – certainly worse for my mental stability. How many romantic side trips had I taken in just a few short weeks? It felt almost like embarking on a whirlwind jaunt through Europe, seeing a new city every three days.

Falling in and out of love with so many men in such a short span of time was like limiting myself to reading picture postcards instead of full-scale novels. Where did I come off even using the word "love"? Like pebbles being skipped across a lake, I barely got to scratch the surfaces of these men before sinking and disappearing from sight.

My fleeting relationship with Steve had been so superficial that after all these years, I can't recall what it was, if anything, that he wanted to do with his life. Steve was so superficial and unmotivated that he probably didn't know the answer to that question himself. At least the doctor served a higher purpose and lived farther above the equator.

Yes, the doctor! And I had a follow-up visit scheduled for the following week.

If I expected anything personal to happen between us, though, then I couldn't risk letting our last meeting be wasted on a quick, routine medical evaluation. Even if Ronny was right, after this final visit he would no longer actively be treating me. Yet if I wanted to be more than his patient, then I would have to stop being so patient.

It was time, I decided, to take action and make some sort of move myself.

Yet I knew myself well enough to recognize that I was far too cautious and reserved to do or say anything remotely overt in person. Anything that I said would have to be subtle, and it would have to be said in a letter.

A letter, in fact, could be extremely subtle, although the one that I ended up mailing to him in care of the hospital that week probably could have been far subtler.

My dear Dr. Bronsky,

A one-year subscription to the enclosed magazine has been entered in your name, compliments (of the highest order) of my department.

Unfortunately, our circulation computers are a little slow and inept. They will take about six weeks to begin spitting out labels bearing your name and address.

To tide you over, expect to receive a personalized copy each week, direct from our editorial offices. This does not pose any serious problem or inconvenience. I don't have to pay for postage, and I get to write you a witty, suggestive note once a week. Let me know when your subscription starts coming – unless, of course, you begin to enjoy the notes.

I concluded this with the safe and highly sanitized salutation "All my best," and sent it far enough in advance of my appointment for him to receive it by the time we met.

That appointment was set for a Monday in mid-March during my lunch break. This time, I managed to arrive on schedule.

"So, how's the hand?" he asked, taking mine in his to admire his handiwork.

"Fine," I replied, my cheeks burning from his touch. "Almost as good as new, thanks almost entirely to you."

"Good, good. No pain or discomfort?"

Only the one in my heart, I thought. "None worth mentioning," I said. "Good, good."

And so the exam continued. He asked about soreness, stiffness, and whether I'd been doing the exercises he'd prescribed to stretch my tendons back to their former state. Everything was as it should be, I assured him.

Was it my imagination, or did he seem distant and more businesslike than ever? Meanwhile, he made no mention of my letter. Was it possible that he hadn't received it? Was it going to end for us like this? Or was I going to have to bring it up myself?

"Oh, by the way," he suddenly began, "thanks for the note and the subscription. That was very thoughtful." He sounded sincere, but his eyes were evasive, focused over my shoulder onto the opposite wall. "I don't find I have a lot of time to read magazines," he added. "But I'll bring them home. My wife, uh – she really enjoys them."

"Oh," I said, "it was the least I could do." Now my cheeks were really burning.

Fortunately, my broken bone had indeed mended. My broken heart might take longer to heal, but I could manage that on my own. I would never have to see him again.

Having taken an extended lunch hour, and having lost all capacity to concentrate, I ended up working a bit late that night. Putting in long hours was nothing unusual at a weekly magazine. Several other staff members were also on hand to keep me company. On my way out, I paused at the end of the office to chat with a small group of stalwarts. Among them was a soft-spoken reporter who was working on a free-lance story.

There was something so gentle about his manner that I'd often wondered about him. I'd long ago even developed a secret crush on him from afar. But we had never met.

It was late, though, and I was beat, so I excused myself and wandered out. Less than a minute later, he emerged from the main office and joined me in front of the elevators. We waited in silence until a car arrived. Then he gestured in a gentlemanly fashion for me to step in first, and we rode down together.

"Do you people always work this late?" he asked.

"Do you people call this late?" I replied.

He smiled. "Well, it's a little late to find a taxi in this part of town."

"It's never too late to take the subway," I said.

"True. I'm usually a subway man myself. Which way are you headed?"

"Up," I said. "And west."

"Go west, young woman," he said.

"West not, want not," I said. "And you?"

"Also a west case scenario."

"Good," I said. "May the west man win."

And so we continued as we strode side by side toward Grand Central Station, where I assumed we would hop the shuttle to Times Square. It actually was late, and I was happy to have an escort. A blustery March wind was blowing against us, though. By the time we had reached the terminal, we were all out of puns and almost out of breath.

"I'm Sam, by the way," he said, as we entered the station annex at 42nd Street and Vanderbilt.

"Yes, I know," I said. "I'm – "

"Patricia," he said. No one ever called me Patricia. Other than to Ronny, I was just plain Pat. He must have seen it on the masthead.

"Nice to meet you, Sam-I-am," I said.

"Sam-I-am," he groaned. "Sam-I am. I do not like that 'Sam-I-am.'"

I grinned. "But do you like green eggs and ham?"

"No ham, please," he said. "I'm Jewish."

"Likewise," I said. "But green eggs are all they're cracked up to be."

"And then some," he said. "I would eat them in a house."

"I would eat them with a mouse."

"I would eat them in a plane," he said.

"I would eat them in a train."

"How about in a train *station*?" he asked.

"Even better," I said.

"Actually, I would eat almost anything right now," he said. "Green, or even blue. I haven't had dinner yet. What about you?"

Racing to and from my doctor's appointment, I hadn't had time for lunch. Why, with all of the day's anxiety, I'd barely touched breakfast. "Beyond famished," I said.

"Well, we'll have to do something about that."

Some years later, the lower level of Grand Central Station would be remodeled to house a smorgasbord of international cafes, replete with foods of every ilk and ethnicity. Now, rather than boarding a subway car in our ravenous state, we settled for two adjacent counter seats at the boisterous Oyster Bar.

There, chatting animatedly over steaming chowder and freshly broiled fish, we discovered that we shared the same quirky passions for almost everything, from books and music to silly, inventive wordplay, to the habit of munching the parsley sprigs garnishing our plates after we had finished our food. Yet our automatic, deep connection went way beyond our relishing the same old movies and various other cultural propensities. Although he was several years older than I was, we felt entirely at ease together, which for me was something rare. I was usually shy with strangers. He was, clearly, shy himself. But we were anything but shy with each other.

There was one important thing, though, that we probably didn't have in common. My friend Suzanne, who also worked at the magazine, had once lamented that he had gotten married. Unless she was somehow mistaken, one of us was no longer available, and the other was setting herself up for another monster of an emotional letdown.

Still, there we were, exchanging furtive smiles, eating off each other's plates as though they were common turf and jabbing each other flirtatiously in the side. When our coffee cups had been refilled and emptied twice, and he asked if there was "anything else my heart desired," I found myself lowering my eyelids as I replied, "If you mean do I want anything else to eat or drink, then the answer is a decided no."

Despite what I'd said earlier, it was now so late that the subways presumably were running too sporadically to consider. He suggested taking the scenic route, a city bus, instead. I knew this was likely to be even slower, but readily agreed. When we had arrived uptown at last, he insisted upon accompanying me home the few blocks from the nearest bus stop to my apartment. Then, seeing me shiver, he offered to let me wear his warm winter hat. As we approached my door, I began to realize how little I wanted him to leave, and how much I wanted to touch him. Instead, he took his hat, bid me a barely audible goodnight, then strolled down my block without looking back and vanished.

It was just as well. I'd already spied the telltale gold band affixed to his left hand.

Lying in bed later, staring at the ceiling, I found myself wondering many things.

I wondered if Sam and his wife were as amazingly compatible as he and I seemed to be.

I wondered why he had asked me to dinner and lingered for so long over it.

I wondered whether, if he hadn't been married, I would have wanted him half as much as I did. That one was easy. The answer was that had he been available, I would have gone to bed with him right away – that night, or the next, or no doubt whenever he asked. If he hadn't been married, I'd have wished that my phone had rung soon after he had left my doorstep, and that we could have continued our conversation in hushed voices before reluctantly bidding each other goodnight as though we were still together.

I had accepted his dinner invitation spontaneously, and with an irrational hope against all probability that my friend Suzanne had been wrong.

Now I could empathize deeply with how my poor friend Ronny must have felt. It had been a while since someone I was so attracted to and wanted so feverishly simply wouldn't have me. To be honest, I wasn't sure that Sam wouldn't have me, except that he was obviously an honorable man. From what I'd heard about him and I sensed about him, inviting me to dinner had been wildly out of character. His kind eyes exuded integrity. An air of gentleness and fundamental decency was evident even in the way he walked. To me, he brought to mind Phil Green, the compassionate journalist who pretended to be a Jew in the 1948 film *Gentleman's Agreement* in order to expose anti-Semitism. Or maybe it was the noble Atticus Finch in *To Kill a Mockingbird.* Had he been a character in an old movie, he would have been played by Gregory Peck.

But this was no movie, and neither Sam nor I were mere fictional characters. This was real and happening to me, another sorry episode in the tragicomedy that was my life. Never had I been so unreservedly entranced by anyone. But this time I would tell no one.

—⟨⟩—

Over the next few days, I found my mood ricocheting like a shiny metal pinball between absolute euphoria and abject pain. There was nothing more exhilarating, or more agonizing, than to sense that a man like him, someone whom I believed to be of uncompromising integrity, appeared to be – against his will, morals, and better judgment – besotted with me.

Yet as casual as my approach to sexuality might have seemed, I was anything but cavalier about adultery. I had watched my mother wonder where my father was on too many nights not to know how demeaning it was to be on the receiving end of betrayal.

All my life, I had been determined not to reproduce my parents' tainted union. Now I was echoing its most unsavory element, except that I'd been cast as the villainess. I was the one threatening the sanctity of someone else's marriage. That is, if I were to succumb to my urges, I was on the verge of potentially becoming "the other woman."

This was something that I would never, ever have allowed to happen had I been my usual scrupulously ethical and relentlessly self-controlled self. But I had just undergone several months of extreme emotional turbulence. Plus, still reeling from my debacle with the doctor, I simply hadn't seen this one coming. I had accepted Sam's impromptu dinner invitation expecting only to have a decent meal and some diverting conversation, not to discover what might turn out to be true love at last.

Continuing to see him would be morally reprehensible and, for the sake of my own sanity, indefensible. Yet such is the frailty of the helpless human heart that I wasn't nearly ready to relinquish the sweet fantasy of our being free to be together without guilt. Or, barring any better alternative, our being together *with* guilt. Yes, try as I might, faced with such a deliriously irresistible temptation, I guess I just wasn't turning out to be quite the pillar of impeccable moral virtue that we would all like to fancy ourselves to be.

And so I'm ashamed to report that over the following days, whenever he stopped into the office to work more on his story, we engaged in a covert game of eye-contact tag. We took turns gazing across the room longingly at one another, both glancing away the instant our lines of vision would lock. Occasionally, when I could only hope that no one was bothering to notice, we hovered in one another's vicinities and dared to briefly speak.

Did anyone see us? If so, they would have had to have been blind to miss my inner feelings, for my face lit up like a golden harvest moon every time he approached. If only we could steal away together without arousing public suspicion, I kept thinking, merely to take a walk or have lunch. I began toying with the idea of daring to suggest it one day, until a coworker wandered over and insisted that I join him for lunch, instead.

This poor fellow and I went to our favorite Greek diner, where I sat across from him trying to make normal conversation, yet was too distracted to focus on a single word he said. It was agony to watch him slowly nibble his tuna on rye, wishing he would just gulp it down so we could pay the check and leave. Ambling beside him on the way back to our building, I suddenly couldn't stand it one second longer. I announced that I had an important errand to run. Then I dashed down a side street, waited until I saw him safely round the corner, then doubled back to the nearest vegetable and fruit market.

There I bought a lush green bunch of the most impeccable parsley I could find. I also spent nearly five minutes poring over a bin of small, ripe pears until I was convinced that I had found the most perfect and appealing one. It was flecked with peachy gold on one side and bore a small patch of rosy pink on the other, like a softly blushing cheek.

At the stationery store on the opposite corner, I marched from shelf to shelf, trying to find a greeting card that would seem light-hearted and amusing. Nothing flowery, sentimental, or heavy-handed would do. The best one I could find was blank inside. On the cover, a bright yellow crayon with splayed stick-figure arms and legs was staring into a tall mirror, only to see its slightly smaller and paler reflection smiling back. It was a capricious image, signifying nothing, or maybe just enough.

After paying at the cash register, I foraged in the plastic bag that held the parsley and picked off a small, healthy, emerald stalk. Then I scrawled inside the card in script:

Sam:
> *A sprig of spring fever for safe-keeping –*
> *unless you would rather destroy the evidence.*

I placed the parsley carefully inside the card and then tucked it into the envelope. I did not sign my name.

I had hoped that he would be away from his desk when I returned so I could leave my offerings undetected and surprise him. Instead, I had to settle for creeping up behind him and placing them quickly on a corner of his desk. He looked up, saw me and smiled.

Twenty minutes later, I saw him pad nonchalantly across the room, wander by me surreptitiously and slap a folded slip of paper beside me. I waited several minutes in case anyone had seen the maneuver. I didn't dare risk having nosy coworkers notice the reaction that might flash across my face. Finally, I could stand the suspense no longer, and I tore it open and read:

Patricia,
> *I did destroy the evidence. And now it is springtime inside my tummy.*

> *Also, as for that pear with all its red and yellow speckles, that's as smashingly, sweetly beautiful as General Foods, or whoever it is, makes them.*

I read those words over and over again throughout the rest of that day, until I had committed them, like a poem or a prayer, to memory. Sitting in a movie with friends that night, I kept reaching into my pocket to make sure that precious missive was still there. When I got home, I took it out, read it over yet again, then slept with it under my pillow.

The next day, we did slip out together at lunchtime, although not at the same time. There was nowhere nearby that we dared to dine together. The frenetic butterflies in my stomach had eradicated my appetite, anyway. So we took a short walk instead, and then, eager to escape public detection and the chilly air, entered the Pierpont Morgan Library.

There, bypassing the exhibits of medieval art, we opted as word lovers to survey the vast trove of literary treasures instead: letters written by famous figures ranging from Marie Antoinette to Albert Einstein; an original, handwritten copy of Charles Dickens' *A Christmas Carol;* and signed manuscripts by the world's greatest authors, from Henry David Thoreau, who had forsaken civilization for life on Walden Pond because he "wanted to live deep and suck out all the marrow of life," to Emily Brontë, who had penned the romance that towers over all others, the heart-rending *Wuthering Heights.*

Then, my allotted lunch hour having passed all too quickly, we left to hurry back. A block before reaching my building, Sam stopped short and turned to face me.

"Patricia?" he said. He still called me Patricia. "You're really enchanting to me. You'd better watch out."

I couldn't eat a bite or sleep that night. I just lay in bed scribbling furiously in my journal, agonizing and deliberating about Sam, and wondering what I was going to do.

How could all of this insanity be happening? For once, it wasn't just another case of my excessively fertile imagination getting carried away. We had spoken openly together that day about our feelings, about the intense emotions which, try as we might to contain them, leaked out of our eyes. I had conjectured to him that I was such a relentless dreamer, such a woman of hopes and hidden passion instead of action, that the majority of my experience unfolded entirely inside my head. Yet he had assured me that anything I sensed he was feeling toward me was real, and not just a figment of my imagination.

How often did you meet someone and have an immediate flash of recognition? You understood every word that he or she said, or perhaps didn't dare say aloud, and you felt completely comfortable and exuberant and alive with that person and lost all interest in everything else you normally did unless you could do those things with him?

Now I realized why I had felt a flash of recognition when I'd chosen that greeting card with the comical yellow crayon. It was like a cartoon parable of our crazy situation. It felt like we were two of a kind, that we were each other's almost exact mirror images. Or maybe, gazing at each other so intently, we had simply become one another's mirrors, and when viewing my reflection in his admiring eyes, for the first time I liked what I saw.

But that was where the analogy abruptly ended. Sam certainly was no stick figure. He was no brutish British writer with a short fuse and a fine-feathered flying menagerie. He was no polished and perfectly coifed news-caster, or up-and-coming doctor who might be the perfect catch. And he was certainly no aimless, muscle-bound beach boy for whom the proverbial cat had gotten his tongue. He was a real, live, three-dimensional man, a good and kind one with countless strengths, but also some real human weaknesses. And if I truly cared about him – or because I truly cared about him – I would have to let him go.

I would have to let him go *now*, before anything further could happen between us. For his sake, for my sake, and because, given my history, it was the only thing I could do.

The week was almost over. The next day was Friday, and when he stopped in at lunchtime, we took a walk together again. The March sky, like both our moods, was an overcast shade of lead gray. Walking along quietly, we brushed against each other now and then accidentally, but didn't deliberately touch. We had never once dared to touch. Finally, when we reached a small court-yard on a nearby street, he faced me and paused.

He looked at me. I looked at him. And suddenly, before I could catch my breath, I was locked in his embrace at last, letting him crush me to his chest, feeling the heat and tenderness of his strong forearms, allowing my cheek to brush briefly, softly against his, then burying my face in his neck. God. I wanted to stay there, clinging to him like that. Just to be close enough to feel him breathing, to be connected to him, to his skin, at last. Yes, that alone would have been more than enough, if only time could have just stopped.

But seconds later, without having to even speak, we both seemed to have the same thoughts at precisely the same time. This was crazy. It was wrong. Someone we knew could happen to pass by at any second and see us. See in an instant what we were doing. See what we both felt.

And so, although I could have stood forever holding him like that, suspended eternally in a moment of ecstasy, of heaven on earth, we both abruptly fell back to earth. Sam released me slowly from his arms, took my hands gently in his and began to speak.

How mournful he sounded as he said all the things that I already knew. We had met each other at the wrong time – not that there would ever again be a *right* time. Even stealing away together like this to be alone in public already felt dishonorable and cheap. We were both too virtuous for the next sordid step, the deceitfulness of sneaking around. He had been truly content within his marriage and owed his wife far more respect and decency than he was showing her now. To proceed further would wreak havoc upon all of our lives, including, or maybe especially, mine. He could not bear to do that to me.

It was hard to listen, although, as usual, I knew almost everything that he would say before he said it. I already had decided that whatever he would say to me didn't really matter. The previous night, I had begun writing him a letter. I'd begun writing it having fully anticipated this meeting. Although I hadn't known him long, I already knew him well enough to know that, like me, he felt horribly conflicted and also unbearably guilty. There were many things I wanted to say about that, as well as about other aspects of the brief time we had spent together – things that I could never have said to his face.

I had plenty of time over the terrible, lonely weekend that followed to complete my letter. The story he'd been writing for the magazine over the past few weeks had gone to press, but I knew that he would probably stop into the office again briefly on Monday. This time, soon after he arrived, I handed the envelope to him directly, knowing that I couldn't risk letting it fall into the wrong hands.

Hand-written on ordinary, lined notebook paper, my letter read as follows:

Sam —

I know that I have no business writing this, but about 40 pages into my journal this weekend, I realized that I was not a misguided woman in search of catharsis, but simply struggling to communicate with you. Rather difficult at this distance.

My fortune cookie at dinner on Friday night had the incomparable chutzpah to inform me that "The best things in life are the most difficult." Ha! (This is just the sort of endless coincidence that convinces me there are supernatural forces at play in my life; either that, or simply from my years as a conscientious English major, I derived an annoying talent for reading meaning into everything.)

Hey, Sam? I feel like I know you, instinctively. We haven't shared much, in terms of actual time or experience together, but somehow I register things about your character and thoughts (spoken or not); I feel naturally receptive to signals and sparks you give off. Chemistry? Must be. My whole electrical system has gone haywire...

This could be the steepest moral incline on which I've ever perched. I'm trying hard to keep my balance. At moments, I tremble and teeter and lean so far backwards that the arch of my back threatens to sever my spine. If I start to skid down, I'm sure I'll scramble up again, but tell me: If you take a sudden leap, what are the chances of landing upright?

No. Never mind. I'm sure that we'll prevail, even as I get carried away with the foolish rhetoric and imagery my mind conjures up inexhaustibly, almost cruelly. This is the bottom line: I could not be the first infidelity in your marriage, and I shudder at the prospect of unleashing chaos upon your life or mine.

I'm just agreeing with you, in case you wondered.

Still, when I reflect on the thought that "no good can ever come of this," I feel outraged. What a ridiculous waste that would be. It scares me to think that you might come away feeling guilty or irresponsible. Don't! You've done absolutely nothing wrong. Certainly nothing to hurt me. (If anything, you've just managed to fulfill my expectations of you, which makes it that much harder to let you get away.)

Even this far (this near?), I've gotten a lot from the experience. Aside from the simple joy of being with you, being anywhere near you, I've gotten something to think about. Call it a spiritual awakening, or a heartening reprieve from my recent emotionally barren life.

As for you — if you don't come away realizing how exceptional you are, how warm and gentle and strong and zany and witty and brilliant and wonderful and perceptive and talented and deep and complex and gorgeous and enchanting you really are — well, then I might as well have been wearing sunglasses the whole time. (Sometimes I'm glad that everything leaks out of my eyes.)

At least we don't get to ruin any of this, to cradle our dreams and expectations of one another and then watch them fizzle out like air through the pores of a balloon. I wasn't up for evasion of risk this time, and uncritical as my glance has been, I would have reveled in watching your foibles unfold as much as I delight in your virtues.

Ah, well. How often in life do you get the chance to do something noble? (I know that's a stuffy, exaggerated, artificial word; nonetheless, there it is.)

Don't hang onto this silly letter. Give it back, if you wish, or burn it. You have nowhere safe to put it, I'm sure, and I wouldn't want to see it in the Pierpont Morgan Library someday.

I saw him leave the building to read it. Sometime soon afterward, he returned and sadly handed it back. Because what I had said at the end was true. He had nowhere safe to keep it. I tucked it into my journal that night, and that's where it remains to this day.

During the next few days, despite endless signs of spring sprouting all around me, from flowerbeds blooming on street corners to the fragrant sweetness infusing even the hopelessly polluted New York City air, what felt like a permanent chill of winter began settling into my soul, the way that the soil up north freezes rock solid come December.

Over the coming weeks, I tried to return to normal life, but couldn't stop myself from thinking about Sam every waking minute. Every time I was talking to someone, I privately would be thinking, "But it isn't Sam," and it would be an effort to pay attention or evince more than the slightest interest. Every time the phone rang, my throat would constrict against all reason as I answered it. I automatically kept imagining that it might be him calling, even though I knew that it never could or would be. Everything I did seemed to be with the express intent of being able to tell him about it afterward. I carried a mental image of him around with me everywhere, and I found myself taking stock of events unfolding around me and feelings unfolding inside me so that I would have small, profound secrets to tell him the next time we met, which would be – when? Maybe never.

Most likely never. How could I already have lost all hope at the tender age of 26?

I had started out determined not to fall in love. Then I had set out to fall madly in love with a man whom I might marry someday. And I had ended up falling madly in love with a man whom I could never marry because he was already married to somebody else.

Unless…

Life has such strange, unexpected ways of unfolding. No one can ever be sure what the distant future might bring. For Sam, I truly wished only the best. And yet, if he was so susceptible to feeling attracted to me, maybe his marriage was not made to last.

So, rather than giving up on him then, permanently and completely, I decided to go on with my life, but to still give the possibility of being with him someday some time. Not too much time. A year, or maybe two. That seemed like a reasonable amount of time.

If during that year, or maybe two, I heard that Sam and his wife had become parents, I would indeed give up on him forever. I had no misgivings about the fact that, just as my background prohibited me from stealing a married man away from his wife, I was absolutely not a woman who could ever consider robbing some children of their dad.

If after that year or two he remained married, I would also give up on him forever. Even though he was worth waiting for, I still didn't have all the time in the world to wait.

In the meanwhile, I would try not to turn husband-hunting into an Olympic Event.

I would go back to spending Saturday nights with Lisa. I would go back to The Plan.

And Then There Were Nins

∾

I was just about to run out when the phone rang in my New York City apartment on an icy Sunday afternoon in early February, three weeks after my twenty-seventh birthday. The caller was my older brother Joel, and, like the blunt, direct fellow that he had always been, and the self-possessed and forthright public prosecutor he had in recent years become, he didn't bother to chat for even two seconds before getting down to business.

"Listen, what are you doing next Sunday?" he asked. "There's someone I'd like you to marry."

Such is the fate of almost any Jewish girl who approaches the overripe age of 30 without having a husband, or at least a conceivable prospect for a future fiancé in sight. Remain hanging on the proverbial vine just a little too long, and your entire family throws subtlety, along with caution, to the wind in the interests of marrying you off.

Mercifully, my one and only sibling wasn't proposing that I marry a complete stranger. Of course not. We would need to get acquainted first. The young man in question was a political consultant he had just met who had three notable things going for him: Like me, he was unattached; like me, he was Jewish; and unlike me, and unlikely as it might be, at the tender age of 28 he was making in excess of a million dollars a year. Having run a successful senatorial campaign or two, he was considered a political genius.

"Hal," this prize catch, was an acquaintance of my brother's closest friend, Artie. Artie was holding a party in honor of his own thirtieth birthday the following weekend. My brother was calling to invite me to this illustrious event.

It presented the ideal opportunity for the unimaginably eligible Hal and the unacceptably still-single me to meet, and perchance to fall in love.

At this juncture in my life, I was all for love. After five years of being wild and relatively carefree in New York City, I was even all for marriage. I wasn't necessarily all that intent on marrying someone who was so wealthy and successful. On the other hand, these were not personal attributes that I would necessarily rule out.

At the very least, it was nice to have potentially romantic plans for Valentine's Day, with which Artie's birthday party would happen to coincide. The thought of ending up spending this sex-and-romance-saturated holiday solo always filled me with dread. It invariably left me feeling like everyone on earth had someone to love and to love them back – everyone, that is, but me. Although I already had a boyfriend, he had just left for a week's vacation at a romantic island resort without me. That made me wonder whether I really had a boyfriend, or would still have a boyfriend, by the following Sunday, anyway.

$$\backsim\!\!\frown$$

The next day in the office, Lucy, a stunningly pretty production assistant at the magazine at which I worked, also happened to ask if I was free the following Sunday. Her new boyfriend, the one who'd gone to Harvard and who was a senior editor at *Time* magazine, had a close friend from Hartford who was coming to the city for the weekend. Lucy's boyfriend had asked her if she had a friend with whom she could fix him up.

Now, I already had committed to meeting my brother's friend's friend on Sunday. I also had been fixed up with enough friends of friends in my lifetime to know that most of the men they fixed you up with ended up being in drastic need of fixing up themselves. But there was another basic thing I also had learned about blind dates. If you let your mother fix you up, as I regrettably had, you ended up being stuck for the evening with a young, male version of your mother. If you let your father fix you up, as I regrettably had, you ended up being stuck for the evening with a younger version of your father.

But if you let someone hot like Lucy fix you up, you were likely to end up with someone hot, because hot guys were the only guys that someone like Lucy would date. And hot guys were the only guys that someone like Lucy thought *anybody* should date.

My only question was why it was worth my while to meet a man who lived in Connecticut. To me, anything outside the New York suburbs might as well have been in another country. Hartford practically *was* another country. It was at least two hours away.

Lucy shrugged. "Why not just meet him?" she asked. She had already done so herself and could attest to the facts that he was really cute and he drove a BMW.

I wasn't much of a car person, and was even less of a status person. I couldn't have cared less whether he drove a Rolls Royce or a beat-up old Chevy. "Really cute," however, was another story. Really cute, by Lucy's standards, probably *was* really cute.

Fortunately, it turned out that Lucy wanted me to meet her boyfriend's really cute friend in the morning by coming to her apartment for brunch. Even though Artie's party would be held out on Long Island, it wasn't scheduled to begin until mid-afternoon. This meant that I could fit in both social engagements, although I might have to cut the brunch a little short. It would be a bit hectic – and more than a bit self-indulgent – to go on two blind dates in one day, not to mention that I already had agreed to go out with my current boyfriend on Sunday night. But after five years of living in a three-ring circus like New York, I was used to juggling. There was no good reason that I couldn't manage all three.

$$\backsim$$

If it sounds like my life revolved exclusively around meeting men, believe me, that was not the case. I was keenly interested in virtually all of the arts. I was keenly interested in world events. And I was most keenly interested in scrambling out of the permanent purgatory in which my fledgling career in publishing now seemed to be stuck. Along with working long hours, I had recently completed a lengthy free-lance writing assignment at the magazine, then quickly proposed another, on which I was hard at work.

OK, so that last story actually had been about dating, my main area of expertise. This had not been executed based on personal experience, however. To help formulate "An Etiquette for the '80s," in view of all the confusion between the sexes that seemed to dominate the social scene, I had spent weeks interviewing a wide variety of single people. I'd probed into their typical dating patterns, exploring habits and customs ranging from whether men were still picking up checks to how quickly new couples were having sex.

" 'In the fifties,' " it began, quoting the late, great Mort Sahl, " 'you had to be Jewish to get a girl. In the sixties, you had to be black to get a girl. And in the seventies, you had to be a girl to get a girl.' And what about the eighties?... Emily Post may never have considered what the proper time is to leave a toothbrush at a new paramour's apartment. Or how soon after your first dinner out with someone you should be sharing breakfast in. But such are the dating dilemmas that face the average New York single. And here are some guidelines for dealing with them."

My current story was on a very different topic, one that I had contrived myself. The premise: Put too many laboratory rats in a cage, and they would tend to become withdrawn, aggressive or even homicidal, turn predominantly homosexual, and begin exhibiting all sorts of antisocial behaviors. Put people into living conditions that were too close for comfort, and they would quickly become typical New Yorkers, with all of the abrasive, uncivilized proclivities that these strange, disagreeable urban creatures seemed to embody and display. To prove my point, I was engaged in interviewing scientists, psychiatrists, and a vast assortment of people who shared tight living quarters: young married couples, old married couples, gay couples, co-habitating heterosexual couples, and unrelated roommates, both friends and strangers who were simply splitting the rent.

I spent much of my time outside the office either conducting these interviews or transcribing the tape recordings I'd made of them. But when Saturday, the day before my dates, rolled around, I found myself unable to concentrate. Maybe it was the suspense of my impending triple-header. Maybe it was the hint of an early spring thaw in the air. Whatever the cause, I decided that after a hard week of work, I deserved a little break. Besides, Artie's birthday party was the next day, and I had yet to buy him a present.

Men, as we all know, are very difficult to shop for. Women appreciate anything, especially anything pretty – a purse, a pin, a nice pashmina to help make them look thin. Men don't know from pretty. They also hardly accessorize or obsess about looking fat. When buying gifts for men, I generally try to avoid neckties – no matter how intimately you may know a man, you still may not get his taste in ties – and go for socks, instead. One size fits almost all, almost all are reasonably affordable, and who among us, given those mysterious disappearing acts in the clothes dryer, couldn't use a few more pairs?

So I headed down to one of the city's most stylish men's stores, Paul Stuart, where I painstakingly selected, in keeping with the impending holiday, a pair of bright red socks, a pair of plain black socks, and a pair of black socks with bright red hearts. Artie, like my brother, was a lawyer, but he was extremely lively and laid-back for a lawyer. I had little doubt that he would be able to take some flashy footwear in stride.

After my errand, I wandered aimlessly for blocks, gazing idly into shop windows, until I realized that it was getting late and I descended into the nearest subway station. Moments later, a car came to a crashing halt, and a pair of doors opened directly in front of me. I stepped aboard, looked straight ahead, and came face to face with Sam.

Sam, the most perfect man I had ever met. Sam, the one man I couldn't forget. Sam, the already married man for whom I had been lugging around a mammoth torch, more like a bonfire, sizzling with a flame that wouldn't die, for the better part of a year.

Over that year, I had considered that maybe Sam was not the flawless paragon of virtue I believed him to be; that for all I knew, he might be hard to live with – demanding or distant or self-involved or moody. I'd tried to convince myself of these terrible things.

But I never had.

I had tried to convince myself that someday soon I would meet someone else, someone who was actually available, and that he, too, would be handsome and brilliant, perceptive, warm, contemplative, and unpretentious, not to mention literary and talented, and that he would make me forget about every other man I had ever met, including Sam.

But I never had.

I also had remained unwilling to destroy a whole family with an extramarital affair, the way my own family had been torn apart when I was young. And so I had resolved that I would abandon all hopes that Sam's marriage might somehow come to an end, setting him miraculously free to be with me, if he ever became a father.

But he never had.

Once, a few months after we had first met and quickly concurred that having a clandestine relationship was unthinkable for us both, I'd found myself unexpectedly alone with him in the office. We had chatted briefly about how we both were. Then he had stood before me, touched his lips sweetly and oh, so fleetingly to mine, and said wistfully, "And now I'm going to keep walking before I do something that I'll regret."

I hadn't laid eyes on him since then. But there he was, standing before me now.

His face lit up instantly to see me. Mine, I could tell, just looked shocked.

Of all the cars in all the subways in all of New York City, I'd had to walk into his.

Over the din of the rumbling train, we exchanged all the news that either of us could bear to report, mostly events of a professional persuasion. He didn't mention any change in his marital status, so I could only assume there was none. But after a short while, as the train screeched and groaned its way uptown, I could stand it no longer.

"God damn it, Sam," I exclaimed, "why don't you guys have some kids already?"

Now it was his turn to look shocked. I had caught him completely off-guard.

"I can't believe you asked that," he said. "We just found out. My wife is pregnant. We haven't told anyone yet." They were going to have dinner with her parents' that very night and reveal the blessed event.

"*Mazel tov!*" I said, blurting out the phrase with which any good Jew greets any good news. "Really, that's wonderful. You must be so happy."

"We are," he said. His eyes, indeed, shone. But gazing at me, he didn't look happy. His mouth looked apologetic and sad.

Seconds later, we thundered into my station and I heard the doors part behind me.

"Well, see you," I said as I stepped out, my eyes still magnetically locked on his. "Take care of yourself. Take care of the baby!"

He smiled in the doorway. I smiled back. Then the doors closed, and he was gone.

I ambled the five blocks back to my building slowly, my arms wrapped around myself, protectively crisscrossing my midsection. I wasn't just huddling against the late-afternoon cold. I felt like I'd just been stabbed.

Throughout that year, I had continued to go out with assorted men, but my heart never had been fully in it. No matter where I went, or whom I met, my real feelings had always been kept on reserve. With my hopes now dashed, my soul had been set free. But this freedom felt less like openness than emptiness. My heart abruptly had been deserted, like a nice, clean house where nobody lived anymore, or nobody, at least, was home.

How bizarre it was that I had ended up in that subway car at that exact moment. Or maybe it had been beyond bizarre. It had been *beshert*, the Yiddish word for "fate."

I lived in a studio apartment on the top floor of a brownstone on West 88th Street. As I forlornly rounded the last of the four flights up, I heard my telephone begin to ring inside. I made myself hurry down the hall, then began fumbling with the keys, struggling to unlatch the door before the phone would stop. I reached it on the eighth ring.

The caller was distinctly male, but I didn't recognize his voice at all. His delivery was a deep basso profundo, with all the resonance of a radio announcer's. He said that he had gotten my number from his friend's girlfriend, Lucy.

He was taking me to brunch the next day and needed my address so that he could pick me up.

Oh, of course. Blind date No. 1! How nice to hear from him, I said. He asked if he could meet me at my place at around ten the following morning. I said that would be fine.

We continued to chat for a few more minutes. His first name was Harlan and his last name Levy, which he pronounced, oddly, to rhyme with "heavy." He said that he was a television news reporter at the NBC affiliate in Hartford. That helped to explain the big voice. I asked if this meant that he stood in front of a news scene each night reading from a prepared script. It was a snotty, impertinent question, but he didn't seem to take it that way. He replied that he wrote all of his own material. I had to admit he sounded nice.

I'm a little ashamed to confess that I'd been on enough blind dates in the past two years to have an entire blind-dating wardrobe. That is, my mother had persuaded me to meet numerous young men of her selection by buying me and plying me with assorted new outfits to wear. I guess she had my number, all right. If I had been one of those poor, out-of-work people whom you see standing by the highway, my placard might have read, "Will Date for Clothes."

The outfit I chose to get me through this action-packed day was selected for both comfort and style. A silk jumpsuit, it was modeled after a garage mechanic's monkey suit but in pale lavender, worn unbuttoned to the waist with a violet camisole underneath. Loosely gliding over my body and cinched at the center by a narrow belt, it was slinky enough to show that I was trim, but loose enough to leave a great deal to the imagination.

Lucy's friend, the TV reporter who wrote his own material, arrived at around ten, as promised, dressed in a faded blue polo shirt and relaxed khaki slacks. With straight, dark hair, brown eyes, and wire-rimmed glasses, he was indeed cute. He looked, in fact, like a Jewish John Lennon. An inch or two under 6 feet tall, he had a muscular yet lean physique. I also noticed that he had two purple marks on his face, one above his right eye, the other high on his forehead. These gave the slightly unsavory impression that he had recently been in a fistfight. He made no effort to explain them, though, and I decided not to ask.

The promised BMW was nowhere in sight, but that was of little consequence. Lucy lived only a few blocks away from me, in the lower West 80s. It was an easy walk.

Chatting with my date animatedly as we strolled along, I quickly formed an initial impression that he was funny and smart, but one of the most nervous people I'd ever met. He cleared his throat after almost every sentence and rarely looked me right in the eye. Maybe he had allergies. Maybe, like me, he was just shy.

Whatever. I never had been much of a look-you-right-in-the-eye type, either.

As we walked, it crossed my mind that I had neglected to ask Lucy what to bring. What sort of a good Jew visits anyone empty-handed? We needed to find a cake, and fast.

I had often noticed a bakery between my building and hers, but never been inside. The fact was that I had never dared to go inside. The place was called The Erotic Baker, and I could only imagine what it sold. Yet our journey took us through a residential area. Every other nearby store lay further west, and we were already too late to make a detour.

As we entered the small bakeshop that I had long avoided on West 83rd Street, I was alarmed to find that my fears about what lay within had been completely founded. The wares inside the glass case were abundant and attractive, but offered little choice. Half the cakes were shaped like a pair of breasts. All of the rest were giant phalluses. It somehow seemed even more embarrassing to suggest that we leave than to choose. I tried hard not to blush as we deliberated, finally settling upon a big chocolate-frosted penis.

"Do you want anything written on it?" the girl behind the counter asked matter-of-factly, as though we had just purchased a traditional, flower-embellished buttercream.

Harlan from Hartford shrugged and looked at me expectantly.

Inspiration overcame mortification. "How about 'I love Lucy'?" I asked.

He smiled broadly and nodded. Now I really blushed. Little did he realize that, as shy as he might seem, I often became almost catatonic by comparison. What if my brainstorm for this risqué inscription gave him the wrong idea about me?

Actually, in the interests of keeping him interested, I could only hope that this bawdy impulse *would* give him the wrong impression about me.

When we finally arrived at Lucy's, our lusty confection was met with raucous laughter all around. Reunited with Lucy's boyfriend, my really cute date began to relax. The more that he relaxed, the cuter he became. When an hour or two had raced by, and it came time for me to bid him goodbye for Long Island, I began to have second thoughts.

"Maybe I'll call Penn Station to see if there's a later train," I said.

When it came time to leave for the later train, I decided to take an even later one.

By the time I had managed to miss three trains, my date must have figured that his prospects were good. When it finally grew so late that I either had to leave or miss Arty's entire party, my date insisted on accompanying me downstairs and putting me in a cab. Then he did something even more polite. He opened the cab door and helped me inside.

"Let me ask you something," he said, crouching down to my eye level before shutting the door. "If I came back next Saturday, would you go out with me?"

"Sure," I said, realizing just as I said it that this meant I would have to break up with my boyfriend, with whom I had a standing date for Saturday nights. But what did it matter? If I'd wanted to keep seeing him, why would I have accepted two blind dates?

Besides, there was something awfully refreshing about having a man commit to meeting me a second time while the first meeting was still underway. During my five years of living in New York, I had discovered that no matter how enthusiastic any guy might feel about you, he still would continue to come across as totally noncommittal. Even if he liked you when you first met, you still would not hear from him again for at least a week or two. New York men just made it a strict policy to remain detached. Meanwhile, I had grown up believing that detachment, not hate, was the opposite of love. And while I slowly had come to expect it, and then even to accept it, I kept wishing and expecting that eventually I would meet someone who would take one look at me and say, "Yes!"

Now one had. Dare I hope that this miracle might strike twice in a single day?

&

By the time I arrived at Artie's party, the cake had already been served. Artie still looked thrilled to see me. My brother, however, did not. Where had I been all this time? He had nearly given up. He indicated my intended date, who looked none too cheerful himself. A pale, stocky fellow with short-cropped, light brown hair, the esteemed Hal sat across the room debating politics combatively with several male guests. He looked nice enough, but a little schlubby, with wrinkled, slightly ill-fitting clothes. I listened to him for awhile from afar, then gave up and wandered off to schmooze with my sister-in-law.

When the festivities broke up surprisingly early, I figured that my brother's scheme had been foiled, until he approached me with my intended mate by his side.

"I'd like you to meet Arty's friend Hal," he said. "He's driving back to the city, and says he wouldn't mind at all giving you a lift."

So I got to sit beside the venerable Hal for more than an hour, trying to make small talk. It wasn't easy. For my brother's sake, I did my best to answer all of his queries with personality. It felt more like being interviewed for a position than flirted with, though. By the time Hal had dropped me home, I had gotten the impression that had I been running for office – a romantic office, if there were such a thing, like the ruler of his heart – I might have won, but only by a narrow margin. I also realized that if he had been running for ruler of mine, he would have been the runner-up. By about a mile. So it was probably just as well that I never heard from him again.

&

I did hear from my man in Hartford, though. He called me every night that week.

I couldn't tell if he was going to great pains to plan the perfect date for the following weekend or just wanted to hear my voice. I also wondered a bit anxiously if he was presumptuous enough to assume that he was going to be staying overnight with me. So it was a relief when he mentioned that he'd be rooming with Lucy's boyfriend, Russ.

Actually, to be more precise, he'd be rooming with Lucy's *ex*-boyfriend, Russ. Just as I had been going on blind dates behind my boyfriend's back, Russ had gone on one of his own behind Lucy's. His date actually had been set up by his mother, but to his surprise, against all odds, he had liked the woman immensely and planned to see her again. He had admitted this to Lucy on Sunday, sometime after I'd left.

It wasn't the sort of confession anyone wants to hear from her boyfriend, especially on Valentine's Day. And so, I'm convinced that had I not gone to meet Lucy's boyfriend's friend from Hartford that Sunday morning, I never would have met him at all. Because by Monday morning, Lucy and her boyfriend had irrevocably broken up.

Just as I had anticipated, I had similarly parted ways with my current boyfriend, a low-key, non-demonstrative newspaper reporter. In fact, it turned out that we had secretly grown so disenchanted with each other that it was as if our eagerness to break up was a breaking story, and we were competing to see which one of us could report it to the other first. This not only relieved any lingering guilt I felt about the previous weekend's dates, but also cleared the deck for the coming weekend, plans for which were forging ahead.

My man in Hartford had continued to call. Once he had loosened up, he was no longer shy. Instead, he was bursting with personality, as well as personal questions. He was curious to know who I was, what I thought, what I liked, and in particular what sports I participated in.

"Tennis," I responded readily. I'd been playing it all my life.

Bingo! It was his favorite sport, too. He'd been on his school teams in both high school and college and continued to play ever since. "What else?" he asked.

What else? Wasn't that enough? I groped for a possible answer. I didn't play golf. Bombed at basketball. Wasn't a fan of football. Was it too wimpy to say Ping-Pong? "Pretty much all racquet sports," I replied.

He asked if this included squash. It did. I had learned to play in college.

"In that case," he said, "I'll pick you up a little before one." He suggested I come dressed to play.

The Princeton Club of New York had several squash courts in its basement, and as a graduate of Princeton and member of the club, he was entitled to use them. Why he wanted to use them with *me* was another matter. Never in all my life had I gone on such an athletic date. I could only wonder whether he was an exercise nut or just wanted to see how I looked in a T-shirt and shorts. He later confessed that it was a little bit of both. My loose silk jumpsuit had indeed left a little too much to the imagination.

After several invigorating games, during which both my shorts and I managed to score some points, I was glad to have brought along a nice change of clothes, because our next stop was The Plaza. Over cocktails in the legendary hotel's posh eatery, The Palm Court, we got to rest up while boning up on the basic details of each other's lives.

With a last name like Levy, he didn't need to tell me he was Jewish, but it was nice to learn that he was primarily of Russian descent, like me. Unlike me, he had gone away to prep school, then Princeton, but he had majored in English, like me. A law degree from N.Y.U. had led to a position in the cable TV bureau of the Federal Communications Commission. Yet after five years at the FCC, based in Washington, D.C., he'd come to the unequivocal conclusion that the entire field of law was too dry.

"It was totally boring, and offered absolutely no emotional arousal at all," he said. "Anything was exciting compared to the flatline of being an administrative lawyer."

Can't say I was about to object.

Through a close friend from his prep school, a Brit named Paul who now worked for the BBC in London, he had managed to land a few radio-reporting assignments, which he found to be infinitely more stimulating.

As a free-lance reporter based in the States, he'd gotten to interview a wide range of celebrities, from The Boss, Bruce Springsteen, to The Greatest, Mohammed Ali. Eventually, he'd managed to propel these random assignments into a full-time stint as a radio reporter and anchorman in a Boston suburb. This, in turn, had led to his becoming a news reporter on TV. He'd worked at a station in Richmond, Virginia, then another in Miami before accepting his current job in Hartford, which happened to be his hometown.

After three months there, he had concluded that dating women in Hartford offered about the same level of excitement as practicing law. And so, courtesy of Lucy, he also had gone on two blind dates in New York the weekend before. The first one had left him cold. The second, he told me, had been "va-va-voom – funny, sexy, verbal, and voluptuous." At this, I blushed deeper than the remains of the Bloody Mary I was sipping. The second had been me.

Just as exciting for me was to discover that he was witty and fun, and that his sense of humor was just as twisted as mine. We also had one other fundamental thing in common. Unlike too many of the men I came across – lawyers, doctors, bankers, and businessmen – he was clearly a creative type. I couldn't picture him trying to practice law. He enjoyed being imaginative and inventive, and especially took delight in doing this with words. He admitted to having won several poetry prizes in high school, and said that the only thing he could imagine that might be more fun than writing a novel, play, or lyrics for a musical was the prospect of doing any or all of these things with me.

But for the moment, he had planned more than enough other things for us to do together. After drinks, we had dinner at a restaurant that had a comedy club, then took in its rather ribald show. Then, the night being barely middle-aged, he invited me to come up to Russ's apartment. Russ, it turned out, was away for the weekend. It was with only mild hesitation that I agreed to this, and then, once inside, settled beside him on a couch.

Up to that moment, as enthusiastic as he seemed, he had yet to lay a hand on me. What, I wondered, was he waiting for? After we had talked for fifteen minutes or so, I could stand it no longer. When he leaned forward to take a sip of soda, I gave in to a sudden impulse and let my hand run down the back of his head and lightly stroke his shiny, dark hair. He later admitted that this was a technique he had picked up over the years. The best way to get a woman really interested was to let her make the first move.

Yet at that point, he barely wasted two seconds before making the second move. Or, for that matter, the third. After about twenty minutes of intense, impassioned, and extremely pleasurable kissing, I felt him begin to fumble with the zipper on my pants.

Now it was my turn to clear my throat. "Heh-hem! Uh, excuse me," I piped up. "Just where do you think you're going, buster?"

I later admitted that this was a technique that I had picked up over the years. The best way to get a guy really interested was to not let him go too far on the first few dates.

I guess it worked, because before I left he proposed yet a third date. But he didn't want to return to New York the following weekend. Now he wanted me to come see *him*.

There he was, in the promised BMW double-parked in front of Hartford's Union Station. The car turned out to be a little the worse for wear, both on its rusting body and in its cluttered interior. His apartment, however, was surprisingly neat. He confessed that he had hired a cleaning service in order to impress me. I confessed that I was impressed.

After quickly depositing my bags at his place, he took me on a driving tour of the city. I had passed through it on the highway perhaps a hundred times, traveling to and from the college I'd attended outside Boston, but until now I'd never had a reason to stop. The downtown area looked grim and sterile, like many a second-string American city, but the surrounding environs boasted stately mansions and well-manicured private homes.

I had arrived early on Saturday afternoon. That night, we went to a party given by a pair of his closest friends, Chris and Marie. Lucy's former beau Russ was also there, up visiting for the weekend with Ellen, the woman he had met on his own blind date. Despite Hartford's public image as the Insurance

Capital of the World, most of the guests turned out to be artsy types – writers, painters, and museum curators – and I felt totally at ease with them almost immediately. But to be honest, I wasn't fully focused on getting acquainted with Harlan's friends. For one thing, he and I had suddenly come down with a mysterious condition perhaps best described as Can't Keep Our Hands Off Each Other. For another, I was wondering what was going to happen that night right after the party, because as I had expected, Harlan's apartment had only one bedroom. And only one bed.

I was wondering about it, but I wasn't really worrying about it, because by this point I realized that I had neither the need nor the desire to continue playing hard to get. Somehow, in only two weeks, this manic man with the deep voice and I had progressed from blind date to dating to no longer dating because we were already in a relationship. How time flies when you want to make love.

Thinking back to that first night, I have no specific memory of any special moves or moments. What I remember most is wondering about one of those "chicken or the egg" equations: Is it depth of feeling that leads you to have sensational sex, or is it sensational sex that leads you to have such depth of feeling?

After a night like that, it was a little embarrassing to be taken to meet his mother. On the other hand, his wanting me to meet her, and her to meet me, was something new for me and extremely nice. In all the years that I had lived in New York, and with all the men that I had dated in New York, not once had I been asked to meet anyone's mother. Yet only two weeks to the day after we had met, I was already being introduced to his.

Afterwards, we went to a birthday party given by another one of his friends who lived by the sea in Branford, Connecticut, about an hour south. Then he drove me to the train station in New Haven. We stood clutching each other on the platform until my train arrived. Then he carried my bag right onto the train, hoisted it onto the overhead rack, and wrapped his arms around me. We stood there until a conductor shouted, "All aboard!"

Then he put his lips close to my ear. "I love you," he whispered, then stepped off.

This was long before cell phones existed. I had to wait two hours before arriving home in New York to call him with my response.

He lifted the receiver on the very first ring. "I love you, too," I said.

—⁌—

It was heartbreaking not only to be sequestered two hours away, but also to know that we wouldn't even be together the following weekend. He was flying to Miami to be an usher in a close friend's wedding. But Monday night, he called me with an inspiration. "Come to Miami with me," he said.

The next night, I decided to go to my father's apartment for dinner. I felt guilty that I hadn't seen him in weeks. Normally, I tried to stop by his place for Sunday brunch. But that, I informed him, wasn't on the upcoming agenda.

"I'm going to Miami next weekend," I said.

"What do you mean, you're going to Miami next weekend?" he asked. "Why are you going to Miami?"

"I'm going with this guy I recently met," I said. "He's going to be in a wedding, and I'm going to be with him."

I thought my father's eyes would pop out of his head. "Let me tell you right now," he said. "You are not going to Miami this weekend with some guy that you just met."

"But *Dad*," I said. How was I supposed to explain this to him?

Then I heard five words come out of my mouth. Until I had said these words out loud, I hadn't even thought them to myself inside my head. "I'm going to marry him."

"You're going to *what*?" he asked.

When I called my mother to report my impending trip to Miami, I had the good sense not to mention the marriage part. Still, she was far more receptive and encouraging. She only wondered if I had something appropriate to wear to the wedding. "If you don't, then go buy something new," she said. "Just make sure it isn't too low-cut."

In fact, I had nothing appropriate for a wedding in Miami, but here's another tip about romance I had picked up over the years: Whatever your mother tells you to do, try to listen carefully. Then, at your earliest opportunity, be sure to do exactly the opposite.

So the next day at lunchtime, I dashed over to Saks Fifth Avenue and bought a summery-looking dress with pale orange, cream, and lavender stripes and gold spaghetti straps. It was very pretty, fit perfectly, and was the lowest-cut dress I could find.

Back at the office, I proudly showed my purchase to famed fashion arbiter Anna Wintour, who was then the style editor at the magazine at which I worked. My ebullient heart withered a bit when she sneered, shook her head disapprovingly, and ventured a professional opinion that this frivolous garment would soon be out of style. Oh, well. Whether she was right or not, maybe she wasn't the ideal person to give me romantic advice, either.

Harlan flew from Hartford, I flew from New York, and a funny thing happened to me on the plane. I ended up sitting with an older couple and their son, who was about my age and worked for his father. "The Feinsteins" were headed for a business conference that they were conducting at a luxurious hotel on Key Biscayne. To their great frustration, several people who had enrolled for the conference had backed out at the last minute, too late to cancel their hotel reservations. Mrs. Feinstein asked where I was staying in Miami.

"All those rooms are already paid for," she sighed. "You might as well use one of them." I politely declined this generous invitation, but she persisted until I would accept.

I had told them that I was going down to meet my new boyfriend and to attend a wedding. I also had mentioned that I worked for a certain prominent magazine in the city.

For many weeks after I returned, I continued to field calls from Mrs. Feinstein at work. If I wasn't willing to date her son, she said, then the least that I owed them was to write an article to help promote their company. As embarrassing as I found these overtures, I kept insisting that I already had a boyfriend and that I owed them nothing. But this wasn't entirely true. I owed them for helping to facilitate the most romantic weekend of my life.

The water licking the beach on Key Biscayne mirrored the perfect azure sky, the sand that it lapped was finer than salt, and the bed linens we lolled in together at night were as cool, white, and inviting as an ice cold glass of milk.

Compared to the frigid clime we'd left behind, it felt like we'd been reassigned from Siberia to Shangri-la. And as hard as it was to drag ourselves out of bed each morning, we also managed, at his insistence, to jog on the beach every day and play a few invigorating sets of tennis.

Not that this was a purely recreational excursion, mind you. I had an extremely low-cut dress to wear, and he had some serious ushering to do. At the lively rehearsal dinner, I was welcomed by Harlan's good friend Arthur and his beautiful bride Sari as though I were a cherished old friend. I also got to meet Harlan's best friend, Rick, whom I had been warned was a demanding and finicky fellow, yet with whom I managed to hit it off instantaneously. Together, we had enormous fun engaging in one of my all-time favorite activities, collaborating on some silly new lyrics to an old tune in order to musically, and hopefully amusingly, toast the happy couple.

Performed to the melody of The Band's "The Night They Drove Old Dixie Down," it had a chorus mixing English with Hebrew and bit of mumbo-jumbo that went like this:

> The night our Art met Sari Kim
> All the bells were ringin',
> The night she first laid eyes on him
> And all the people were singin',
> They went, *Sh'ma na na na na na*
> *vitzy vahnoo, mah nishtanah!*

At the lavish wedding that followed the next day, Harlan and I danced and got caught up in the spirit of romance. Then, before we flew home, I got to introduce my new beau to someone of incalculable importance to me. Although he hadn't yet met my parents, in Hollywood, Florida, just north of Miami, there lived an even higher authority.

My mother's mother, Grandma Mary, had never seemed too fond of any boyfriend of mine she had ever met. In fact, just being around almost any man seemed to turn her from fairly merry into "Mary, Mary, Quite Contrary." I can't say that she particularly cared for this one, either. But she was so happy to see me, and to see me finally happy, that she somehow forgot to give Harlan from Hartford a hard time.

The only one having a hard time was me. Later that day, waiting for my plane to board, I decided that what I'd said to my father about him hadn't been all that crazy. But if I had to keep leaving him, week after week, then I soon might be crazy myself.

—❦—

The very first day that we had met, I had severed ties with my official boy-friend. But there still remained about ten other men I also had been seeing casually on the side. The week after spending the weekend in Hartford, I had begun phoning all of these men. I called to announce that I had met someone. I had decided that I was finished with them. Every one of them but one.

I didn't call this last person because it had been a long time since I had completely cleared the decks for anyone. Pinning my hopes on just one man seemed awfully risky.

I didn't call him because I was used to having people, and men in par-ticular, let me down repeatedly, and to having promising situations turn unex-pectedly disastrous. I didn't call him because I wanted to wait just a little longer, until I was really sure.

I also didn't call him because I couldn't quite imagine telling this man that I never wanted to see him again. I couldn't imagine this because I still couldn't quite believe that he had asked me out in the first place.

As a present for the birthday I had celebrated the previous month, my father had graciously paid for me to spend a week at Club Med. Never before had I been to one of these resorts, notorious for their raucous singles scenes and the free-spirited guests who bathed nude on the beach. Arriving in Guadeloupe, I'd quickly come to the conclusion that the name Club Med, presumably referring to its mostly Mediterranean locales, was instead short for "medical." Nearly every man I met there was a physician of some kind.

Most of these doctors seemed socially inept and rather desperate to meet women. One in particular, though, made a decidedly different, much more favorable impression. "Dr. Barry Seidel" was an adorable, dark-haired, Jewish pediatrician from Long Island. He seemed bright, quick-witted, and sweet, and I became infatuated with him right away. As it turned out, he had read my magazine story about dating, which had appeared on newsstands the previous week. He even came to my room to have me autograph his copy. Yet he rapidly homed in on another female guest, a curvaceous brunette who always seemed to be popping out of her bikini top and who struck me as a bit of a bimbo.

I could only conclude, despondently, that as amused as he seemed whenever we chatted, he just didn't find me attractive. So I was shocked when, the morning that we left the resort, he had sidled up to me in the hotel lobby and asked me for my phone number. Then, shortly after we had returned to real life, he'd shocked me even more by using it. We had been seeing each other with some frequency ever since.

Maybe I was his physical type, after all, and he, certainly, was mine. The more that I got to know him, though, the less that I believed he was remotely right for me. Most unsettling was the time that he called to ask me out for dinner the following week. He was coming in from the Island to take a class at The New School for Social Research.

When we met, he told me all about the class over dinner. Its name was a play on the title of a popular Paul Simon song. Not "Bookends," "Graceland," or "The Sound of Silence." The name of the class that he was taking was "50 Ways to Meet Your Lover."

Now, it seems to me that as a pediatrician, he might have wanted to explore, say, "50 Ways to Make Young Patients Comfortable," or "50 Ways to Treat Strep Throat." But to take a class with a name like that, and then have the nerve to tell me about it? Well, let's just say that he seemed to be suffering from a terminal case of tackiness.

Yet isn't it always the case? Just as my attraction toward him began to wane, his interest in me started to expand in an inversely proportional way. Or maybe he was just practicing one of his 50 new lover-locating techniques on me. One night, shortly before the weekend of the two blind dates, he had called to tell me about a popular band that I had mentioned I liked. I think it was The Waitresses, but it might have been The Go-Gos. He had heard that they would be playing Madison Square Garden the following month. Hoping to surprise me, he had already taken the liberty of buying us two seats.

This upcoming concert was scheduled for the week after I returned from Miami. It seemed rather insensitive to tell him before this occasion that I was no longer available. It also seemed a little callous to disengage myself from our once-promising relationship over the phone. I figured that I would go to the concert, behave like I was appreciative, and then tell him soon after, the next time that we met. But by the night of the concert, in view of my newfound passion, I had begun to have extremely intense feelings of regret.

I couldn't imagine letting someone pay for a pair of expensive concert tickets and dinner out, and then not even kissing him goodnight. I also couldn't imagine kissing him. The thought of having physical contact with another man made me almost physically ill.

Under the circumstances, I was not too upset when he was late to pick me up.

Then he was very late.

Then, at last, he called to say he was somewhere on the Long Island Expressway. "I'm so, so sorry," he said. "I had a bad car accident driving in on the L.I.E. I'm still here waiting for the cops to come." He wouldn't be able to make it in for the concert, he said. He wouldn't be able to make it into the city that night at all. "I'm fine," he assured me, "but I think my car is probably totaled."

Assuming that this story was not an L.I.E. itself – and he sounded so shaken that I believed it – I felt terrible for him. But also terribly relieved. Even better than having escaped a dreaded obligation was to realize that it had helped me crystallize my feelings. If I was so sickened by the prospect of kissing Dr. Barry Seidel, I must really be in love.

And so I met him for coffee soon after, over which I let him down gently. He seemed genuinely disappointed, which I must admit was nicer than having him seem genuinely happy for me. "If anything ever changes, you know where to find me," he said.

I nodded. That was nice to hear, too, although I couldn't imagine ever calling.

Only one month earlier, there had been ten men in my life.
Then one day, I'd met Harlan from Hartford.
And now there was only one.

—ↀ—

As deeply as I cared for him, the name "Harlan from Hartford" was getting
to feel like quite a mouthful. Not that I had ever used this moniker directly to
his face. The fact was, I didn't know what to call him, so I usually didn't call
him anything. Although he told me that he had been named after a former
chief justice of the Supreme Court, Judge Harlan Fiske Stone, "Harlan" struck
me as a pretentious, stuffy name. Nearly every TV soap opera had a character named Harlan. He, in the meantime, was having a hard time calling me
Pattie, which just didn't seem to suit me. It was too perky, a cheerleader name.

"I know," he finally said. "How about if I call you by your Hebrew name?"

And so, by the time that we had reluctantly returned from our weekend
in Florida, he had begun referring to me as Penina. But somehow, I couldn't
see calling him Chaim, the Hebrew name that had been given to him at
birth. The old rabbi at my family's temple had been a Chaim. I knew that
Chaim. I'd been bat mitzvahed by that Chaim. My new boyfriend, by comparison, was certainly no Chaim. He was too free-spirited and randy to be
a Chaim. And so, for want of a better option, I simply took to calling him
"Mr. Levy."

The "Mr." part was probably modeled after a funny tradition in my family.
I often called my brother Joel "Mr. Joelly," and he, in turn, would refer to me
as "Mr. Sister." And we both called our father "Mr. Daddy." (No, my mother
was not "Mr. Mom.") But calling my boyfriend "Mr. Levy" felt extremely
formal, and was more than a little odd. He happened to be a little more than
a decade older than I was. And as a former preppie and former Princeton
man, he tended to wear tweed sport jackets almost everywhere, even to the
supermarket. Anyone eavesdropping on us in public might have gotten the
misguided impression that I was a grad student dating her professor.

Let them think what they wanted. I'd always wanted to date a professor, anyway.

The closer we got, the more agonizing it became to be separated by such distance. I found myself living mostly for the weekends, which soon fell into a regular routine. Every other Friday, he would drive down to visit me in New York City. On the alternate Fridays, I would take the train north to see him. These rendezvous always raced by much too quickly. Still, while we were together, we managed to make the most of them.

I quickly had come to recognize that he was far from the shy, earnest fellow I had taken him for at first. Rather, he was eccentric, quirky, and a bit of a buffoon, someone who did the chicken dance at parties and often paired an orange shirt with blue shorts, purple socks, and bright red athletic shoes. Yet I had been right in my initial impression that he could act like a hyperactive maniac. Brimming with energy, he tended to jog everywhere, rather than to walk. And if he happened to run into a friend along the way, then while having a long conversation he would just continue to run in place.

But that always-on-the-go quality could be fun and invigorating, especially when we were desperately trying to pack an entire life together into two days every week. Besides, I found his idiosyncratic qualities to be refreshing, captivating, and delightful. Or so I indicated in one of the letters I wrote to him during my long train rides up:

> *I wish you would relax and stop wondering when I'm going to discover what's "wrong" with you — your weird eccentricities. Do you really think that you keep things under wraps? Or not realize that I'm in this because of all the weird things, not despite them?*
>
> *It's been about twelve weeks (is that all?) and I still think you're perfect and extraordinary and one of a kind, and I love you (yup)...*

Since he worked the night shift at the TV station, which meant he didn't get off until 11 p.m., when I went up I would take a cab from the train station and let myself into his apartment. One Friday night, while waiting for him to return, I began foraging in his living room to see if I could find some old photographs. I was still curious about those marks on his face, yet still hesitant to ask. He had yet to mention them, and they had yet to fade. Had he been in a terrible accident? Or were they something he'd been born with?

The first packet of photos I found included mostly shots of a former girl-friend. Several of these showed the woman stark naked. Nothing overly kinky. Just naked. Oops! Well, at least I thought that I looked a little better than she did. I put those pictures back.

The next photos I found were of another girlfriend. At least this one was dressed.

The only childhood photographs I could find were old black-and-white snapshots. They were so old and small that it was impossible to tell. So the next morning, as gently as possible, I finally got up my nerve to ask. He said that the two marks were a kind of birthmark known as port wine stains. It seemed like an apt enough name; they were the color of red wine. Even as a kid, he said, he had never been self-conscious about them. The only thing that bothered him now was that his TV job required him to cover them with makeup whenever there were close-ups of him on the air.

I just nodded, happy to have an answer at last. They didn't bother me at all, either. If anything, they just made his face a little more uniquely his.

Besides, with his birthmarks, he looked a little on the outside the way I felt inside. Scarred from birth. Scarred for life.

⸺☙⸺

To optimize the weekends on which I went to visit him, he quickly convinced me to always stay over for a third night, until Monday morning. Then he would awaken with me before dawn and drive me to the station. The return trip to New York took a full three hours, but if I made the train that left at around 6 a.m., I could get to work just past 9. Unfortunately, I was then so exhausted that I'd be almost useless by the time I got there.

He tried to extend the weekends that he came down, too, departing to see me after work on Fridays at 11 p.m. This didn't truly give us a third night, though, because by the time he arrived it was often after 2 a.m. As strange as it may sound, after he got off work in Hartford, he would go pick up his widowed mother and bring her to the city with him. All of her relatives lived in New York, so she had people to visit there and places to stay.

While breathlessly awaiting his arrival, I managed to keep busy. We had gotten into the habit of exchanging small, quirky gifts every week including strange stuffed animals and figurines. It was nice to finally find someone who enjoyed giving gifts as much as I did and was willing to put in the extra effort to find just the right one for me.

Having discovered that Mr. Levy was a chocolate lover, I also always stopped by one of many fancy confectioners on the way home and purchased a box of something special – Godiva, Teuscher, Neuhaus, or Ghirardelli, the more extravagant the better.

Capitalizing on another of his passions, I would cook something special as well. Of all the women he had ever dated – and evidently there had been many – nearly every one with whom he had gotten involved had been of another religion. He seemed to revel in the fact that I was a fellow Jew. He also relished eating many Jewish delicacies. And so, while waiting, I would prepare a large bowl of his favorite, chopped chicken liver. (The recipe is simple: Lightly broil a pound or so of chicken livers. Dice and fry a yellow onion in vegetable oil until it begins to brown. Puree the liver in a food processor with two hard-boiled eggs. Add onions, salt, and mayonnaise to taste. Chill before serving.)

If I had time left, I would construct an inventive and often suggestive sign to place beside my buzzer in the lobby to welcome him when he arrived. These were elaborate creations mixing bits of poetry and phrases with drawings and letters cut from magazines to form crazy collages or mobiles joined together with string. Most were written on the heart-shaped sheaves of a pink memo pad I owned, then embellished with kisses made by a lip-shaped, red-inked rubber stamp I'd bought for this express (and expressive) purpose.

One such note was written mostly in French. (It seemed romantic, and he spoke the language fluently, even though mine was pretty rusty and highly ungrammatical.) This challenged him to choose between two tiny pen-and-ink drawings that I'd cut from *The New Yorker*, one of a lovely rocking chair, the other a beach chair under an umbrella. Beneath them, I typed:

Pas de différence. Je préfère faire rien avec toi que faire les choses avec quelqu'un.
  (*It makes no difference. I would rather do nothing with you than something with anyone else.*)

Another note spoke a far more universal language. "Please take your clothes off immediately!"

Unfortunately, he couldn't take action on such suggestions quite so quickly. When he arrived, I'd run down, and together we would drive his mother to the apartment of whichever one of her sisters she was staying with. Then we would drive back to my place, where he'd devour the entire bowl of chopped liver and savor some of the chocolates, after which we'd both collapse. (Is it any wonder that during those months, his lean frame put on nearly 20 pounds?) With luck, we would awaken refreshed in the morning. And even if we didn't, it didn't matter. We'd spend nearly half the day in bed.

Then we'd go jogging and play squash or tennis, often a lively game of mixed doubles with Russ and Ellen, who were still dating.

At the end of the weekend, since he didn't need to get to work until 3 p.m., I would leave him behind in my apartment when I departed for work on Monday morning. Then, before he departed to retrieve his mother and return home, he would compose some sort of farewell note or other missive, often complete with drawings, to leave me.

Most of these were composed on the large pieces of cardboard discarded from the button-down shirts he had pressed at the dry-cleaner's. All were exceedingly romantic.

"It almost happened in Miami," read one, "it didn't happen in Richmond, and not yet in Hartford… only in NYC – when I became a Love victim."

Then there was the one that said only this:

morning becomes you,
afternoon desires you.
And I want you.

He signed that one "Love, Harlan." That was unusual, though. The Hebrew name by which he called me had gradually morphed, from Penina to P'nini to just plain Nini (which rhymed with "genie.") Meanwhile, I had begun calling him, for lack of any better idea, *Mr.* Nini. That is what we were calling each other the day that he left this silly note:

May 1, 1982, the year of the frog & broccoli

Dear Nini,

Now, be a good nini and write your articles, and don't be late to work, and don't forget to call your boyfriend, and make sure nobody gets under the covers but one nini and one Mr. Nini. Also, don't spill your noodles on your new blouse and don't dribble your banana daiquiris on it … and remember, Mr. Nini will be lonely without you, so come to Hartford and meet him next week, and tell your mother to send chopped liver –

Love,

Mr. Nini

The mention of my mother came in the wake of my having taken him home for Passover. Thrilled to meet the man she now surmised might become her son-in-law, she had welcomed him warmly with a big hug, homemade matzo ball soup, and a large bowl of chopped liver that was evidently even better than mine. He still had yet to meet my father, however. To introduce him at this point seemed premature, considering that my father continued to express some reservations about our relationship. To put it mildly.

Being the self-made man that he was, my father didn't find the field of TV news reporting to be particularly impressive. Although he had always made it a practice to stay well-informed, creativity and literary prowess were not among his priorities. Money was. He probably would have preferred if Mr. Nini had remained at the FCC. No, scratch that. He would have preferred if Mr. Nini had *owned* the FCC.

Other misgivings related to age. If my dad was concerned about my "getting on" at the age of 27, then Mr. Nini was beyond the pale in terms of acceptable bachelorhood. He was nearly 38.

My father remained doubtful that a marriage between us would ever materialize. "A man of 37 who has never married doesn't want to be married," he warned repeatedly.

Like the rest of the litany of dire predictions and pessimistic decrees relentlessly issued by both my parents, this one did little to intimidate me. "You're wrong," I replied each time. "A man of 37 who has never been married *needs* to get married right away!"

Our budding relationship encountered no such resistance from Mr. Nini's family.

The first time I'd met his mother, Harriet, she had struck me as extremely formal. Not only did I fear I'd never feel comfortable enough to call her by her first name, as she had suggested; she was so austere that I thought I'd never manage to feel comfortable with her at all. But soon after Mr. Nini and I began to date, I realized that I'd won her over. As stiff and proper as she might seem, in her own reserved way she had already warmed up to me.

I also realized that, although her husband had died 15 years earlier, while Mr. Nini was in law school, this 78-year-old widowed mother was not the true head of the family. The apparent head of the family, as far as I could tell, was the crusty, elderly dowager who lived directly across the hall from Harriet, a woman named Anna Smith.

Anna Smith, or "Aunt Smith," as my mother mistook her name to be, had several unspecified ailments that she delighted in harping about whenever she had a visitor. "With kidneys like these, who needs enemies?" she'd remark, mawkishly sipping her tea. Good fortune, a little finagling, and a colorful personality had led her to prosper in earlier days as an insurance broker. She had never been married, to my knowledge, although this was not for a lack of interest in the institution, I surmised. At least she took more than a passing interest in almost everyone else's affairs of the heart. Especially Mr. Nini's. During the 15 years that Harriet had been her neighbor, either she had come to view him with great affection – like a favorite nephew or a surrogate son – or she was just incorrigibly nosy.

"You're the fifty-eighth girl he's brought home," she told me the first time I was paraded into her living room. "I've actually been fond of one or two. I want to see how you measure up."

She then proceeded to ask me what she considered to be all the right questions. Did my father have money? Had I done well in school? Was I Jewish? (She was, apparently, despite her Anglo-Saxon-sounding name.) What was my political affiliation? Was I a good cook? Was I fond of children? Vacuuming? New England? And Harlan?

Hesitant to offend her in front of her other guests – Harriet and three more beaming octogenarians from the building – I replied to all of these queries with polite candor. Apparently, my answers were satisfying enough, for on all subsequent visits to Harriet, I was invariably marched across the hall in order to show Anna Smith my new dress or to taste her casserole and also invariably to answer even more pointed questions.

"We're not getting any younger, you know," she'd chide me with feigned irritability. "When's the date? Where are the grandchildren? I can't wait forever!"

Although of indeterminate age and health, Aunt Smith was right about the last bit. She couldn't afford to wait forever. If we dared to ring her doorbell unexpectedly, she'd receive us propped up in bed with obvious effort and considerable discomfort. When our visits were anticipated, I'd find her seated on the stiff, somber Victorian-style couch in her living room, her plump body swaddled in a quilted bathrobe, her scowling face a crinkled, powdery white except for two round dabs of rouge ... and still in obvious discomfort. But even in this compromised state, she always gave a semblance of vigor, like a queen tempestuously holding court, or a five-star general preparing to do battle.

"Believe me, dear, you're doing something wrong," she admonished me once. "Men don't want to marry Emily Dickinson these days."

On other days, she abruptly dispensed with such hints and proceeded to offer not just personal philosophy, but also specific strategies to help ease us toward matrimony.

To my own discomfort, this advice became progressively more and more graphic. "You don't want to end up alone," she pronounced with authority once. "Take it from me. But if you give him *everything* he wants – not to be crude, but you understand me, I'm sure – you'll never get anything in return."

Wait a minute. What had happened to my image as Emily Dickinson, prim maiden poet, scribbling alone in a garret? Apparently, Anna Smith had a network of spies helping to keep tabs on us. She seemed to know all about our lodging arrangements, our every move, even our every meal.

"You went to your mother's for dinner last weekend," she reported one afternoon in April. "He likes your mother. She makes a good brisket. So what are you waiting for?"

What *was* I waiting for?

I guess I was waiting to get to know Mr. Nini a little better. And waiting for him to get to know me better. Or maybe I was just waiting for conniving old Anna Smith to come up with some new ploys a little more practical than my withholding sexual favors.

⎯⎯⎯ ᧒ ⎯⎯⎯

One weekend in May, Mr. Nini's good friend Rick came up to visit from Miami. He had a girlfriend in tow and wanted to give her a quintessential New York experience. A recent cover story in the magazine at which I worked had pronounced singles bars to be all the rage. Never mind that they were mostly the rage with the so-called Bridge and Tunnel crowd. Rick wanted to go to the trendiest one, and he wanted us to go with him.

On the way to Grass, an action-packed watering hole in the East 70's, his date and I had an inspiration. To help get fully immersed in the scene, wouldn't it be fun if we women went to the bar alone and the two guys came over and tried to pick us up? We joked about the terrible pickup lines they might use. "Hey, baby! What's your major? What's your sign? Wanna make like a tree and leave?"

Insisting that they were far smoother than that, they agreed to take the challenge.

It was a little early in the evening for things to be in full swing, and to our surprise Rick's date and I managed to find two seats at the bar. Meanwhile, the guys went to the other side and tried to order some drinks. It took a while for them to get the bartender's attention, though, and by the time that they finally approached us, cocktails in hand, someone else had already come over to me and tried to strike up a conversation.

I told this man that I was with someone else, but this did little to discourage him.

"Oh, yeah? Where is he?" he asked, sounding skeptical.

I indicated Mr. Nini. This man, who was closer to my age and a bit of a brute, did not seem impressed. Even when Mr. Nini had come over and sheepishly settled at my other side, he showed no intention of leaving.

"I don't want to scare you, but my boyfriend is a champion boxer," I told him. "You'd better clear out while you can."

He just smirked, then laughed. We four were the ones who finally cleared out.

Walking back to my apartment, I tried to shrug it off. But Mr. Nini wouldn't let it go.

"Tell me something," he said, once Rick and his date had bid us a good night. "How often does that happen to you?"

"I don't know," I replied.

"*About* how often?" he asked.

I actually had never been to a singles bar before in my life.

"All the time," I lied.

He didn't seem to like this answer. We walked another block in silence.

"We're going to have to do something," he said, "so that never happens again."

"OK," I said. "What are we going to do?"

"I don't know," he said. "Something."

We walked another block.

By now, he was almost sputtering.

"What if…" he said. Then he said it again. "What if…"

It was as far as he could get with that thought.

By now, we were only a block away from my apartment building.

"What are you trying to say?" I asked.

"I'm trying to say, um… I mean… What if we were to get married?" he said.

"That would be something," I agreed.

That would be also something, I agreed, that I would want to do.

When we got up to my apartment, I went straight to the refrigerator. I pulled out the bottle of champagne I'd been saving for years in case I ever had anything to celebrate.

I proudly brought this out, then returned to the kitchen to get glasses.

"Actually, I've never really liked champagne all that much," he called after me. "Do you have any chocolate milk?"

I didn't. I also didn't stop to think whether I really wanted to marry a 37-year-old man who would prefer to toast our impending marriage with a glass of U-Bet or Bosco.

As time wore on, I began to realize that "impending" was a bit of an exaggeration, anyway. The only things that were impending for us were countless more hours of travel.

Before we could even consider getting married, we needed to be living in the same city. There had been a time in the not-so-distant past when, as the woman, I would have been expected to simply pick up and join him wherever his occupation required him to live. I had a good job, though, even if I wasn't advancing quite as rapidly as I would have liked. I wasn't about to quit before locating at least a comparable job to replace it. Meanwhile, whenever I visited, his friends' wives, many of whom were imported brides, warned me not to move to Hartford.

"You don't want to live here. It's too boring," one told me. It would be foolish to consider coming, even on a temporary basis, she said. "Remember, his mother's here. You'll never get away!"

We had already ruled out the possibility of Mr. Nini moving to New York to be with me. New York was the top television market in the nation. And as much as I thought he was the greatest man to ever live, he was unlikely to find a job there.

And so, heeding his friend's wives' friendly advice, I asked him where else in the country he might like to live, in the event that we were to compromise and both relocate.

His first choice, by far, was Washington, D.C. Although he had once opted to flee the FCC, this had been due to no fault of the nation's capital. He'd loved living there.

By a stroke of luck, a brand new national newspaper had just been launched in Alexandria, Virginia, a Washington suburb. I sent clips of my few published articles, was flown down for an interview, and on the spot was offered a job as a feature reporter there.

I would be replacing another reporter who had left abruptly, so the paper, *USA Today*, needed me to start at once. I trusted that Mr. Nini would find a position nearby before long. So I accepted and gave notice at the magazine immediately.

It's a funny thing, giving notice. When you aren't happy working somewhere, the only thing that keeps you going is fantasizing about getting to tell your boss off someday. But when the day finally comes that you're ready to leave, you can't tell him or her off. Just in case the new job doesn't work out, or they happen to talk to others in the industry, you have to suck up to them even more than you did while you still wanted the job.

As it is, I had never been too good at sucking up, even when I still wanted the job. Once, about a year before meeting Mr. Nini, I had gotten so frustrated that, instead of sucking up, I had actually practically told off my boss's boss.

My boss's boss was the head editor of the magazine, and although he may have been a good editor, he wasn't a particularly nice editor. At least, he wasn't nice to me.

Sometimes he would summon me to his office and blast me for various mistakes I had made. At other times, he would call me in and proceed instead to tell me a joke or anecdote. It filled me with terror, having to go in there never knowing what to expect.

After a few years of this, and of going nowhere fast, I had heard that newswoman Barbara Walters needed a new assistant at ABC News. I went for an interview and was very encouraged. In fact, I was led to expect that she might actually hire me. When I called the next day, however, my hopes were destroyed. Her current assistant told me that Ms. Walters had deemed me over-qualified and feared I wouldn't stay in the job for long.

The editor of the magazine, who was an inveterate name-dropper, claimed to be on a first-name basis with Ms. Walters. And at this point, I was so frustrated working at the magazine that I barely wanted my job anymore. And so I sent him this crazy letter:

Dear _____,

Life isn't fair. That is, I'm caught in a rare bind. What do you think I should do?

I applied for an opening as Barbara Walters' assistant. My prospects seemed good, and the woman screening applicants seemed impressed.

Barbara, though, upon reading my resume, decided I was (they say) overqualified: too intelligent, too creative. She even liked my clips.

I told them the people here don't have trouble seeing me as a secretarial type. But alas---

You know her. Don't you? So, would it be too much trouble to put in a <u>bad</u> word for me? It just might help.

He fired back a letter saying that my asking him to "peddle" me to someone else was strange and inappropriate because I was a "valued staff member." He had never made me feel like a "valued staff member." I had been made to feel more like a worthless lackey or abused indentured servant. And after sending the note, I felt even more worthless and abused, because he found many ways to retaliate over the next few months.

By the time I went in to give my notice, though, we had managed to make peace. So I tried to be as gracious as possible. I told him where I'd be working, and said that the main reason I had taken the job was that I was getting married.

"May I ask what they're paying you?" he inquired bluntly, almost right away.

I had wondered if he would even try to make a counter offer. The fact was, though, that *USA Today* was paying top dollar to lure young journalists from throughout the country, and I had been offered more than a 50 percent raise. I expected there was no way the editor would up the ante that much. I was right. He just whistled in obvious amazement. Instead, he suddenly became curious about whom I was going to marry.

I told him my fiancé was a TV reporter in Connecticut. This made him even more curious. He had a weekend home in Connecticut and watched the news there all the time.

He wanted to know what city in Connecticut. Then he asked what station.

"He's a reporter at Channel 30!?!" he cried incredulously. "Don't you know that Channel 30 is the third-rated station in Hartford, Connecticut? Nobody marries a reporter at the third-rated station in Hartford, Connecticut."

I guess that I was nobody, then. "*I* do," I wanted to say. In fact, there were a lot of things I wanted to say. But remembering what everyone says about burning your bridges, and regretting that we already had butted heads over my overly outspoken letter, I simply thanked him for having let me work there all those years, and then I promptly walked out.

‿⌀

I moved down to what residents of Washington D.C. tend to call "the District" two weeks later, confident that Mr. Nini would follow shortly after. But week after week, rejection letters kept rolling in. Openings in television reporting jobs are relatively rare, especially in competitive markets. By the time a month had passed, he had already been turned down at every station in the area.

A month was also more than enough time to settle another matter. Although I was thrilled to be a reporter and writing for a living at last, I detested working at *USA Today*. Designed to cater to the busy modern reader, it took an approach to news that was slick, short and sweet. Its stories were succinct to the point of being shallow. Its high-tech format favored graphs and statistics over depth and good quotes. And even though fashion, the beat to which I was assigned, may not have been the deepest subject in the world, I couldn't seem to write anything of substance in the limited space I was allowed.

Even so, I'd already made some great friends there and I liked and respected my editors. I also considered it unethical and imprudent to leave a new job so soon after I had arrived. The decent and responsible thing to do, I thought, was to stay for at least a year.

And so, Mr. Nini and I fell into a new routine. We still got together every single weekend – partially because we wanted to be together, and partially because, to be perfectly frank, I didn't trust him on his own. But this required traveling by plane. Although I had been given a substantial boost in salary, much of this went to airfare. And with all of the constant flying around, our time together flew by even faster.

Halfway through this second year of our serious relationship – we hadn't missed a weekend since the day that we'd met – my mother finally seemed to grasp the intricacy of finding two acceptable journalism jobs in the same city. At least, the endless *noodging* about employment efforts ceased, as she seized upon a new and surprisingly modern tack.

"Keep commuting, if you must, but get married now!" she urged. "Why not? You have the best of marriage already, and none of the problems."

A lot she knew! What we really had was the worst of marriage, and none of the tax advantages. It wasn't simply that our commuter arrangement meant single-handedly subsidizing USAir instead of saving for, say, a house. (After all, we each had an apartment and a home away from home already.) Nor was it that we hadn't run a single errand in over a year. (When you have fewer than 24 waking hours together per week, time is too precious to spend it shopping for dental floss or repotting plants.)

Perhaps we did enjoy some advantages denied traditional couples who cohabitate; a certain romantic urgency weighed deliciously over the weekends, and the freedom to watch television programs only of our own choosing prevailed during the week. But along with this silver lining came a vast accumulation of clouds that might have precipitated stormy weather in an alliance less sturdy than ours.

To wit: It is generally assumed by the vitally interested parties – parents, that is (especially hers) – that preparing for marriage is in no way akin to training the Amtrak way. Even a willingness to make long-term commitments ("supersaver" fares required that reservations be made at least seven days in advance) does little to allay their anxiety. To parents, apparently, nothing, including a potentially derailed career (especially hers), is of real concern when there are important things at stake, like grandchildren (the only chance they have that someone in the family will turn out better than you did).

Buildings at airports, we discovered, are not called "terminals" for nothing. Although it has yet to be reported in *The New England Journal of Medicine*, frequent exposure to jet fumes can probably do more to kill off carnal inclinations than Viagra and Cialis do to enhance them. OK, maybe we weren't having any trouble in that department. Yet with all the lugging of luggage, taking of taxis, and paying of long-term parking fees, whenever the arriving partner made a beeline for the bedroom in our case, you could be sure that it was not for romantic purposes, but just to take a much-needed nap.

With all the money we were spending on travel and the telephone bill, we were beginning to feel like we were being taken to the cleaners. And with any luck, we were. It isn't ideal having to be seen in clothing that has traveled 332 miles squished into the overhead compartment of the plane under someone else's skis.

Even more awful was having the separation anxiety begin on Sunday mornings, when we awakened to realize that what may have been our first full day of the week together would also be our last. This always seemed like the best time to repack. It was distracting. It got some of the unpleasantness out of the way. And if he was staying at my place, I might get out of doing the dirty laundry he had brought with him before he left.

Meanwhile, my father continued to call and harangue me. He didn't get to see me much anymore, and he didn't believe that he would ever get to see my wedding day.

"You're engaged?" he would scoff regularly. "Really? Where's the ring?"

The fact was that I didn't have a ring. In over a year since we'd become engaged, Mr. Nini hadn't gotten around to buying me one. Maybe, I worried, my father was right.

◟᷄

It may be easy to joke about in retrospect, but that whole year, I was miserable. Even when I managed to join coworkers for dinner, I still would soon come home to an empty apartment knowing that my fiancé was hundreds of miles away. As wimpy and pathetic as it may sound, I began crying myself to sleep there almost every night. I missed my old friends. I missed my whole family. And I desperately missed Mr. Nini.

By this time, actually, the names we called each other had shortened even more. Maybe it was a way to economize on the limited time we had on the phone and in person. But he was now calling me, simply, Nin. And so he had evolved into, simply, Mr. Nin. Or, when I was being lazy, just plain Nin.

Along with seeing each other every weekend, we also talked every single night. One night, I began calling him shortly after he finished work at 11, but he wasn't home. The later it got, the more anxious I became. Although I had to be up for work early, I persisted in calling repeatedly. By the time he answered, it was around 1 a.m.. I started gushing on the phone about how worried I'd been, then began to tell him about my day.

It was obvious that he was edgy about something, though, and in a short while he said he had to go.

Suddenly, I realized what a fool I was. "You're not alone, are you?" I said.

"Umm, actually, no," he admitted reluctantly.

"It's so late," I said. "Who's with you? Anyone I know?"

It was a woman he'd gone out to dinner with. They were just talking, he said.

"Oh, Mr. Nin!" I said.

"Sorry, Nin," he said.

He assured me again the next weekend that nothing had happened. And as far as I know, he never saw her again. But I began to realize that I had better do something fast.

Before moving to Hartford, Mr. Nin had worked in Miami and still had his old friends Rick and Arthur there. So when I heard about a new fashion section being introduced at *The Miami Herald,* I instantly applied for the job.

As the fashion reporter for *USA Today,* I had covered the semi-annual fashion shows held in New York by all the prominent American designers, from Calvin Klein and Ralph Lauren to Oscar de la Renta. My credentials easily put me in the running. *The Herald* flew me to Miami, where I was subjected to a battery of tests, then taken out to lunch and interrogated by four editors at once. The job entailed not only being the editor and main writer for the new section, but getting to do reporting for the rest of the paper, too. So I was thrilled when I received a call back soon after and they offered me the job.

Determined not to make the same mistake twice, I tried to delay my response, until Mr. Nin could canvas all the TV stations in Miami to see if he could get a job, too. Not only were there no immediate openings, but not a single station even anticipated any. *The Herald* was now pressuring me to make up my mind. I didn't know what to do.

I called all the airlines that flew between Connecticut and Florida and compared all their schedules. That's when I realized the truth. It was impossible to commute between Hartford and Miami. If I took the job, we couldn't see each other on weekends. There was no way to make it work.

"Are you insane?" my father asked. "You're already having a hard time as it is. Why in God's name would you want to move a thousand miles further *south*?"

I'd been resisting and ridiculing almost everything he'd been telling me for years. But for once, I realized, he was right.

So I called and turned *The Herald* down. They called and offered more money. But no amount of money was ever going to make it work. So I turned them down again.

Then I flew to Hartford and cried, harder than I had ever cried over any man.

Soon after that, Mr. Nin bought me a ring at last.

~⸙~

By November, I had finished my year at "The Nation's Newspaper," as I had resolved to do. I still had no other job alternative. But I was beginning to think that it might be much easier all around if, rather than our trying to find two new jobs in yet another city, I just moved to Hartford, after all. When I heard that a feature reporting position had opened at the city's only newspaper, *The Hartford Courant*, I hurriedly applied. The applicants were narrowed down to two. I was one. They took the other.

Now I was all out of ideas. But one day soon after, Mr. Nin ran into the editor of *The Courant*'s award-winning Sunday magazine, *Northeast*. This man had formerly been the editor of *Tropic*, the Sunday magazine of *The Miami Herald*. Mr. Nin had met him in Miami, when a reporter he'd been dating had taken him to a party at this man's house.

Mr. Nin told this editor about me and asked if I could come in for an interview. He seemed receptive and suggested that I call his office to set one up. I concocted an excuse to take an extra day off from work and went in the following Monday morning.

I arrived early for my appointment, but this editor didn't take me early. Neither did he take me on time. He sat in his office conducting meetings and phone conversations with countless other people. Every once in a while, he would come out of his office and ask someone else to step in, but that someone was never me. I just kept sitting there for what felt like two hours, and may even have *been* two hours. Seeing this, many of the other staff members looked embarrassed. I felt embarrassed to keep sitting there, too. But I had no alternative. I wasn't going anywhere. This man was my only hope.

Finally, I was ushered into his office. He spoke to me for only a few minutes, flipping absent-mindedly through the copies I'd brought of articles I'd written. I had also prepared some stories ideas, but not one of them intrigued him. He said that his staff was so small that jobs opened rarely, if ever, and that he had absolutely nothing to offer me.

Rejected and extremely dejected, I flew back to Washington that afternoon.

At this point, I was all out of prospects. I had no clue where to go from here.

Early the next morning, my phone rang at work. That same editor was calling. Now, however, he was charming. "How soon can you be back in my office?" he asked.

I later learned that this editor had not particularly liked the reporter Mr. Nin had been dating, and she had attended his party uninvited. Mr. Nin, as her date, had been guilty by association, and the editor had reluctantly agreed to meet me only to be polite. But after I'd left, he had started to read my clips. He'd liked them, especially my fashion stories. He had long been dissatisfied with his magazine's fashion coverage. He wanted to fire the woman who was covering fashion for them and to hire me instead.

I flew back to Hartford the following weekend so I could meet with him again.

It would be only free-lance work, and not pay much, but more might crop up, he said.

"If you go to work for a man like that, and it doesn't work out," my father said, "don't come crying to me."

I wouldn't, I assured him. I was a big girl. Besides, I would have a husband now. If necessary, I would go crying to him.

—⸎—

I moved to Hartford two weeks later, just in time to celebrate New Year's Eve. The job worked out and we were married the following July, on a perfect, gloriously sun-drenched day, six months before my thirtieth birthday and one month after his fortieth.

The wedding was held at The Water Club, a restaurant overlooking the East River in New York. Although we were now both firmly (and, as it would turn out, permanently) ensconced in Hartford, most of the guests were not. All of Mr. Nin's relatives lived in or near New York. All of my relatives lived in or near New York. And as my father said, "My whole family is not going up to Hartford, Connecticut, to see you get married."

I readily agreed, although I personally felt that after all the trouble I'd gone through and all the traveling I'd done, they should have been willing to go to the moon.

Of course, it cost at least three times as much to hold it in New York. Even so, it was easier for everyone to converge there – easier for everyone but the two of us… and Anna Smith. Her kidneys and other maladies precluded her from attending the festivities. She did, however, send us a nice check tucked into a pale blue, flowery card. There was no marital advice inside. It was signed, simply, "With much love, Anna Smith."

Grandma Mary flew up from Miami, though. She led the wedding procession, escorted by my brother, who proudly walked her down the aisle. Arthur and Sari, who were expecting a baby at any minute, were unable to make it. But Rick came to serve as best man. Unable to choose between my oldest friend, Lisa, and my college roommate, Hallie, I defied convention and decided to have two maids of honor. It was just as well. Unable to choose between ten of his closest friends for ushers, Mr. Nin had them all.

My parents, united again for the first time in years – united in their relief that I was getting married at last – walked me down the aisle together, beaming luminously on either side. Russ and Ellen, now happily married themselves, looked ecstatic as well. All of our friends from Washington came up. All of our friends from Hartford came down. Even Lucy, who had more than earned that cake inscription, showed up to take a bow.

And next to me, standing under the *chuppah*, a traditional Jewish wedding canopy, was Mr. Nin. Harlan. Whatever I called him, he was the only man I had ever really loved. And I realized that my heart was no longer empty, with nobody home. It was a full house.

Red, Red Wine

⟿

THE NAMES HAVE NOT BEEN changed to protect the innocent. Believe me, there are no truly innocent characters in this case (although just how much anyone actually did, I'll never know for sure). Besides, I couldn't invent a more fitting name for "the other woman" if I tried. This rose by any other name would still be covered with thorns.

Her name, you see, was Juliet. She was the new girl at the station, and it didn't take me long to notice her because Channel 30, WVIT, was the only local TV news station that we ever watched. This had nothing to do with Nielsen ratings, or special news reports, or even the anchor people's attempts at heart-warming rapport and witty repartee. We only watched the news on WVIT because my husband worked there, too.

It also didn't take me long to notice Juliet because she was young (fresh out of college, no doubt) with honey blond hair (fresh out of a bottle, no doubt), and because she had a practiced, overly dramatic way of enunciating words that made me think she wasn't really a news reporter, she just played one on TV. "Here I am, LIVE on the STEPS of the STATE CAPital," she would intone emphatically, "where the GOVernor has just announced his CANdidacy for a THIRD conSECutive TERM!" A slight dip of her chin or fetching toss of her flaxen hair accompanied each stressed syllable, of course. No, I couldn't possibly have not noticed Juliet. The surprising thing to me was how little time it took for Juliet to notice my husband.

I found this surprising for several reasons. For one, my husband was just that: my husband. How dare any other woman take an active interest in him?

Why, having been married for just over two years, our official status as new-lyweds had barely yet expired.

For another, although he was my husband, I failed to see the irresistible attraction. We may have celebrated a mere two wedding anniversaries, yet our status as new parents had catapulted us straight from newly wedded bliss into a murky, moody, irritable phase of almost chronic bickering. We were going through what you might term a "rocky" period in our relationship – if you consider Mt. Vesuvius a rock.

Then there was the delicate but inescapable matter of age. Although I was a relatively mature bride, I had chosen to link my life with a man of distinctly riper vintage. At 32, I packed nearly a decade more of wear and tear on my bones than my rival, and my husband had an additional solid decade on me. A fanatical routine of jogging, tennis, and other daily exercise managed to keep him fit and looking deceptively youthful. Yet if this modern-day Juliet was inclined toward romantic encounters of the extramarital kind, why couldn't she at least pick a prospective Romeo closer to her own age?

At least I had no reason to suspect that my husband reciprocated her affection – not initially, at least – but there could be little doubt that there was something going on between them. First, her name began creeping into his daily dinner conversation. "You won't believe what Juliet told me today," he'd say, when what I really couldn't believe was that he thought I'd want to hear about it. Then, soon enough, gabbing with him during working hours was no longer enough for her. Juliet, who lived in a ground-floor apartment only four blocks from our house, began finding frequent flimsy excuses to phone him after work, presumably for advice. Who were the best dry-cleaners in town? Did he know of a good local restaurant that served Sunday brunch?

Just what did she think my husband was – a public service? The Yellow Pages? And how long would it take before she stopped talking and let her fingers do the walking, all over my husband?

When he finally suggested that the three of us have dinner one night, I readily accepted. This was not because I put one iota of faith in his oft-repeated assertion, "You have to meet the new reporter. You two have so much in common." ("Yes," I'd think snidely to myself, "we're both women, and we both want *you*!") No, I wanted to meet her mainly because I could no longer contain my curiosity. I also had at least one ulterior motive. Several years earlier, at one of my own first journalism jobs, I had instantly recovered from an office crush on an older man the moment I'd met his wife.

I'm ashamed to admit now that I had been well aware that this man was married. Having grown up in a household in which marriage was regarded as less than sacred – and having vicariously suffered through my mother's heartache at being openly betrayed by my dad – I could never in good conscience actually have conducted an affair. I was still painfully aware of the infinite pain that this sort of illicit pleasure could inflict, particularly on the people who were peripherally involved. Yet somehow, seeing my co-worker exclusively at work, it had been hard to envision him ensconced in a domestic scene involving a wife and children. (Yes, I shudder to admit, he had a few of those, too).

Certainly, around me, he'd never acted as if he were married. Besides, his wife had never seemed real to me until we had been introduced at an office party. That night, I had been mortified to discover that she was not only real, but also witty, accomplished, intelligent, affable, and far worthier of my respect than her roving-eyed husband was.

Given my hard-to-camouflage hostility toward Juliet, I had no delusions that she would like me enough to instantly relinquish all designs on my spouse. Nor did I remotely aspire to have her choose me as her preferred confidante (although as our family's designated shopper, I was eminently more qualified to serve as her consumer guide). I could only hope that seeing me in the flesh would trigger in her some sisterly sympathies or moral sensibilities.

Fat chance! I tried to act charming. I tried to be nice. But it became immediately clear during our dinner that this little vixen did not possess one sisterly bone or moral sensibility in her body. I also trembled to notice that her body, lean and taut when viewed in person, might pose more of a threat to my connubial contentment than I'd anticipated. That thing that they say about the camera adding 10 pounds is absolutely true.

I was similarly distressed to detect that my suspicions were not merely the products of a paranoid imagination. Her response to me was openly adversarial. The moment we met, she looked me over critically, from my wavy auburn hair to my black leather ankle boots, as though sizing up her opponent in a wrestling match. After that, she barely spared me a glance. For the duration of the meal, she sat there smiling brazenly, coquettishly, and adoringly at my husband.

The situation was enough to make me sick, and probably would have if I'd had a moment of spare time to sit down, catch my breath and obsess about it. Mercifully, I suppose, I didn't. I had a full-time reporting job of my own at a local newspaper. I also had a household to run and an infant son to raise. Yet, unfortunately, what they say about pregnancy adding inches to your waistline is also true. So maybe I should have worried.

Instead, I continued trying to look the other way until one evening in late October. I'd been phoning my husband all afternoon. Finally, I reached him at home just past 5.

"Where have you been?" I asked. "It turns out that I have to work tonight." I'd been assigned to cover an exclusive party being thrown by a local investment bank that did most of its business with countries in Africa. "I was hoping you could meet me there and bring me my black silk dress. Beth, the magazine's food editor, is helping to cater it, and she said it's fine if you come, too."

"That sounds great," he said, barely stifling a yawn, "but I think I'll pass."

"Oh, come on," I pleaded. "It'll be fun. There are going to be all sorts of foreign dignitaries. Bishop Desmond Tutu's daughter will be there. I *love* Desmond Tutu."

"I love Desmond Tutu, too," he said. "But I'm too-too tired."

I laughed plaintively. "Too-too tired to chow down on incredible, exotic food? Beth says they're serving goat."

"Goat? Sounds ba-a-a-a-d!" he said, braying hoarsely. "Anyway, I'm not only tired, I'm also stuffed." He hesitated briefly, then blurted it out. "Juliet's car broke down today when she was returning from doing a story. I had to go help her out, and by the time the tow truck finally arrived, she was so upset that I took her out for a late lunch."

So I had to suffer through this deadly party all by myself, in casual pants, no less. I also had to spend the whole night imagining my husband consoling that helpless hussy in some cozy roadside café. And wondering how much she had consoled him right back. Now, that got *my* goat.

This incident made me queasy enough, but it was just a tasteless morsel compared to the foul feast served up to me a few months later. My husband mentioned that a pair of young reporters from the TV station were throwing a holiday party. Usually, when it came to socializing with his co-workers, I tried to beg off. Shy and introverted by nature, I didn't share his passion for parties, or, frankly, his admiration for television personalities. (It was a matter of long-standing journalistic rivalry. TV stars may have all the glamour of constant public recognition, but we print people had the moral high ground because we worked much harder for less recognition and much less pay.)

This was one party, however, that I was not about to let my husband attend alone. Instead, I went out and purchased a slinky, slenderizing new outfit just for the occasion. Then I arranged for my mother-in-law to baby-sit.

The night of the event, nothing seemed to be going right. When you have a baby, getting ready to go out for the evening feels like preparing to invade a foreign country; the enemy doesn't have the slightest interest in cooperating and doesn't even speak your language. It didn't help that we had set up a ridiculous routine soon after our son had been born. Whenever we went out, my husband's elderly, widowed mother babysat, but I would cook her dinner first. By the time I had finished feeding both our infant and my mother-in-law, I would have only minutes left to shower and dress. My makeup would have to be applied shakily in transit by the faint glow of the passenger side lighted mirror.

On this ill-fated night, when we were finally ready to leave, I discovered that my mother-in-law, who was 82 at the time and severely hearing-impaired, had inadvertently left her hearing aids at home. We had to repeat all of our obsessive instructions about bedtime routine three times, then finally gave up and resorted to writing them all down.

—ᐊ—

Our destination was a short drive away to the outskirts of the neighboring city. Still, by the time we had located a parking space and entered, the apartment was crowded and deafeningly noisy, the festivities in full swing.

Fending off teasing catcalls from co-workers, my husband propelled me through a narrow foyer into the kitchen so we could greet our young hostesses for the evening. Then I followed him as he made a beeline for the bar. Typical of informal parties given by young, single people, "the bar" consisted of a card table strewn with six-packs and a motley assortment of bottles supplied by the invited guests. Declining the can of cut-rate domestic beer proffered by my husband, I poured myself a cup of wine from an open, magnum-sized bottle. Then I began wandering through the packed apartment in his wake.

Considering how much television work takes place behind the scenes, and how rarely the so-called top "talent" socializes with the rank and file, most of the revelers were relative strangers. I had glimpsed them before on previous occasions, when stopping by the station or attending the office holiday party, but I didn't know their names. Evidently, my husband wasn't particularly chummy with any of them either, because he bypassed the chance to chat with them all. Instead, we kept roaming until we poked our heads into a small, dimly lit den off the living room and encountered Juliet.

The way her face flushed as we entered, there could be no doubt about two things: She felt considerably better to see that we had arrived, and she was considerably the worse for drink.

"Oh! Um, well, hi!" she said, sounding about as casual as she might if Tom Cruise had just walked into the room.

"Hi, yourself," my husband responded, then turned to me. "You remember Juliet."

Sure did. "Of course," I said, drawing a deep gulp of vino.

Her cheeks echoed the hue of the cheap rosé her hand cradled in a plastic tumbler. "So, you finally made it over," she said. "I was beginning to wonder."

Some people, under pressure, have the good sense to shut up. Not me. I babble.

"That's right, we finally did," I replied. "And don't imagine even this was easy! We had planned to be here an hour ago, but someone refused to gobble down their gruel and creamed spinach."

"You feed your baby gruel and creamed spinach?" she asked, spitting out the last words as though she could taste them.

"No, my mother-in-law," I said with a dry laugh. "She's watching the baby."

My husband glared at me.

"*Really*," she said, narrowing her eyes, not quite sure whether to laugh. Then she turned to face my husband, brushing her hair back nervously behind one ear (a sure body-language sign of physical attraction, I've been told).

The dubious pleasure of accompanying your spouse to an office party is that you become privy to all sorts of shop talk, primarily gossip about all the people who didn't bother to come, mostly people you've never met. I had no idea what they were talking about at the time, so I certainly don't remember any of it now. What I can still picture pretty clearly, though, is the three of us standing there, posed in a perfect triangle. There were an assortment of chairs and a lumpy-looking sofa in the room, but not one of us made a move to sit down. We just stood there in our places, sipping and talking, talking and sipping. Awkward, yes, but fairly uneventful, until Juliet's little faux pas.

"Guess what!" she suddenly piped up, "I finally found it."

"Found what?" my husband asked.

"My sweater," she said.

"What sweater?"

"*You* know," she said. "The one I was looking for the other night, when you stopped by my apartment while you were out for a run." She stated this jubilantly, then her face fell and her empty hand shot up to her mouth. She pressed three fingertips to her slightly parted lips, as if feigning horror. "Oops," she squealed giddily, dumb-blonde style, with an openly mischievous grin, "I wasn't supposed to say that, was I?"

If our bodies were endpoints, then the shape they formed was a perfect equilateral triangle – three equal sides. I stood as close to her as I did to him, yet in an instant I made a snap decision. Gripping my wine glass firmly in my hand, I swung it toward him in an abrupt, underhand arc, splashing its remaining contents across his shirt and tie. Unfortunately for him, I had been sipping slowly and sparingly. I had also bypassed Juliet's cheap rosé at the bar, and strayed from my usual preference for pale Chardonnay. The wine he was now wearing was a deep red Cabernet.

"Hey – " he began. Presumably, something more expressive followed, but that's as much as I heard. By the time my husband had summoned any further thoughts to add, I had stomped out of the room, pushed my way furiously through the crowded foyer and begun flying down the stairs.

Although relatively mild for December, it was a nippy night, and I realized soon after hitting the street that I had neglected to wear a coat. Even worse, the outfit I had purchased for this occasion had been chosen expressly to compete with a young vamp. The clingy, black top bared a sliver of my midriff. The faux fur skirt in black and white zebra stripes gripped my hips like a second skin. As for the spiky black heels, they may have accentuated the curve of my calves, but these shoes were definitely not made for walking.

In this tarty get-up, and a seething fit of pique, I had to stride nearly two miles home, much of it through a seedy, urban neighborhood. Several cars slowed down as they passed so that their male drivers could roll down their windows and call comments to me. Most of these were comments I would not care to repeat.

The last car to stop was my husband's.

"Nin!" he called, using his usual pet name for me. "Nin, get in," he said.

"Get lost," I replied, and kept walking.

"Oh, come on," he pleaded, letting his red Saab glide so it matched my gait. "What the hell are you doing?"

"What am *I* doing?" I asked, quickening my pace. "What have *you* been doing?"

"Nothing!" he replied. "What are you talking about? I haven't done a thing!"

By now, other cars were veering around him. I could sense this through the corner of my eye, although I refused to glance in his direction. I couldn't bear to look at him.

"Come on, will you cut it out?" he yelled through the passenger window. "Seriously. Have you gone crazy? You can't walk all the way home."

In fact, I didn't want to walk all the way home. I didn't want to go home at all. But my infant son was there, and everything I owned in the world was there. The closest relative I had in the vicinity was my mother-in-law and, at this point, even *she* was there. I had nowhere else to go.

By now, my husband had given up pleading with me, but he still refused to drive away. Instead, we proceeded side by side in the darkness, his lipstick red sedan rolling languidly down the street, me strutting on the sidewalk frenetically, as fast as my wobbly spiked shoes would carry me, until we finally reached our modest colonial.

Flinging open the front door, I peeled off my heels and burst into the living room. My husband, having parked in the driveway, followed, panting in close pursuit.

My mother-in-law was settled on the sofa, reading a hardcover library book. Peering through her bifocals, she looked up, startled. Without her hearing aids, she hadn't heard the door.

"My, you're home early," she exclaimed, closing her book. "How was your party? Did you have a nice time?"

"Nice?" I replied icily. "Oh, yeah. Sure. We had the time of our lives."

"The what?" asked my mother-in-law.

"Ask your son," I said.

"Nin!" said my husband.

"Don't you 'Nin' me!" I answered.

"Nin, wait a second," said my husband.

"What did you say?" asked my mother-in-law.

"Oh, shut up!" I said.

"Don't tell my mother to shut up," said my husband.

"I'll tell her whatever I want," I said. "But actually, I was talking to you!"

Beneath his black leather jacket, I could see that the wine stain had spread from his tie to his shirt, as though he had been stabbed in the chest.

"What exactly happened back there?" he demanded. "How could you do that, in front of practically everyone I work with?"

"What's wrong?" asked my mother-in-law. "Has something happened?"

"Oh, so you feel embarrassed?" I asked him, ignoring her. "Well, you should be. I'm your wife!"

"I'll tell you what you are," he shouted. "You're crazy!"

"I may be crazy," I fired back, "but I also happen to be the mother of your child!"

"What?" asked my mother-in-law. "Is there something wrong with the child?"

"Oh, shut up!" yelled my husband. I'm not sure which of us he directed this to.

"This is awful," my mother-in-law said. "I can't hear a thing. What are you saying to him? What is he saying to you?"

"You want to know what we're saying?" I asked her. "Fine, I'll tell you. Do you want to know what your son has done?" And pacing back and forth agitatedly, I proceeded to relay the whole damn story, almost loudly enough for the neighbors to hear. It's amazing I didn't wake the baby.

"And then he has the nerve to deny he did anything!" I concluded. "This girl may be a little witch, but am I supposed to believe she made it all up?"

"Made *what* up?" asked my husband.

"You know what up," I said. "Stopping by Juliet's on a snowy evening."

He looked at his mother. He looked at me. He looked as if he'd been caught red-handed. "All right, I did stop over there, once or twice," he said. "But it was just to say hello. I swear to you, nothing happened."

"I don't care what happened!" I yelled. "You shouldn't be visiting other women's houses. When a man tells his wife that he's going running, he's supposed to go running. And only running."

"God, do you actually think I'm messing around with Juliet?" my husband asked, sinking into a chintz-covered armchair. "Do you think we're having some sort of affair?"

"What is he having?" asked my mother-in-law.

"An affair!" I said.

"I'm not having an affair," my husband said.

"I almost had an affair," replied his mother.

"What did you say?" howled my husband.

"You had a *what*?" I asked.

Our voices had finally grown loud enough to indeed wake the baby, who had begun to wail. "Calm down," my mother-in-law said. "One of you had better go upstairs. When you come back down, I'll tell you everything."

That night, I may have set a world record for the fastest diaper change ever. I didn't even stop to exchange my excruciatingly clingy clothes for a cozy nightgown. I was so eager to hear this story that I almost forgot about the scene I had just created.

You have to understand something about my mother-in-law. She wasn't just so elderly that it was hard to envision her as the object of anyone's unbridled passion. She was also, by nature, an exceedingly prim and genteel person. Her stiffness was not just a product of advancing age. By all appearances, she had been born with it. With the haughty bearing of a woman born to wealth, she had a tendency to condescend to almost everyone and to overdress for every occasion. I'd been painfully aware of this ever since the first time we'd met, when my husband had taken me to her apartment for a casual Sunday brunch. I had shown up in jeans and a sweater. "You're wearing that?" he'd asked me anxiously. She came to the door in a somber, tailored black dress and pearls.

Her only son seemed to be as eager to hear her tale as I was. I returned to the living room to find him, stained tie removed, sprawled on a rattan chair across the room. When I plopped into the corner of the couch opposite her, he leaned forward, propping his elbows on his knees.

"As you know," she began, addressing my husband, "Daddy and I met at the Griswold Inn, down in Essex, many years ago. I had traveled up from New York to spend a weekend in the country with my cousin," she said. "Your father happened to be there, having dinner with a friend."

This part of the tale I'd heard several times before. The second youngest of eleven children, my mother-in-law had been in her late 30s when she'd met her husband in the midst of World War II. Having seen how regal she looked in her 1940s wedding photo, almost movie-star pretty in a short white dress and elbow-length gloves, I still wondered how she had nearly become what in those days would have been labeled "an old maid." Presumably, after finding suitable mates for most of her ten elder siblings, her parents had simply run out of steam.

"We became engaged almost immediately," she said. "Then we got married, and we stayed married for nearly 25 years."

My father-in-law, once a traveling concert violinist, had settled down and become a stockbroker after they wed. It was a less gratifying profession for a man of his talents, but far more lucrative and better suited to family life. "Times then were so different from what they are today," she observed. "I worked as a teacher for years, but my husband handled all of our finances. I never paid a single bill."

So along with feeling devastated when he suffered a heart attack and died suddenly, late one November night while my husband was away at law school, she had also felt helpless. "I tried to manage on my own, but I had no idea what I was doing." It had been especially difficult that first year when it came time to pay her taxes.

"But you remember my good friend Gertrude, don't you?" she asked. "Her husband was so successful, the top executive at a large firm. He said that he was worried about me and offered to help sort things out."

"Homer?" my husband asked, sounding a bit incredulous.

My mother-in-law nodded. "Yes, Homer. He came over after dinner one night. How very nice of him, I thought! We sat down together at the dining room table. 'Show me everything,' he said. So I did. Files, checkbooks, stacks of bills. There was so much paperwork to go through." By the time he had finished reviewing it all, it had grown late.

" 'Oh, I don't know how to thank you!' I told him. I knew he wouldn't let me pay." No matter. He had an idea. "I still remember how he came over to my side of the table and stood right behind me. He put his hands on my shoulders, and then…" She paused and shuddered, as though being touched by ice. "Well, he said all these things – how he had always found me attractive, and did I feel the same way about him? And then he —"

"Homer?" my husband interrupted. "You're kidding! Homer did that?"

"Oh, my God," I said. In fact, I had never met him, but I had certainly met Gertrude. She had been cut from the same mold as my mother-in-law: stiff, prim, and proper. So maybe it wasn't that hard to imagine that she'd had a husband inclined to philander. But a husband who philandered with my mother-in-law?

"What did you do?" I asked.

"Do?" she asked. "What could I do? Gertie was one of my very dearest friends. Homer and my husband had also been close. And even though I was all alone, I was deeply in love with someone else."

"You were?" my husband asked, with fresh horror.

"Yes, of course," she said. "You must know that. I still very much loved Daddy."

No wonder, as my husband had often told me, she hadn't been out on a single date since the day his dad had died. "So you gave cheating Homer the old heave-ho," I said. "But that was a good 20 years ago. Didn't you ever go out with anyone else?"

"Go out? No, I didn't," she said. "Not even once." She reached down to change the stretchy bedroom slippers she'd been wearing for her street shoes, a pair of pumps. "It's not that I didn't have any potential suitors," she said. "I may not have been young anymore, but believe me, I did."

"Then why didn't you – well, you know?" my husband asked.

"Why? I didn't for the very same reason that I never married anyone until I met your father," she said. "I had never met anyone else who had such fine qualities before. And I never met anyone who had his qualities again. He was the only man for me."

Just as I always cooked dinner for my mother-in-law, it was part of our standard routine that my husband always drove her home. This gave me time to change out of my party clothes at last. By the time he'd returned, I was already in bed. I considered pretending to be asleep, but knew he wouldn't have let me get away with it anyway.

"Good night, Nin," he said, climbing in beside me and flicking off the light.

"G'night," I muttered back gruffly.

"All right, I'm not going to try to kiss you," he said in the darkness. "It's just... Well, you know what my mother said about my father? 'I had never met anyone else who had such fine qualities before?' Well, that's how I feel about you," he said. "Really. You're the only Nin for me."

"Me, too," I said quietly. Then I gave him his kiss.

He never mentioned Juliet to me again, and shortly after that she left the station, for a bigger market, no doubt.

Neither did I ever again set eyes on the necktie my husband had been wearing that night. He knew better than to ask me to apply spot remover or bring it to the dry-cleaners. I assume that he had the good sense to simply throw it away. I thought about it recently, though, when I noticed some tips for removing red wine stains in an advertisement promoting a magazine published by another honey-blonde hussy, Martha Stewart. The instructions called for salt, rubbing, and plenty of hot water, but I doubt they really work.

The fact is, there are just some stains that never quite come out, no matter how hot the water is, no matter how hard you rub. They may fade, but there's still a discoloration, a telltale trace. Then again, what marriage, even a good one, is totally free of stains?

In the grand scheme of things, though, I think we all got off pretty easily. Shakespeare's tragic tale of Juliet ended with three young lives lost, two grief-stricken families, and enough heartache to deeply sadden centuries of audiences worldwide. All that was sacrificed in my case was a necktie, a bit of pride, and an unadulterated sense of marital trust. But in the process, I gained something too. I learned that I had the strength deep within me to defend my own borders, without weapons, threats or even harsh words. So I guess, as far as I'm concerned, my wine glass was still half full.

The Wooden Lobster

FIVE MINUTES AFTER MY TRAIN passed through the 125th Street station, the last stop before the last stop, I fished a pale green plastic compact out of my purse to check my hastily applied makeup. I could no longer bear to survey the scarred, skeletal remains of the South Bronx, real-life ruins that never failed to plunge me into middle-class guilt. I also knew that my time in the sun was numbered. Within moments, I would lose the day's last rays of natural light as the train descended into the soot-scented tunnel for its subterranean approach to Grand Central Station.

Why I bothered about my appearance, I can hardly say. I had no one to impress, and little to impress anyone with, unless you count the bags beneath my eyes, fleshy protrusions the size and shape of red globe grapes. And these were not the only bulges in my physique ready to betray my beleaguered condition. The careworn mother of a lively toddler, with new life visibly well on the way, I was fleeing my husband of five years and my humble home in Central Connecticut.

OK, "fleeing" might be a mild exaggeration. A bit of dramatic – make that melodramatic – license. The small suitcase I was lugging contained only enough clothing to last a couple of days. That was about as far into the future as I could clearly focus. Besides, no matter how much psychic good it might do me to try running away for the weekend, I was obliged to be back at work early on Monday morning.

Running away? God. That sounds so trite. So juvenile. But yes, I have to admit, that's just what I was up to. I'd been doing it most of my life. Growing up, whenever my parents' constant battles had grown boisterous enough to swallow me like a raging beast, I'd often run right out of the house. As a teenager, I'd typically found refuge by visiting Lisa, who was not only my closest friend but also the nearest in terms of proximity. Once, instead, I'd "run away" by hiding under the flowery, floor-length skirt of the antique dressing table in my own bedroom, curling my body into a tight cocoon for hours while my frantic parents searched the neighborhood by foot and phone and even called the police. How ironic it seemed now that running away meant returning to one of them.

To be honest, I don't remember exactly why I was headed to see my father. Perhaps I was just thinking that his apartment was a free, available place to stay in New York City. My mother, from whom he'd been divorced for a decade now, would have welcomed me eagerly, but she lived an hour out of the city in the dull, small-town suburb in which I'd grown up. Besides, she would have reacted in her typical motherly mode: total hysteria about my marital woes, mixed with well-meaning but useless advice based on her own past experience. (My mother maintained this warped worldview that led her to interpret all human predicaments by relating them tangentially to herself, her parents, her late sister Gloria, or the family sexpot, her Cousin Leatrice.)

But that, to be perfectly honest, is not why I was descending on my father instead. Rather, even as a grown, married woman of 34, I still harbored a hefty dose of that little-girl instinct that says if you're in trouble – particularly man trouble – Daddy should be there to rescue you and try to make things right. And given my distended physical condition and my distressed mental state, this was just about the worst man trouble in which I'd ever landed.

It certainly beat every problem I'd ever had with difficult bosses or boyfriends. If a boss was a total bastard, you could easily attempt to find another job. And you could always give up on a boyfriend who treated you callously or had already given up on you. But how could you simply wander away from a troubled marriage when you and your spouse had one small child together and another on the way?

The part that made my rescue plan downright irrational was that my father had rarely been around or available to me, emotionally or otherwise, when I was a little girl. Why in the world would I imagine him to be there to kiss away the tears or torment now? I didn't really expect I could count on him, although there was always that needle-slim ray of hope. As I hailed a cab outside the station and uttered his Upper East Side address, the most I hoped for was a home-cooked dinner and a couch on which to spend the night.

—✺—

Pausing now in memory in the hallway outside my father's door, I find it almost as difficult to enter as I did that day. The décor of his apartment, from its muted recessed lighting and dull earth tones to a tacky, potbellied Buddha statuette stationed on his coffee table, never failed to depress me. Casting a greater pall over the premises was the fact that my father shared them with his second wife, Elaine, the woman for whom he had many years earlier virtually abandoned my mother, along with my older brother and me.

It didn't boost my confidence much that I was now arriving on his doorstep in abject need and personal disgrace. Yet I had phoned him the night before, and he was already expecting me. So I took a deep breath, gritted my teeth and did what I had to do: reach out, ring the bell, and put on a happy face.

"Coming!" Muted sounds of adult male feet plodding across plush carpeting. Then the door swung open and my father uttered one of his favorite nicknames for me as he folded me somewhat stiffly into his arms.

"Ah, Flutonia!" The name stemmed from the brief time in which I'd played the flute back in fourth grade. I had given it up within a year because I was thin and frail, and prolonged blowing into the mouthpiece tended to make me dizzy. But my father had always liked the gentle, feminine image that flute-playing evoked – a docile, dainty attitude that never had or would quite suit me – and so decades after the instrument had been abandoned, the name played on and on.

"Hope I'm not too late," I said, returning his hug and pressing my cheek awkwardly to his to avoid implanting his face with a temporary lipstick tattoo.

"Not at all," he said, kissing me back. With his still-lean body and year-round tan (thanks to frequent excursions to his condominium in Palm Beach), my father always managed to look handsome and prosperous, even now, in his early 60s. Several years earlier, when I had still been single and working at a magazine in the city, he had come to my office one day to take me out to lunch, and the somewhat older woman who was my direct superior had spied him from across the room and breathlessly exclaimed, "Introduce me!"

By comparison, I was now looking old beyond my years, the result of chronic sleep depravation and preoccupation with my young son to the point of neglecting personal glamour and hygiene. Realizing this, however, did little to lessen the sting of his next three inevitable words. "You look tired."

"Do I?" I asked, setting down my suitcase and purse in a corner near the closet. Running my fingers through my scalp to smooth my disheveled hair, I caught a glimpse of my profile in a smoked-glass mirror. At least he hadn't stated the even more obvious: "You look fat."

But I could tell he was thinking it as he nodded vaguely, looking me up and down. "Was the trip bad? I still don't understand why you took the train instead of driving in. You could have parked right in my building."

"I know," I said. "But I hate driving in the city, especially anytime close to rush hour." Train travel was so much more civilized and relaxing. Besides, my husband had offered to pick me up on Sunday, I told him, so it made no sense to bring in my own car. "That way you'll get to see your grandson."

I was glad to see his face light up at this news. "That would be grand!" he said, using his favorite word. "Really grand! Now go get washed. Dinner's almost ready."

⎯⎯⎯⎯ ᧙ ⎯⎯⎯⎯

In fact, I had only shrugged silently when my husband had offered to retrieve me. But I was tired and pregnant. Getting picked up and driven home would be so convenient. I also welcomed the idea of my father getting to see my little boy, too rare an occurrence.

Born and raised in a New York suburb, I had been led by serendipity to meet and marry a man from Connecticut, but it was not by pure chance that we had chosen to live in his hometown. I didn't mind keeping a comfortable cushion of psychic and geographic distance between my relatives and me. Too many of them still treated me as though I were a child. The down side was that the distance deprived my little boy of having an extended family. It isn't easy to maintain a relationship with a 3-year-old by phone.

And even if my father did not seem capable of loving me (I mean the real me, moles, moods, and all) the way I wanted to be loved (consistently, despite moles, moods and all) I could not bear or accept the notion that he would not totally and limitlessly love my little boy (whom, as far as I could see, was absolutely perfect, moles, moods, and all).

⎯ᕃ⎯

"More potatoes?" my stepmother asked in her distinct Brooklyn accent, hovering beside me wielding a Teflon spatula and an oven-stained Corningware serving dish.

"No thanks. I'm so stuffed." I watched as she dished two onto my plate anyway. "Well, all right, thanks."

"Take another leg, too," she said. "Please! It's a shame to throw them out."

Dinner turned out to be not nearly as awkward as I had anticipated. Elaine, I must admit, was a fairly adept cook, especially with homey food like roast chicken. And face it, when you're pregnant, eating is always a pleasure. The conversation also managed to stay innocuous enough, between some humorous anecdotes I offered about my son and their usual never-ending supply of gripes and gossip about relatives and friends. By the time the dishes had been cleared and my stepmother had passed around the small tin box she always kept filled with homemade cookies, I was feeling sated and almost content.

So it was with some ambivalence that I heard Elaine excuse herself to go indulge in her nightly evening bath. I was beginning to have serious doubts about baring my soul to my father, but if I was going to go through with it, it was far better to do it in private.

Apparently, he felt the same way.

"It's so good to see you. Really, really great," he said, having settled opposite me on the taupe leather sectional sofa. "But I have to say, I've been wondering something." I kicked off my frayed sandals and curled one bare foot nervously under the opposite thigh. "What exactly brings you here?"

Just like a businessman to get right down to business.

"Nothing, really," I answered, a bit too quickly. "What makes you ask?"

"Nothing much," he replied. "Just a hunch."

"Oh." I hadn't thought I'd said or done anything to give myself away. And I hadn't thought that my father was someone particularly given to having hunches. "Everything's fine," I insisted. "I'm fine. We're fine. The baby seems like it'll be fine."

"Good," he said. " 'Fine' is good. What about work? You're still bent on staying on after the baby is born?"

Oh, please don't make me debate this again. "Yes, that's definite, as I've told you," I said. "I really want to keep working, and they've pretty much agreed to let me go half-time after I come back from maternity leave."

"All right," he said. "At least you're cutting back. But if it's a matter of money – "

"It's not," I said, cutting him off. "I wish you could understand. It's more about wanting to accomplish something – something worth something – while I can. It's also a matter of… well, self-sufficiency. I want to maintain my independence."

"Independence?" He said the word with less distaste than bewilderment. "You already have one child at home. If you're so concerned about 'independence,' why, for God's sake, are you having another?"

"Why?" I asked. "Seriously? You've got to be kidding. I want this baby more than I've ever wanted anything in the world!"

It was true. About my maternal condition, I had no regrets. I had become so determined to divide and multiply during the previous year that when months of attempts to conceive had failed, I had resorted to using every over-the-counter remedy available. My eagerness had nothing to do with foolish schemes to stabilize my tumultuous marriage. I was well aware that most of the turbulence had arrived in tandem with our first-born, and that having another helpless entity to care for was less likely to calm our domestic seas than to unleash more monstrous waves. Yet there was no denying my innate urges. The S.S. Mom had a new passenger on board and was all ready to pull out of port.

"Good," my father said. "I'm glad to hear it. Do both of you feel that way?"

Interesting question – one I preferred not to answer.

"I'm sure he'll be happy after the baby is born," I replied. "Right now, he's not too happy about anything. As far as I can tell. We aren't exactly speaking."

There, I'd said it.

I don't know quite how my father reacted because I didn't dare meet his gaze.

"And why is that?" he asked.

"Because," I said.

How could I begin to explain what it felt like to be gigantic, far heftier than you'd ever been in your entire trim and supremely self-controlled life, yet at the same time, somehow, invisible?

"It seems to me that you don't sound particularly happy, either."

Happy?

"It's weird," I said. "From what I can see, most women love being pregnant. *Love* it. Morning sickness? No problem. Swollen ankles? How sweet! The way some of them gush, you'd think hemorrhoids were heaven." I laughed self-consciously – people in my family didn't usually mention distasteful bodily functions.

To my relief, he gave a sympathetic chuckle back.

"I can't expect you to imagine personally what this is like," I continued. "The problem is, if I'm supposed to feel like all those other women, then I don't get it, either. The first time around, I had moments of ecstasy just waiting for the baby. And don't get me wrong – I was totally thrilled after he was born. But the process itself wasn't a thrill. It was almost... I don't know. Suffocating."

In fact, my husband had been the one in a rush to procreate that time. I thought he'd just been eager to keep up with his friends, many of whom had wives who were expecting. "Just have the baby," he'd begged. "I'll do everything else." Finally, I'd agreed to try getting pregnant on the theory that it took an average of six months to conceive.

Or so I'd heard. Six months? Surprise! For us, success came in a single night.

After that, he'd been so ecstatic, it seemed, that he'd obsessively doted on me. "The first time around, when I arrived home from work exhausted, he used to serve me dinner in bed. He'd carry up cold drinks, bring me magazines to read. That was great, but there was also a downside: He turned into this nervous wreck. I couldn't drive anywhere, even to the supermarket, without phoning to reassure him that 'we' had arrived safely. The thing is, I could never tell whether he was worried about me or only 'it.'"

"Actually, that sounds nice," my father said. "I'm pleased he worries about you like that."

"Yup," I said. "I'm sure. But that was then, and this is now: I still work full time. Long hours. And when I get home, instead of getting to lie down and rest, I have this lively, little munchkin to take care of. Plus dinner to cook and a house to clean. I'm lucky if I get to bed by midnight. I'm nearly six months pregnant, with a husband who's never home."

"Why is that?" he asked, his voice sounding an alarm. "Why is he never home?"

"Because he's working," I said.

"Working," he repeated skeptically, and I remembered who I was speaking to. "Are you sure he's actually… working?"

"Oh, yeah," I said. "I'm sure."

Frustrated by his modest salary and the demands of his longtime job as a television news reporter, he had become completely absorbed with his struggles to start a new business, a video production company, with a colleague. He wasn't quite ready to commit himself to this new risky venture, however. This obliged him to keep his usual full-time job while putting in countless hours on the side.

His partner was a talented genius by my husband's account. I had my own views. "The main problem is Damien," I explained. He was temperamental, demanding, impossible to please, and bossy to the point of tyranny. Having no children, and a tempestuous marriage of his own, he also had little desire to spend any time at home. Instead, he was determined to devote all of his evenings, weekends, and any other spare time to the new business – *their* new child – and he expected my husband to do the same.

This made Damien my enemy. We battled endlessly for my husband's attention, and I could never tell whose side my husband was on. That made him my enemy, too.

Under my current circumstances, I was not actually prepared to leave my husband; I was just at my wit's end because I didn't want to be married to him anymore. A few years earlier, we'd been so hot for each other that we couldn't remain in the same room without touching. Married life and parenthood had managed to put out the flames.

"When he's home, which is rare," I said, "he's usually on the phone. One recent night he got home after 9, then took two or three calls from Damien while he was reading a bedtime story to the baby. By the time he hung up from the last one, our poor boy had fallen asleep."

"That's no good," my father said gruffly. "You know how I believe in hard work. But that certainly doesn't mean he should be neglecting the child."

"Neglecting?" I asked. "He *totally* neglects him. And that doesn't begin to cover what he does to me." I stopped to try to soften my voice, which I knew was getting shrill. "I'm sorry. I don't mean to sit here and complain to you. It's just that… I don't know. We have no time alone together. By the time he gets home at night, we're both exhausted. And he seems so preoccupied with work that he never even looks at me."

I stood to shift my position, then grew self-conscious looking down at myself. "Maybe that's good," I said, "since I'm beginning to resemble a baby hippo." I laughed. "But I don't think that's the problem. The problem is he doesn't seem to know I'm alive."

My father seemed more annoyed than amused. My mother had always warned me not to confide in him. Hearing I wasn't happy never failed to make him angry.

"Maybe you should talk to him," he said. "Are you sure he knows how you feel?"

"Oh, yes," I said. "He knows. Earlier this summer, I gave him an ultimatum. We needed to take one last, relaxing family trip before the baby was born or else. I suggested Martha's Vineyard. It's one of his favorite places. 'Fine,' he said. 'Book it.' So I did. I took a room at a new hotel in Edgartown for last week, right on the beach. Then, just before we left, he scheduled a meeting with clients in the middle of our vacation."

It took five hours for us to get to the Vineyard, counting the drive and a 90-minute ferry ride. My husband couldn't have attended the meeting and returned in one day.

So much for our respite. All three of us had ended up returning on Tuesday, on the only ferry available on such short notice. Our much-needed "week off" had been whittled down to a long weekend, with the first and last days devoted entirely to travel.

"Yesterday, he went to the meeting," I said. "Damien wanted him to be on hand when they aired their new video, just in case the clients had any questions or complaints. Well, guess what. They didn't! The viewing went great. When the video was over, everyone broke into applause."

"That sounds excellent," said my father.

"Does it?" I asked. Listening to my husband describe his moment of triumph, all I'd been able to think about was the sound of the surf crashing at dusk, and how purple the sun looks melting into the horizon from the sands of Menemsha Beach.

"This morning, I told him I needed a few days alone," I said. "Then I called a sitter, packed my bag, and got on the train to see you."

"I see," he said. "And so here you are."

I nodded.

My father had never been a man of few words. Just as long-winded as he was short-fused, he possessed the vociferous, rock-solid certainty of a successful man accustomed to having those who were less successful than he was (virtually everyone) seek his counsel about matters he presumably knew more about (virtually everything). This made conversation with him resemble sitting in one of those cavernous, echo-filled lecture halls at college. Your only permitted role was to sit there listing at rapt attention, and shouldn't you be taking notes?

This evening, I had to admit, the tables for once had distinctly been turned. I'd been permitted to hold forth for more than half an hour, with only minor interruptions. Now, drained of words, as well as energy, I sat back, folded my arms self-protectively across my chest, and braced myself for the lecture to end all lectures.

It never came.

Was he, for once, at a loss for words, or did the sound of water draining from the tub in the adjacent room remind him that the hour was late and it was time for bed?

"When the two of you first met and were seeing each other, however many years ago, I have to admit that I felt certain . . . well, reservations," he began.

"I realized that," I said. Many, I had always assumed, were based on my father's preoccupation with financial security. As someone who valued money beyond all else, how could he be enthusiastic about having a son-in-law who didn't earn much of it?

"But I didn't get the impression you would have welcomed hearing any of them then," he said. I shook my head silently. "And I don't believe it would help matters if I voiced any of them now."

"No," I said softly, and shook again.

"The question is, what are you going to do?" he asked solemnly.

"Do?" I asked. "What *can* I do? I can't possibly go back to him. And I can't possibly *not* go back to him. Between those two options, do you have any bright ideas?"

He sat there silently, and for the first time I noticed that his hair had grown as spare and wispy on top as the brittle reeds alongside sand dunes.

"Only one," he said. "It's getting late. You could probably use some sleep."

⌇

In fact, it was amazing how much good a night of uninterrupted snoozing did me, even in a narrow, makeshift bed created on his leather sofa. Evidently, it also gave his brain time to rebound from my unsettling revelations. By the time my father had finished polishing off two sliced bagels laden with glistening morsels of pink smoked Nova Scotia salmon, he was ready to brainstorm.

"I wish there were something I could do," he began, wiping a stray dab of cream cheese from one corner of his mouth.

"Like what?" I asked, helping myself to seconds on creamed herring.

"I don't know, exactly," he admitted. "Maybe I could talk to him."

"Bad idea," I said.

"Well, then, what if I talked to his mother?"

I shook my head violently and winced. "*Really* bad idea."

"OK, then. What if I hired someone to break his legs?"

"Now you're talking!" I replied.

"Maybe not," he said, when we had both finished laughing, in my case so hard that there were tears in my eyes. "Well, if I'm not going to talk to him, and I'm not going to have someone else relay the message for me, that really leaves me only one choice."

"Yes?" I asked expectantly.

"I'm trying to remember... What is that thing you always used to say?" he asked. "When the going gets tough... the tough go shopping?"

"What?" I asked.

"Yes, that's it," he said. "Your motto. Or was it, 'I've only begun to shop?'"

"Either way." I grinned. OK, so shopping had been a favorite teenage pastime. Almost an obsession. In recent years, budget problems had provided a miraculous cure. "My credit cards and I don't get around much anymore."

"That's exactly what I was thinking," he said. "Here you are, alone in New York. If you don't have any particular plans, I thought I might treat you to a new outfit or two."

In truth, I had no plans. I also didn't own a single presentable article of clothing in my current size, enormous. Besides, my first child had been born in late summer. With the new baby due in December, I owned almost nothing to wear once fall weather struck. So he didn't have to ask twice.

My father happened to live on the Upper East Side. The nearest maternity shop was so classy that its wares were stylish enough to make even normal, non-bulging women drool. After nearly an hour, I had narrowed my choices down to several irresistible options. There was a riotously bright pullover sweater in multicolored checks; a funky green and black mini-dress trimmed with black buttons the size of poker chips; an elegant, skirted business suit in navy blue pinstriped silk that made me look like a gangster (albeit a pregnant one); and a pair of nifty, pre-faded jeans with a hidden expanding waistline. "We'll take them all," my father told the saleswoman.

On the walk back home, he treated me to a hearty Chinese lunch out. Not the best culinary choice for my fragile digestion, perhaps, but a bowl of steaming wonton soup and seconds on General Tso's chicken did my soul immeasurable good.

So did the ensuing evening spent visiting one of my college roommates. Having failed to find a marriageable mate in more than a decade since graduation, she never failed to remind me that the unencumbered life might not be all that we disenchanted married folk cracked it up to be.

⎯⎯ᗰ⎯⎯

I heard their voices before the buzz the next morning, and made it to the door first. Smothering my son in ardent hugs made me wonder how I'd managed to leave him, even for a day. The extended greeting also excused me from having to kiss my husband. His mother, who had accompanied them, though, warranted a quick peck on the cheek.

"Grandpa! Grandpa Stu!"

Seeing my father sweep my child up into his arms brought some long-lost color back to my face. Then I noticed the bag my husband was holding, a bulging paper parcel with a long stick protruding, and my heart plummeted to my knees.

Having a lively toddler in tow, we had spent most of our abbreviated Martha's Vineyard vacation cavorting on the beach. Only on our last afternoon, before returning home, had we driven into Edgartown to buy some souvenirs. Primary on our list was a present for my father, whose birthday had fallen a few days before we'd gone away. Our choices, however, proved slim. It was late August, the tail end of the tourist season, and the merchandise, which had been on sale for weeks, was clearly well picked over.

If you've spent some time in any seaside resort, you know what the scene is like. In Edgartown, along with the usual assortment of ice-cream parlors and tacky T-shirt shops, there were several weathered-shingle shacks chocka-block with knickknacks, an upscale jeweler or two, and a few offbeat women's boutiques. None of these offered anything remotely appropriate for my father.

One sporty men's store I wandered into showed some promise. Here, I briefly considered a nautical-looking jacket interspersing blocks of navy blue with patches of bright primary colors. Even the sale price was exorbitant, though, and it didn't look all that special. I began foraging for something less ordinary and more affordable when our son, who had recently been toilet-trained, announced an urgent need for a bathroom. This sent us dashing frantically among nearby shops and eateries to find public facilities fast.

It was returning from this excursion that we noticed an unusual store-front. Actually, our son discovered it first. A gift shop specializing in carved wooden wares, In the Woods featured birdhouses, baskets, chess sets, beads, and an appealing variety of softly polished cutting boards and bowls. In the back was stationed a small display of rustic furniture, and even a few canoes. The specialty of the house, however, was its imaginative assortment of wooden animal toys.

Most of these beasts, in keeping with the beachside locale, were related to the sea. There were puffins and ducks, and chunky blue whales. Each of these critters came attached to a long wooden pole on which to push it around. All were also equipped with floppy rubber feet fastened to small wooden wheels, so that the feet flapped furiously as you propelled the push toys along. The ducks' webbed feet, as I recall, were especially large and amusingly loud. The most appealing members of this mechanical menagerie, by far, though, were unquestionably the wooden lobsters.

Lobsters may be among the least cuddly of all God's creatures, but they held the softest of spots in my heart. My all-time favorite food since I first tasted one at age 3, these fierce-looking crustaceans instantly evoke a life-time of fond memories. When I was small, my beloved maternal grandparents often treated me to lavish shore dinners at legendary Lundy's in Brooklyn, my bon vivant grandfather broadly beaming (and my disapproving, kosher grandmother visibly shuddering) as I passionately devoured my ruddy-shelled prey, tentacle by tentacle. In later years, my family had often celebrated special occasions at colonial-style restaurants such as Patricia Murphy's, dining by candlelight as we dipped rosy morsels of succulent lobster flesh into ceramic bowls of melted lemon butter. And who could forget the raucous dinners enjoyed during seaside summer vacations with our relatives when, alongside my aunts, uncles and cousins, we had feasted al fresco at casual wooden picnic tables on the world's best culinary bargain, lobster in the rough?

In light of this family history, buying my dad a lobster, even a comical, wooden one, seemed clever, almost inspired. No, it was not an extravagant gift, but at $20 apiece they were the priciest toys in the shop. And although a toy might not be the ideal choice for a grown man, I figured he would derive some joy from using it to amuse the grandson he rarely got to see. After all, in my father's sophisticated, sedately furnished New York apartment, it would be the first and only juvenile amusement.

At least it was a good start, I figured, approaching the cash register, wallet in hand. Later, we could buy something else. The line was long, however, and by the time we had reached the head of it our son had erupted into wild sobs, long overdue for a nap. So we had hastened back to our hotel.

Early the next morning, we boarded our ferry. We never got to buy anything else.

⟳

The lobster was the object poking out of the bag my husband toted under his arm. Given my abrupt departure and the item's unusual size and shape, it wasn't even properly wrapped. Seeing it now, I cringed with regret but had little choice. We settled down for a visit in the living room, and at the first lull in the conversation I gestured toward my son to convey the bag over to his grandfather.

"What's this?" asked my father, looking delighted to receive a gift, then visibly bewildered when he opened it.

"A belated birthday offering," I replied, doing my best to muster a smile.

"I see," he said, lifting the lobster end into the air. "But what *is* it?"

"What do you mean?" my husband asked. "It's a lobster."

"Wooden lobster!" my son exclaimed.

"Oh. How... interesting," my father replied.

"Here, wait," I said, taking it from his grasp and handing it across to my husband. "Show him how it works."

Remaining seated on his end of the sofa, my husband lowered the lobster to the floor and rolled it gently across the carpet. My son giggled as the claws, attached to the front wheels, rotated forward and clacked.

"Oh, my!" exclaimed my mother-in-law.

"Wherever did you find *that*?" my stepmother asked.

Reaching for the stick, my father tentatively rolled the lobster back and forth on the carpet. My son giggled and clapped as its claws wriggled and slapped. Soon they were racing from room to room, my father chasing my son with the rolling crustacean, then my son chasing him, my father's face lobster red, my son shrieking with pleasure.

"Maybe that wasn't so bad, after all," I remarked to my husband, as our exhausted youngster dozed in the back seat beside his grandmother during the long drive home.

"What do you mean?" he asked. "You had a good visit?"

I hadn't thought about it until then, but he was right. "Yes," I said. "I really did." It was then that I also realized I'd forgotten to offer my father the other part of his gift. Not a traditional present, exactly, but an announcement I knew would please him more than any mere thing. We had finally settled on a name for our unborn child, whom I had recently learned was going to be a daughter. She would be called Francesca, in honor of his late, adored father, Frank.

⎯ᘓ

I was sitting in my office late the next morning when my phone extension rang. Hearing my father's voice, my mood brightened instantly. "Hi there! Everything all right?" I began. "You know, I really can't thank you enough – "

"Listen, I have something I want you to do for me," he interrupted, speaking in a voice so loud and stern that I snapped to immediate attention in my chair, like a dutiful soldier at a drill sergeant's barked command. "Something important. Are you listening?"

"Yes," I said. "Of course."

"Good. I'd like you to write this down. I want you to go to a tennis shop today, buy two white tennis shirts, put them in a box and mail them to me. Do you understand?"

"Understand? I guess," I said, although I didn't really. His dresser drawers in Florida (and, no doubt, New York) already overflowed with barely worn athletic apparel. "You need tennis shirts?"

"No, not particularly," he said. "But I want you to send me some. Two of them. Size medium. Make sure they're white, 100 percent cotton, and as plain as possible."

"OK," I said, scribbling down the details, as he had requested. "Sure."

"I'd like you to do that today," he added forcefully.

"Fine," I said. "I'll do my best to get to the post office after work before it closes. But, if you don't mind my asking, well… Why?"

"Why?" he asked. "I'll tell you why. I've never been so humiliated in all my life!"

"Humiliated?" I asked. "What are you talking about?"

"I'm talking about your gift," he said with disgust. "That… that *thing*. What sort of present is that for a grown man? You embarrassed me in front of your mother-in-law!"

I could almost hear his blood beginning to simmer on the other end of the phone.

"My mother-in-law?" I asked. My mother-in-law was 85 years old. Quiet, sweet, and extremely hard of hearing. I doubted she had given the matter a moment of thought. "You must be kidding," I said. "Harriet's just happy when we take her along for the ride. I'll bet she didn't even notice."

"Didn't notice?" he barked back. "I can't imagine what you were thinking! After the way I treated you this weekend? You embarrassed me in front of your mother-in-law! You embarrassed me in front of my wife!"

Embarrassed him in front of his wife. *His wife?* He was referring to a woman in her mid-60's who still dressed like a teenager in clingy jeans and cheap, skin-tight tops. He was referring to a woman who routinely spouted baldly racist remarks, and who'd conducted an affair with my father for a dozen years while he was married to my mom. How deeply offended her sensibilities must have been to watch him receive a slightly cheesy birthday gift. But I didn't imagine it would help matters to point any of that out.

"I'm sorry," I said. "Really. I thought you could use it to play with your grandson. I mean, it's not as though your apartment is exactly brimming with toys."

"Toys?" he repeated. "I'm 62 years old. Why would I have toys?"

"I don't know," I said. "I'm sorry! I'd be happy to send you something else."

"You do that!" he roared. "I want those shirts. I want you to send them – today!"

I did send the shirts. Two of them. White. Size medium, 100 percent cotton.

I put them in a box and mailed them that day. I followed this up with a letter.

In it, I repeated my apology, then went on to point out every unwelcome gift he had given me during the past 34 years, all of which I had graciously chosen to overlook – until that moment.

Take the night of my 25th birthday. There I had been, still as timid as a teenager, yet proud to have finally reached a milestone that made me feel like I was all grown up (so grown-up that I was secretly dating a man of 51). What did my father do? He marked the occasion by presenting me with a reasonably tasteful, delicately designed wristwatch. Then he undercut it all by whipping out my "real" present: a gigantic stuffed Snoopy doll.

In more recent years, he had phoned one day to ask if there was anything in particular I wanted for an upcoming birthday. When pressed for an answer, I'd reluctantly confessed that I was dying for some decent kitchen equipment.

Cooking was among my greatest passions, yet I didn't own a single respectable pot or culinary gadget.

"Kitchen equipment?" he'd scoffed. "That's no kind of present!" Instead, he had arrived at our house bearing a heavy, garish, gold bracelet – something I would never have any occasion to wear. At the time, we were struggling desperately just to pay the mortgage. So imagine my added horror when my stepmother followed me into the kitchen to confide how many hundreds of dollars he had spent on it.

Worst of all, however, was the white polyester nightgown. The year before, my father had completely forgotten my birthday. It had come and gone without so much as a call. Then, while I was visiting him about a month later, it had abruptly sprung to mind. Embarrassed, he had hastily summoned Elaine, who went into her closet and came back with a shiny, white, floor-length nightgown that was hideously frilly and distinctly low-class. This was heaped haphazardly in an unwrapped, slightly crushed yellow gift box, without tags, and wreaked unmistakably of her usual scent. I could only conclude that it had belonged to her and was the best thing she had on hand to mark the missed occasion.

Neither were his foibles limited to *giving* gifts, I charged. He was equally as awkward at accepting them. No matter what I bought him, he never managed to force out more than a tepid, half-hearted reception. I had long ago concluded that I had no talent for finding anything that would please him. In fact, I reminded him, several years earlier, after one too many unfortunate choices of necktie, he had firmly requested that my brother and I refrain from buying him clothing again; he preferred to pick his own.

Housewares, evidently, were also off-limits. Just consider the case of a large glass salad bowl I had given him as a wedding gift when he had married Elaine. I had presented it filled with Chinese fortune cookies and a note saying, "Marriage is a fragile thing. I hope yours is filled with good fortune." A year or two later, he had lent it to me for a dinner party, then suggested that I keep it, noting, "We never use that thing."

I could only assume that my venomous missive arrived safely, because I eventually received a response. Hand-written on two pages torn from a lined, yellow, legal-size notebook, it provided a thorough self-defense, point by point. I still have it in the top drawer of my desk, folded neatly in four and tucked into a plain white business envelope postmarked November 8, 1989.

It reads precisely, odd capitalization and all, as follows:

It is 6 weeks since you wrote me and now I think I can answer.

Your general conclusion appears to be my lack of interest in you, my lack of consideration for your needs and a general disregard for your problems.

I never asked or hinted to Joel and you to refrain from buying me clothes or anything. On the contrary I always appreciated whatever was given and felt I showed the satisfaction I really felt. My not taking back the bowl you once gave was more an expression that we hardly do any entertaining and you could make good use of it.

I have given you many things over your lifetime and always to please and help you. It was a real satisfaction to give you things of all types, and a Father does this gladly. Only now I will not accept that my choices were hurried or casual with no real effort on my part to give you something really nice that you would enjoy.

The gold bracelet I bought may not be your taste but I looked very long and hard and spent a great deal of money trying to delight you. I have purchased gifts for Elaine which she returned (exchanged) but never with the thought I really didn't care what it looked like.

Now the nightgown.

Elaine bought this in Alexander's and I liked it so much I asked her to go back and get one for you. It was just a small gift for no occasion. She bought a second one in another color for herself (it is in Palm Beach) and since Alexander's does not gift wrap she just put it in her drawer (sachet or cologne scent was picked up on the gown). It was purchased for you, never for anyone else, and never never used. You have given a strange twist to a simple event. Once again it may not be your taste – of course – but it was bought spontaneously to please you. MY HAND TO GOD.

The wristwatch was your considered 25th birthday gift – chosen with Love. The Snoopy was our inside joke. It was not trying to put you down. I never have knowingly done that.

Against your several charges or criticisms I hold up a continuous record of being in touch with you, listening carefully to your remarks, worried about your problems. Always showing a strong Fatherly interest in your welfare and Happiness. For every one lousy story you mention I have 1000 instances of ongoing concern, love, caring, responsiveness to you.

Am I perfect? Of course not, but I am a loving Father and nothing changes that record because I always felt that way.

I am not trying to win an argument but rather remind you to see my total record and let the chips fall where they may. If you feel you need more detachment from me then you shall have that also. Send me a signal of what you want and it is yours.

For my next birthday get me either 5 good cigars or a white tennis shirt.

Love,

Dad

P.S. Please return the bowl when convenient.

I read these pages. I read them twice. Then I placed them back in the envelope. The only signal I sent to him was silence. It went on for nearly six more weeks, until the morning I gave birth. I had just returned from a holiday party wearing one of my new dresses – the green stripe with the huge black buttons – when I suddenly went into labor.

When my husband began broadcasting the good news from the maternity ward, my father was the first person he phoned. He and Elaine began driving up from the city almost immediately. Photographs of them huddled around me in my hospital bed, my little boy clowning, my father beaming madly, make us look like any normal-ish, happy-ish, Jewish family. And from that moment on, as much as could be expected, we were.

We never discussed either of our letters or mentioned the wooden lobster again. But for the rest of his life, on special occasions, I lavished on my father a parade of absurdly extravagant gifts. It wasn't enough to buy him an elegant shirt from the finest haberdashery in town. I would also enclose a matching sweater or pair of coordinating slacks. Tennis shirts, a safe fallback, would be accompanied by shorts (all 100 percent cotton, size medium), as well as socks, wristbands, a hat, or even a warm-up suit.

Financially, I could hardly justify such excess. Yet psychologically, I couldn't afford anything less. I didn't want to risk insulting him and resuming our cold war.

For his part, he stepped up his show of appreciation for my generous offerings. More often than not, whenever we met, I'd find him decked out in an assortment of them. If contemporary Italianate men's wear wasn't exactly his taste, he certainly never let on. At least I know he treasured a funky, flannel bathrobe I sent him one Father's Day that was covered with cowboys striking various manly poses (riding horses, lassoing calves). Even Elaine admitted to me that on most nights, as soon as he returned from the office, he would quickly shed his somber business attire and slip it on. It might have appeared comical to anyone else, and no doubt it looked foolish on him. But he loved cowboy novels and I knew the second I spied it that it would appeal to his romanticized, heroic vision of the wild, wild West. I also believe he cherished it because it came from me.

That's about as much mutual forgiveness as the two of us could ever muster. At first, I felt so wounded and appalled by his utter callousness toward me that I changed my mind about my infant daughter and, instead of naming her after my grandfather, gave her an "A" name, Allegra, after my late father-in-law instead. But I see my father's behavior differently now. For a parent to turn on me at one of the lowest points in my life may have been cruel and against human nature, but it was very much in keeping with his. My father was a man of many strengths. Empathy just wasn't one of them.

My brother, in fact, recalls a similar experience with him that occurred at around the same time. As a young criminal defense attorney, my brother had accepted a client with a nearly hopeless case. Even so, he had grown determined to win against all odds. He'd spent months working late into the night preparing for the trial. Devastated when he lost it anyway, he had wandered over to my father's office, arriving just before noon.

My father, you must understand, had long run his own company. A typical man in his position would have insisted on taking his son out for a nice meal and probably a beer – anything to cheer him up. My father told a secretary to have sandwiches sent up from a deli downstairs instead. When they arrived, he gulped his down in a matter of minutes, then looked impatiently at his watch and announced that he had paperwork to do.

"That trial was the worst professional setback I'd ever had in my life," my brother said. It was unmistakable that he felt like a failure, hopeless, despondent and worthless. Yet it wasn't within the barren landscape of my father's makeup to notice or try to help.

In certain ways, you see, he was probably something of a crustacean himself. Demanding, imperious, and intolerant toward incompetence or any other form of frailty, he wore an impenetrable skeleton on the outside. He was not, however, a wooden lobster. No one could push him around.

That weekend when I was pregnant and lost at sea, a dispirited emotional refugee, was the first and last time I ever dared to fully open up to my father. It was also – despite his claims to "1000 instances of ongoing concern, love, caring, responsiveness to you" — the only time I remember managing, however briefly, to truly break through his shell. And for that I ought to consider myself lucky. My brother never cracked it at all.

Having a hole in his heart doesn't make the way he treated either of us excusable. Still, in retrospect, I wish he were still around to thank; for I realize now that in my moment of abject need, he actually did come to my rescue, in his own inadvertent way.

He did it by temporarily becoming the chief villain in my life, an ogre more monstrous to me than my neglectful husband appeared at the time. I can't explain why, but there's a peculiarity of human nature: Just as no one can sing two separate notes simultaneously, it's almost impossible to actively despise two different enemies at once. On the contrary, contempt for a common adversary can often forge unlikely alliances between warring factions. A prime example of this was my son when he grew to be a teenager. He would viciously denounce me as a she-devil, then summon me to his room to conspiratorially divulge, "You know who I *really* hate? Dad!"

That's precisely what happened the morning my father demanded those shirts. Outraged, I telephoned the one person I knew who could fully grasp my predicament. Having been present on the fateful shopping odyssey, my husband was not just privy to all its peculiar pitfalls; he was an actual accessory to the crime. He shared my guilt. He shared my indignation. And by that night, he was back to sharing my secrets and my bed.

Over three decades of marriage later – and counting – he still does.

I sometimes wonder what might have happened had my father not been there to help boost us over that hump, one of the steepest mountains in our marital history. I'm also still curious to know what became of the wooden lobster. Did he cart it to the trash room in his apartment building minutes after we left? Did he fling it furiously down the incinerator shaft, or break it in two first? Or did it get stashed permanently in the back of a closet, like a pair of new shoes that are too good to toss out but hurt too much to wear?

I thought about it recently again when my stepmother died, having outlived my father by several years. One of her children, who had inherited their apartment, called to ask if there were any items inside that I might like to have. I thought of asking if I could visit, just to have a look around. I considered inquiring if anyone had noticed a wooden lobster on a stick. But there's really nothing I could do with it, now that my children are grown, and think how foolish it would sound. "Some photographs would be nice," I said.

So I never did see that lobster again, and I guess I never will. But I often think of that terrible weekend when I get into a jam. When it comes to big trouble – man, money, or otherwise – I still feel twinges of that natural, little-girl instinct that wishes my father were around to save me. Then I remember what happened, and I remember he's gone, and I get busy saving myself.

Set in Stone

~

IF I WEREN'T SUCH A perfectionist, everything in my life would probably be easier, but nothing would be nearly as nice. Sure, I've tried to lower my standards over the years. Sometimes, you just have to accept the idea that doing your best is sufficient – that "good enough" really *is* good enough. Yet some things are simply too important for that. They deserve the obsessive effort it takes to make them turn out just right. So one balmy day in May of 1999, I drove to the Berkshires to plan our summer vacation... in person.

Why peer at publicity shots online when I could see it all up close and personal by driving a mere three hours roundtrip? Besides, after a long, frigid winter following what had been the worst year of my life *ever*, I needed a fleeting glimpse of pleasure to come.

What I ended up finding in those majestic Massachusetts mountains was far beyond pleasure, though. It was my own personal Shangri-La: rambling, elegant old inns nestled amid lush green hills that would soon come alive with the sights and sounds of music, art, theater, dance... and best of all, my own children's laughter. Afterwards, driving back through budding trees and breathtaking tranquility, I felt the tension begin to lift from my bones like a large, screeching bird taking flight into the calm country air.

This tour of oblivion came to an abrupt halt the moment that I walked through my door. Awaiting me on the telephone answering machine was a message from my brother.

"I'll get right to the point," he said when I returned the call. "I have a favor to ask. You need to get a gravestone for Dad."

—⟆—

Throughout the endless year that our father had been ill, my brother Joel had unquestionably borne the brunt of his care. Living in close proximity to New York, where our father had resided with his second wife since our parents' divorce, my only sibling – despite the demands of a busy law practice – had visited almost daily. He'd escorted our dad to doctors' appointments, made grueling decisions about his medical treatment, and even helped him update his will when it became clear that the chemo wasn't working.

My role had been more of the kind that gets nominated for best actress in a supporting role. Situated hours away and having two young children, I'd done as much as seemed humanly possible. This included calling my father daily and conferring often with my brother by phone, sometimes several times a day. I also had begun making the five-hour roundtrip trek to visit my father weekly. And while my brother's visits were short and efficient, mine were long and languorous, lasting the entire day. I'd sit beside him babbling away for hours, often in the hospital, where I'd do my desperate best to distract him while a toxic, orange potion slowly drip... drip... dripped into his veins.

Yet all my chitchat didn't do all that much to help. Neither, sadly, did the potion. If anything, it poisoned every second of his life, far worse than the actual disease itself.

—⟆—

The night before my first hospital visit, I was unable to sleep, so much did I dread the horror that I was certain lay ahead. I envisioned myself holding a plastic basin beneath my father's head while he doubled over with nausea. The scene I encountered upon arrival was much more civilized, although almost as chilling in its own way.

My father lay stretched out in bed 719A, his pale blue cotton hospital gown open wide at the neck to reveal a translucent plastic tube attached to a large needle embedded in his chest. The clear liquid coursing through this, dripping out of an IV bag hanging from above, was just a harmless saline solution, I was told, meant to keep him hydrated.

Yet even when the actual chemotherapy – a toxic-looking, tangerine-colored weapon of liquid warfare – finally commenced, he betrayed no signs of discomfort. Resting contentedly atop the sheets, he proceeded to flirt flagrantly with every nurse who entered. If anyone appeared to feel at all uncomfortable, it was his wife, my 73-year-old stepmother Elaine, who sat planted in a chair at the foot of his bed, a watchful gargoyle engulfed in mink, dutifully enduring this discomfiting scene in sullen silence.

When my brother phoned mid-morning, promising to visit the following day, my father objected valiantly, to the unmistakable amusement of the two young women in faded aqua scrubs who were attending him at that moment, one stationed on either side.

"No one is allowed in this room who isn't wearing high heels and lipstick!" he roared into the receiver.

"I can do that!" was my brother's wise-cracked response, repeated by my father for the benefit of his female audience with such raucous laughter that the IV bag suspended above him began to swing like a low-hanging melon swaying in the breeze.

From where, exactly, were they summoning this eerie reserve of good humor? Sure, it always had been a family habit to make light of even the grimmest situations, the customary Jewish manner of coping with history, with hardship… in other words, with life. My own best lines may have been inspired by my parents' long, messy divorce. But now I was feeling amazingly *un*clever. Something about cancer tended to dull my wits.

⟿

It seemed hard to believe that a year had already passed when I received my brother's call about the stone that day in May. As you can gather from my painstaking approach to planning a mere vacation, I was the right man for the job. Except for one rather crucial detail. My brother and stepmother both lived in New York, not far from where my father was buried. How was I supposed to select a gravestone long-distance?

Then again, how could I refuse? My brother was now busy back at work, and I certainly didn't want my wicked stepmother in charge of something so sensitive and significant. So I contacted the cemetery and got the phone numbers of some reputable monument companies nearby. Not surprisingly, most had nice Jewish names like Horowitz and Schwartz. And a quick call to each yielded a wealth of information.

Those of you who have been obliged to do it yourselves know how unnerving it is to pick out a casket in which to bury a loved one, regardless of the phenomenal expense. Well, choosing a headstone is no picnic, either. Nor bargain, for that matter. You have to deal with everything from size, shape, and finish to the variety of rock from which it will be hewn. And that's before you even consider the all-important inscription.

My father hadn't been buried in a restricted area, I learned, meaning one in which all of the markers had to be uniform in size. So I had a lot of leeway – within reason.

Nearly every cemetery has its share of mammoth monstrosities, no doubt. People who had the means to show off in life are just as eager to show off in death. The typical monument made to mark a grave, however, is far from monumental. "Usually, the normal size is two feet by one foot," I was told. That was for a single stone. There was also the option to buy a double header instead, with a base wide enough to support two separate headstones. That way, my father and his second wife could share one marker for eternity after she was gone. A nice thought, or so it would've been had my dad still been married to my mom. Under the circumstances, I said thanks anyway, but a single would do just fine. Elaine's kids could deal with their mother's final arrangements when the time came.

Then there was the issue of color, or what you might refer to as "the gray matter."

In case of you've never noticed, nearly every stone in any graveyard is some shade of gray. And contrary to the popular erotic romance, there are no 50 shades of that.

"Gray is gray," I was told. There's dark gray, light gray, and a small spectrum of shades in between, but in the end it's all just your grim and grainy, ordinary mouse shade.

There are also various brownish grays that have a ruddy, copper cast to them. The only other real choice is black, which for grave markers is anything but basic.

"Black stands out a lot more," one stone salesman ardently assured me.

It also came with a more imposing price tag, essentially double the rate for its concrete-hued cousin ($3,000 for a single stone at the time, versus $1,495 for mere slate).

Then there was the issue of the finish on the stone. It could be rough or smooth, polished or matte, or something referred to as "steeled." I had no idea what that might be. But my father had been an importer of stainless steel for his entire adult life. He literally had been a man of steel. So I figured that was unquestionably the obvious way to go.

Yet hearing all of these options, I was even more anxious than I originally had been about trying to make so momentous and permanent a purchase from afar.

"Buying something over the phone sight-unseen is not a good idea," a salesman named Charles at a monument company called Schwartz Brothers heartily concurred.

He didn't deem it necessary for me to make the exhausting drive down, however. All I had to do, he advised, was head to the nearest graveyard and have a look around.

So the next day, I did just that. I drove the mere mile or two to Fairview Cemetery, on the outskirts of Fern Ridge Park – a popular, tree-lined public area with a swimming pool and playground – where I went shopping for a gravestone for my father.

─ ᧒ ─

From the time he was a toddler, my father had been known for his keen wit, fierce bravado, and a feisty temper that had landed him in hot water repeatedly long before it had allowed him to succeed. Born in Brooklyn in 1927, the third of four children of Frank Weiss, a humble dress cutter, he always had seemed bent on making sure he got his own way and his due share of anything available in his family's poor, Jewish household.

"No fight, Stuie! No fight!" his beleaguered mother Sadie would admonish him every time he went out to play. Nonetheless, someone almost always ended up with a bloody something, and that someone was rarely him.

Maybe that feistiness was something he'd inherited from her. Her long-suffering husband, my upbeat and mild-mannered Grandpa Frank, had done his level best to make light of her penchant to explode regularly with unfettered rage, like a cauldron of her incomparable chicken soup boiling over onto the stove. "Call up my insurance agent and increase my fire coverage," he'd joke to his kids. "Your mother's burning up again!"

Or perhaps at the root of my father's volatility was a frustration that, with so many kids to please and mouths to feed, there was never quite enough of anything to go around. Given my Grandma Sadie's well-known prowess as a true *balabusta,* or great homemaker – not once do I recall seeing her without an apron at her waist – I find it hard to believe that anyone in their cramped Borough Park apartment ever went hungry. Yet young Stuie not only never had a room of his own, but had to share a small bedroom with his two brothers, in which he had only one dresser drawer to himself and barely enough belongings to fill it.

Among his favorite stories was one that he told relentlessly when I was growing up. It was about a club that he and his older brother Gerard had formed with a few other boys. One day, one of the other kids proposed a hike in the weekly dues, from one cent to two. When his own brother voted in favor of the measure, my father took Gerard aside in horror.

"Do you have any idea what you're doing?" he chastised him furiously. "That would be only one penny extra for everyone else, but for us it would mean two!"

Yes, I know that a penny was actually worth something once. But not *that* much.

My mother's favorite tale about their youth skipped many years ahead, however, to one wintry night soon after they had begun dating. It had started snowing so heavily that when my father brought her home at the end of the evening, her parents had begged him to stay there overnight. But when he phoned home to report the invitation, his own mother had said that she wouldn't hear of it and ordered him to come home at once.

After trudging dutifully for nearly half an hour through the ice and snow, he'd arrived home to tell her that my mother was a respectable girl from a good family. What's more, he said, he loved her and intended to marry her. Hearing this, Grandma Sadie was so afraid to insult her future *machatunim* (Yiddish for your child's in-laws) by having even insinuated that there had been any impropriety underfoot that she put his pajamas into a bag and made him walk more than a mile back to her house through the blinding blizzard.

—⟨⟩—

My parents had met at the beach at Coney Island during the summer of 1945. "You know Stu," their mutual friend Joe had noted to her in his best Brooklyn accent. Recognizing him from her French class the previous year, my mother eyed the "skinny marink" before her appreciatively, noting how pale he looked in contrast to her own well-tanned skin. Could he really be the guy her class soon would designate most likely to succeed? Either way, she knew not to get her hopes up because he already had a steady girl, Rhoda Fenster.

Their next notable encounter, many a month later, occurred at a school dance held by Arista, the honor-student society, during their senior year at New Utrecht High. Poor Rhoda was now out of the picture, and my mother, decked out in a deep red velvet dress from Orbach's, heard my father begin to sing along with a Frank Sinatra record. Then their eyes met over the punch bowl and he dared to ask her to dance.

By then, she'd long harbored a secret crush on him and was mortified to hear herself blurt out, "What took you so long? I've been waiting for you to ask me all night!"

There's no telling how serious it became initially, given their tender age and total lack of sophistication. The steady stream of letters flying between them the following year, while my father did a stint in the Navy, were long on information and short on *schmaltz,* so cordial and undemonstrative that they could have been exchanged between cousins. Most that he wrote began with the basic, blandly generic greeting "Dear Bunny," and ended awkwardly with no closing term of any kind. He simply signed his name.

But by 1948, when my mother took a summer job at a camp for diabetic children, the once-reserved tone had substantially heated up. So had the substance and salutations.

"Dearest Baby-Doll," begins one mushy, four-page missive he penned that June. "…I love you, Fat Soft One. Anyone at the dinner table could tell you were away – I had onions with the [smoked] salmon. I'm sorry I can eat them. I'd so much rather hold you."

Another even steamier example, directed to "Dearest Plumpy Cheeks," went on to declare, "I would be very contented if you would love me with all your glowing heart."

Then there was the lengthy note that began "Dearest Honey-Bunch" in early July. "If you want to know whether I miss you, I'll tell you straight from my heart.

I'm like a lost puppy, like a body looking for its soul, like a right shoe looking for its left. Sometimes when I read your letters the tears come to my eyes, and my heart pounds when I think of you and all you are to me.

I miss you terribly all day long and even more at night… I'm constantly thinking about you and picturing once again many past scenes. Well, you know now how much I worship you (because I do <u>worship</u> you and all you represent)… your pretty brown arms and plumpy cheeks, and all the nice and naughty things that make you so delicious…

What an appetizing and successful wife you ought to make! That's a proposal. Would you, please, huh, please?

All my love,
Stuie

I doubt this was his very first mention of marriage, and it was clearly not his last. He wrote to her every single day that summer and came to visit most weekends, and one night shortly after she had returned he phoned and insisted on coming over, even though it was late. She watched for him through the window and met him at the door before he could knock, since her family had already turned in for the night. Then, only seconds after they had settled on the living room couch, he whipped out a teeny blue velvet box.

Their plans to actually get hitched would have to wait, though, and would not go off without a hitch. They each had one more year of college, which they spent socializing with other young couples. One night the following spring, my mother invited my father to a fancy party at Brooklyn College for which she was in charge of "hospitality."

She spent much of the night replenishing the refreshments and serving tea from a large silver samovar. Then she suddenly noticed that my father was nowhere in sight.

"You won't believe it," her best friend Nada confessed reluctantly when my mother inquired frantically about his whereabouts. Nada and another classmate had seen him slip away with a freshman girl. "We heard her boasting that she would be wearing your engagement ring before the night was over," Nada divulged. He never reappeared.

My mother phoned him the next morning, and he came over to her house at once. "What kind of fool do you take me for?" she asked. "Did you think I wouldn't find out?" Then she twisted the one-carat diamond ring off her finger and flung it at him.

He buried his face remorsefully in his hands and begged for a chance to explain. "Last night was like a bachelor party for me," he contended. "You know – a last fling." He truly loved her, he declared, and wanted to spend the rest of his life proving it.

Soon they were both in tears, or so she'd later claim. Within an hour, the ring had regained residence on her fourth finger, and they were planning a wedding in earnest.

They said their "I do's" on the 5th of June, 1949, followed by a meal of roast chicken that began with "Supreme Fruit Tricolor" and ended with petit fours and fancy ices in Melba sauce. Now-faded photos show my father beaming in a dove-gray tailcoat. My mother, all aglow beside him, is radiant in a short-sleeved gown with a lace overlay, nearly three dozen buttons cascading down its bodice and a 3-foot train swirling around her feet like the foam of a crashing surf. And although I obviously wasn't there, it would be safe to say that the groom stepped on the glass and the bride later threw her bouquet.

I also believe it would be safe to say that, yes, my father did take her for a fool. And as clever and capable as she may have been, it soon became clear that she *was* one.

My mother once admitted to me that, although she may have been president of Arista, the honor-student society, she was not actually the smartest girl at New Utrecht High, class of 1945. That would be Bunny Shenensky, followed by Jeannie Fierstein, who would marry my father's friend Joe, the fellow who'd introduced them. But even at No. 3 in a cast of hundreds (maybe even thousands), my mother was one smart cookie.

In the classroom, that is. How could she have been such a fool for love?

Part of the problem, no doubt, was that, with the exception of that summer she worked at the camp, she lived at home all her life, up until the day that she was married. Far from being a woman of the world, she barely had ever set foot outside of Brooklyn, beyond the occasional family trip to a Jewish bungalow colony upstate in the Catskills.

Then there was the solemn vow she'd made, as a nice Jewish girl and so-called good girl, which she dutifully if not scrupulously kept, to "save herself for marriage." Having to hold back during the many years in which they dated before tying the knot helped fan the initial spark between my parents into a raging inferno. As she wrote:

Sweetest Baby,

Darling heart, angel of my dreams, I love you. I feel so very close to you and warm. Once again my heart beats to the same rhythm that yours

does. Oh, to love and be loved is the greatest thing on earth... I have so
many kisses just ready to explode!

But within six months of their wedding – according to my father, anyway – the once-roaring flame that had ignited at that dance had already
definitively gone out.

Gone out, at least, on his part, only to be replaced by the ever-burning
torch that was my father's uncontrollable temper.

―❦―

The first thing I noticed after passing through the cemetery's cast-iron front
gates was that the place was apparently nondenominational, even though, like
most things in this country, it was vastly dominated by Gentiles. I based this
deduction on the liberal use of crucifixes and Madonnas and prevalence of
names like Mancini, Potter, and St. Pierre.

There were low stones and towering stones, fat stones and flat stones,
angular stones with sharp right-angle edges and others that flared gently at
the bottom like a bell.

There were stones with rough-hewn sides as pock-marked as the face of
the moon, stones chiseled as flat as a board, and ones polished to such a
gleaming sheen that they caught the brilliant rays of the afternoon sun and
mirrored my reflection.

There were single stones, double stones, and towering headstones bearing family surnames rimmed by constellations of miniscule markers where
generations of husbands, wives, sons, and daughters had been laid to rest en
masse, like members of a cult.

There were stones inscribed strictly with names and dates, and others
bearing ornate embellishments, typically flowers. One bore a police badge,
another a dog and cat. But the most common adornments consisted of crosses,
with an occasional rosary too.

Still, I searched for Jewish signs and saw there were some *landsmen* here
too.

In fact, the stone that stood out most prominently bore a name I instantly recognized. It belonged to a prominent car dealer, a pillar of the local Jewish community who had passed away within the previous few years. I recalled seeing him regularly in the dining room at Tumble Brook, my mother-in-law's country club. I even knew his sons.

The reason his stone captured my attention was not just its ample size, but its color. That salesman I'd spoken with had been right. Unlike the run-of-the-mill gray shades that abounded, this stone was jet black, accented with a halo of crimson geraniums carved into its border. The family's surname was inscribed in bold letters across the top, while the bottom offered spaces for seven names, only one of which was filled in so far.

In between was a concise motto, inscribed in florid script:

Live well.
    Laugh often.
        Love much.

As gravestones go, I kind of liked it. And in many ways, it even fit.

—

Not too long after they were married, my father began traveling abroad for work. And that journeying forth into the world led to a wandering eye.

The letters written on onion-skin that he sent home to us spoke of the cultural events and tourist sites he visited in the world's capitals: Buckingham Palace, Westminster Abbey, an opera at La Scala. But that was clearly not all that he saw or did.

The sepia-toned pictures in their now-tattered honeymoon album capture a devoted young duo with their arms lovingly intertwined like inextricably tangled vines. But these blissful images soon gave way to a very different photo montage.

Within three years my brother came along, followed two years later by me. A telltale outtake from that turbulent era shows my brother, age 4, in a fringed cowboy suit, his outstretched hand clasping my mother's shoulder, not with affection but protectively. Both gaze anxiously outward toward the impatient tyrant with the hair-trigger temper clearly taking the shot, a worn-out, world-weary expression clouding both of their faces.

Barely a toddler at that point, I presumably was safely napping inside. But by the time I had fully entered the picture and begun to bear witness to their ever-sputtering skirmishes, I had that wary, prematurely wizened look tattooed onto my face, too.

The many letters my father sent home from his European jaunts still betray an occasional note of warmth and concern for our welfare I never truly witnessed in person. Scrawled on crinkled, tissue-weight paper and sent from distant cities like Copenhagen and Cologne, some even make it sound like he may have genuinely pined for my mother.

I miss you dear, very much, and often look at my watch to calculate the time in New York and imagine what you must be doing... My love to you, darling, and squeeze the kids for me.

But during these frequent overseas trips, which often lasted for weeks at a stretch, I'd hear muffled crying emanating from my mother's room at night, not only because she missed him, although I know that she did, but because she knew what he was up to.

Everybody did.

As I said earlier, Elaine was far from the first "other woman" that my father saw. She was simply the last.

And that, my friends, is how the "smart cookie" crumbles.

—ᴄᴏ—

With the start of my father's chemo came an abrupt end to his appetite. Even when he wasn't succumbing to nausea, that Tang-colored concoction tainted everything that touched his tongue with a bitter, metallic taste. Within weeks it became painfully clear that he was rapidly wasting away. As a lifelong tennis fanatic, he'd always been remarkably fit-looking and trim, a quality considered to be almost universally desirable. Yet that's only true until you all but stop eating and it comes back to bite you in the *tush*.

On one of my daylong visits, now a weekly occurrence, I decided to see what I could do to remedy the situation. Wracking my brain for what might whet his appetite, I picked up some corned beef and hot pastrami, traditional Jewish foods that he favored. Never mind that they weren't exactly the easiest things to digest.

But even better, I figured, would be anything homemade.

So I prepared some fresh chicken soup, far better for an ultra-sensitive stomach. Then it occurred to me that there was one major advantage to living in the stultifying suburbs, and that benefit could be summed up in a single word: grilling. So I also barbecued some juicy chicken. It might not be as luscious by the time I had transported it to the city as it would have tasted fresh off the hot coals, but it would have to do.

This being summer, I also baked some fluffy biscuits for strawberry shortcake, and packed separate containers of hand-whipped heavy cream and plump sliced berries, to be assembled into elegant towers on the spot. To keep it all fresh during the long drive, I bought a small Styrofoam container at the supermarket, one of those deep rectangular receptacles with a scalloped-edged removable lid.

My father immediately dubbed this cheap, white, disposable vessel "the urn," which struck me as rather strange. For one thing, it didn't in any conceivable way resemble an urn, or certainly a Grecian one, the kind to which an ode might be written.

For another, the word struck me as a bit of a double-entendre. Throughout his life, my father's main priority had been to "earn." Earn his keep. Earn more than anyone else. Earn his way out of poverty to achieve a sense of security, or, better yet, superiority.

Because I was "just a girl," he never had expressed any expectations that I'd be a high earner or achiever, as he volubly maintained for my brother. Yet perhaps these visits were my one remaining chance to attain some shred of value in his eyes – to earn my way back not into his heart, where I believe I already had a firm hold, but into his high regard.

Despite the lengths I'd gone to with my preparations, hoping that at least one of my provisions might strike his fancy, I didn't dare hope for the best. Yet the moment I set a plate before him, he hesitated only long enough to place a napkin onto his lap before hacking off a sliver of chicken leg, then seizing the bone with both hands and taking another, far less tentative bite.

"Where's mine? Where's mine?" squealed Elaine, who during my father's illness mysteriously had begun to wither away in girth as well, transforming into a haggard apparition that haunted the premises like a Halloween ghoul, thanks to the raccoon-like kohl band she invariably etched around her almond-shaped eyes. So frail had she become that you might have thought she was a starving waif, or the actual afflicted party herself.

But in this case I was delighted to hear her whine, certain that her childish envy would help egg him on to eat faster, the way dogs often do in the presence of other dogs.

"Coming!" I replied, hastening to fix her a duplicate array of delicacies.

They each even made a decent dent in their respective shortcakes, piled as high as a miniature Mount Everest, stray juice from the wilted berries bleeding into the peaks of thickened cream like rivulets of rust-tinged rain streaming down a snowy mountain.

"Don't forget your urn," my father chided when it was time to bid him goodbye, which made me hope that he wasn't simply objecting to added clutter in his apartment, but actually appreciated my offerings and might look forward to my bringing more.

And so began a new weekly ritual. Each time I visited, I would fill the receptacle anew, selecting a wide assortment of treats – Jewish or not, nutritious or otherwise – hoping to spark his interest and restore some bulk to his shrinking frame.

I would leave some of my offerings stored safely in the fridge and return a week later to find that they had disappeared over the ensuing days, although I had no way of knowing whether they actually had been consumed or simply tossed out in the trash.

One night, though, when I was taking my leave, I couldn't find the urn anywhere.

"Oh, that white thing?" asked the temporary nurse's aide filling in for his customary caregiver that day. Thinking it was just a disposable container for one-time use, she had thrown it out with the garbage.

I hastened to the incinerator closet down the hall from their apartment, hoping that it might still be resting on the floor with the recyclables, but it was nowhere to be seen. And although it had been inexpensive, and I easily could have bought another, this seemed like a bad omen, as ominous as if I had found a lifeless bird on their windowsill.

Perhaps it was, for I never got to replace it. That was almost the last visit I'd pay.

One morning that June, I woke up at 2 a.m. with a tickle in my throat and a bee in my brain. In the middle of a dream, I had become improbably possessed with a strange, unshakable thought – that I could bargain with God for my father's soul. Here was the deal, in what sounded even in the middle of the night like a rather nutty nutshell: If I could think of one truly selfless, kind thing my father had ever done, then God would cut him some slack and spare, if not his life, then at least a little of his terrible suffering.

The judgment, somehow, had been placed in my hands. Or to be more accurate, God was the judge, but I was the lawyer who had been designated to plead on his behalf. In this case, though, I didn't need to prove his innocence. I merely needed to demonstrate that there had been one pure, decent moment in his life – evidence that, however flawed he may have been as a human being, and a dad, deep down he was perhaps good at heart.

The first thought that came to mind was about how much he had loved his mother. "Worshipped" might be a better word. While my Grandma Sadie had been alive, he had called her every single day without fail, to cheer her up or perhaps just hear her voice.

When she eventually grew too ill to speak on the phone, having been felled by one stroke after another, he did more than even the most devoted of children would do. He visited her almost every night after working all day, making the substantial trip from midtown Manhattan to Brooklyn before traveling another hour home to us.

When he came home, he would speak of having to carry her to the bathroom, then lift her off the toilet and carry her back. My grandfather was too old and frail to do it, and she refused to have a full-time nurse. As a young girl of 12, I was horrified by the image of a man having to lift his own mother off the toilet half-naked and possibly have to wipe her bottom clean because she was too weak to do even that herself. Horrified and yet also moved and indelibly stamped by such a stark demonstration of absolute filial devotion.

His willingness to rise to such a grim yet noble occasion, despite the indignity to them both – wasn't that among the ultimate gestures of inner decency and righteousness? Decades later, I still recall the terrible sounds of my father weeping afterwards in his bedroom each night, sobs that in my memory were tremulous enough to shake the house. Surely they had been genuine enough and pure enough to elicit a grain of God's mercy.

At the very least, this had demonstrated to me in the most graphic of ways and at a highly impressionable age a lesson about the duty owed to family. And yet, when it came to showing fatherly duty and devotion to my own family, he had done anything but.

As a mother myself now, I was understandably moved by memories of my father having honored my grandmother by tending to her most basic needs in her desperate final days. Yet that is far from how those months had impressed me when they were occurring.

Rather, it had become glaringly obvious to me as a child that my grandmother's illness became one more excuse for my father to not come home until late at night and withdraw further from our family, neglecting us even more than he had done previously.

He was rarely if ever home then, since in addition to working long hours during the week, he felt obliged to spend evenings and weekends with his mother... or was it his girlfriend? Maybe both. And on the rare occasions that he was around during our waking hours, he was distracted, distant, and despondent. Even in retrospect, I can still summon the sense of dual pain: We were losing my grandmother and my father all at once.

And in fact that double loss indeed came to pass. For almost as soon as Grandma died, my father's decade-plus-long and barely discreet affair with Elaine began in earnest.

Perhaps he threw himself into it with such abandon to offset the agony he felt at losing the mother he so adored, particularly in such a prolonged and painful fashion.

But my mother had another theory, and despite her customary wildly distorted perceptions about human behavior, I can't help but give it some credence. She claimed that my father launched into his adulterous fling with such little restraint because after Grandma Sadie died, for the first time in his life he felt truly free to do as he pleased.

Up until her precipitous decline, my iron-willed and fiery-tempered grandmother had been the undisputed matriarch of her family. She also always had served – more like ruled, rather – as my father's conscience and external moral compass. While she walked the earth, he wouldn't have risked unleashing her wrath by letting her learn of his affair. And had she ever found out about it, she simply wouldn't have allowed it to continue.

With her death, though, all danger of being exposed and chastised evaporated. He didn't even feel any compulsion to be circumspect just to keep up appearances at home. He had been legitimately afraid of his own mother, but he wasn't afraid of mine.

And before I drifted back to sleep, I came to a sudden and startling realization. Maybe my father didn't need God's forgiveness at all. What he really needed was mine.

—◦—

One hot night, when I was preparing to leave my father's apartment to make the long drive back home after my weekly visit, he got up with obvious effort and pain to kiss me goodbye, then had an apparent impulse and bid me suddenly to wait.

I watched as he pivoted and walked slowly to the front closet.

It was mid-June, a few days before my husband's birthday, which he invariably forgot. Perhaps, I figured, he would forage on a shelf as he often did for some unused generic item bought in his travels, like gloves or a hat, to offer as a gift. But no.

He soon came back with a light jacket on, grasped my elbow, and said, "Let's go."

"OK," I said. "Great. But... where are we going?"

He stopped and faced me, the closest thing to delight that he could muster lighting up like a beacon in his eyes.

"The Palm," he said, referring to one of his favorite city restaurants, the sort we'd gone to years earlier for major celebrations. "You can have the lobster. I'll have the steak. I'll have a steak this big!"

He held up his hands in the air, two feet apart, to indicate a colossal slab of beef.

By this point, he'd already lost close to half his weight. He could barely stand up. Was he losing his mind?

But what the heck. If he was up for it, fine. Why the hell not?

"Are you kidding?" I asked, letting him lead me toward the front door.

"Yes," he said, stopping. Then I saw that the glow in his eyes wasn't delight at all. It was just the reflection of a lamp in his tears.

—❦—

The night after my dream about bargaining with God, we attended a dinner at our temple with other families to help us prepare for our son's upcoming bar mitzvah. By chance, the senior rabbi ended up at our table, and after the meal, on impulse, I leaned over and whispered in his ear, asking if I might come and talk to him someday soon.

"What about?" he asked, instantly curious. I'd never requested a meeting before.

I explained that my father was gravely ill and likely to die any day now – my brother had expected it to happen that afternoon – and I was finding things very difficult.

"In my office. NOW!" he ordered so firmly that I flinched.

I protested that he had a roomful of congregants and I could wait. He said that this was much more important. So I dutifully followed him out of the social hall and through the labyrinth of hallways and office cubicles that led to his spacious private chambers.

Once there, settled beside him on a sofa, I began to recount the progression of my father's dramatic decline, noting how ill he'd become and how distraught I was about it. Then I shocked him, it appeared, by blurting out that my father had been, throughout most of my childhood, a terrible father. I chose not to go into any great detail about the particulars of his failings, but noted in almost the same breath that I had begun to fear that my father's illness was a bizarre form of punishment that God was inflicting on *me*.

What had I done to deserve this? I wasn't sure, but I felt overwhelmed with guilt about the fact that I'd never been able to forgive my father for being unfaithful to my mother, and for the incalculable collateral damage done to my brother's life and mine. I felt pressured to do it before he died. Yet it was something I neither could nor would do.

I paused at this juncture to retrieve a much-needed tissue from his desk, but even if I hadn't, it was clear that the rabbi would have cut off my monologue then and there.

"First of all," he said, "God does not punish people by making their parents ill." Where in God's name had I ever gotten a convoluted idea like that?

As for my need to forgive my father, he asked a simple, straightforward question. Had my father expressed a desire to be forgiven, or did he appear to seek this from me?

Hmmm... On the contrary, I had to confess, he seemed so consumed with his own discomfort that being forgiven by anyone seemed like the furthest thing from his mind.

The rabbi nodded and took my hands firmly in his. Under the circumstances, he asserted, my expressing forgiveness was simply not that pressing or even necessary. What I had already done and continued to do – treat my father with the honor and affection befitting a parent, be attentive to his needs, and even tell him that I loved him – was truly more than enough.

I was a little embarrassed to emerge from his office with red eyes and puffy lids. But I also felt flooded with relief and slept through the night for the first time in weeks.

Dear Mr. Bunton,

In keeping with our conversation today, I am writing to request a proposal for a monument to mark my father's grave.

We would like to purchase a single stone, despite your advice to choose a double. It should have a polished face with rough edges, as well as a top that curves gently upward in the center. (I believe you used the word "serpentine.") We would also like a small Star of David imprinted in the center on top.

In terms of the inscription, my father was born in 1927 and died in 1998. We will contact you shortly with the additional words we wish to have inscribed.

When Father's Day approached, I knew that the usual gifts would never do. A new necktie? Fishing equipment? A box of fine cigars? What could you buy for a once wildly successful businessman and avid outdoorsman who now rarely got out of bed?

Like millions of daughters everywhere, I was wracked with indecision. But this was not a question of which scent of aftershave to choose. It was an unsettling conviction that whatever I might select had to be almost perfect, not because my father was perfect but because I knew it would probably be the last gift for him that I would ever buy.

That meant it had to be something that might actually please him for once. So I needed to come up with an item that was thoughtful, personal… and preferably returnable. For before he got to ever use my present, there was a good chance he would die.

I asked the two comely young saleswomen behind a counter in the men's department at Lord & Taylor if they had any pajamas that looked like a business suit. They seemed to find this hilarious. The only funny part to me was that they answered yes.

The muted blue PJ set with dark pinstripes was only still available in size small. And being that it was 100 percent cotton, they warned me that it probably would shrink.

"That's fine, my father probably will too," I replied flatly. They seemed to find this uproarious as well. With luck, they even had a matching bathrobe. I had to go to the women's department, though, to get it wrapped in one of the store's traditional gift boxes featuring a long-stemmed red rose, a nicety upon which for some crazy reason I insisted.

What does it mean when maintaining life and civilization as you've always known it consists entirely of getting stuff you buy put into the right cardboard box?

This was the first Father's Day, or any other such occasion, that we would ever celebrate in the hospital. It was also the first time that it became clear that my father was now unable to hold up his side of the conversation, let alone dominate it.

I sat at his bedside awkwardly making inane chitchat with Elaine, my father paying little if any attention, until he piped up to complain that it was "freezing" in there. Of course it wasn't, but that made me realize that I had yet to proffer my presents. Also that, although my father was impossible to please, for once I had made a perfect choice.

"Hand it over!" he exclaimed when I mentioned that one of the boxes contained a bathrobe. Even over a hospital gown, its crisp tailoring lent him a faint aura of dignity.

To my surprise and grave doubts, he actually managed to return home once more and presumably wear those PJs as well. I still remember visiting him there the following week and getting a sinking feeling to discover how far his daily routine had degenerated. Once a shrewd man who held court ruthlessly at the office, he now lethargically watched Judge Judy hold court on TV, followed by back-to-back episodes of *The Golden Girls* – the not-quite-madcap misadventures of "Maude," a.k.a. Bea Arthur, her feisty octogenarian mom, and two other post-menopausal matrons cohabitating in Miami.

To me, this pretty much signaled the end of my father as I had always known him. But of course there were far worse things to come. And one July night a week or two later, my brother called to report that Elaine had been obliged to call for an ambulance. We proceeded to phone hospitals throughout the city until we found the one to which my father had been rushed, and from which he would never return.

⁓

By that time, I must confess, I already had scrawled out on notebook paper the eulogy I would give on his behalf. I'd dreaded not having the right words to say when the time came. I wanted to be able to speak for him properly. And I'd like to think that I did.

The pews at my brother's Long Island synagogue were full to brimming with relatives and friends that humid afternoon in July when I strode grimly up to the bima and did my best to remain composed so that everyone there could understand me.

My father wanted, above all, to be a success, and a great success he was!

He was a driven man, a meticulous man, a man who demanded the highest standards of himself — and others.

And so every time he came to visit me, I would begin preparing a week or two in advance, as if I were about to receive royalty — sprucing up my house, sprucing up my children, and buying or cooking the foods that he relished and loved.

In the same way, I have been getting ready for this moment for the past year or two, ever since we learned that he was sick. I've been preparing for it, dreading it, and steeling myself against it, as any good daughter of a steel magnate would.

But I see now that, just as it was impossible to prepare adequately for his coming, it was impossible to prepare adequately for his going.

Like all of you here who knew him, I am only beginning to fully realize now just how much I loved Stuie… and how much I'm going to miss him.

I barely have the "kuyach" to stand up here, to use one of my father's favorite Yiddish words, but I feel a need to put in my own two cents worth, or what may actually amount to 2,000 cents worth. In the end, fight it though I might, I am truly my father's daughter.

My father was, in his own way, a loving father to Joel and me, and generous to a fault. But as everyone who knew him well knows, he was not the easiest of men. He could be testy. He could be temperamental. And that's when he was in a GOOD mood. He didn't just like to have things his own way. His way was the ONLY way.

My father wasn't the president of his own company. He was its king! Whether in the office or at home, he liked to be in control. He had an ardor for order, a passion for punctuality. But there is an upside to having such strong convictions. He was also a man of passion.

He had a boundless ability to enjoy the best things in life. To him, those things were tennis, and fishing, and family. He loved getting away – to Montauk, the Catskill Mountains, Florida, Caneel Bay, or fishing camps in the great outdoors. But he also just as deeply loved gathering at the homes of family and relatives, particularly for a big Jewish holiday feast.

My brother and I often joke together about the way he'd describe these favorite occasions. After pouring over the juicy details – the big fish he'd caught or the gefilte fish he'd eaten – he would get a thrilling note in his voice and declare that it had been "GRAND!" That, to him, was the ultimate endorsement. "Pattie, Joel… it was GRAND!"

That is also my ultimate endorsement of him. He was GRANDpa Stu. I wish that he had lived to be a great grandfather. But in a way, he did. He spent more time with my nephew and niece, Charlie and Suzy, since they lived so much closer, but he always looked forward to seeing Aidan and Allegra too, as well as Elaine's grandchildren, and he loved to tell them stories. Perhaps he's the real reason that I became a writer. My father was a man of many words.

He told me a story a couple of weeks ago. He prefaced it by apologizing if he'd told it before, but it was actually one I'd never heard.

Fortunately, I knew it was one of the last times we'd ever talk, so I had a tape recorder rolling.

He recalled a time when my husband Harlan and I stayed overnight in New York years ago, and he came to take care of Aidan, who was only a baby at the time. These are his exact words:

"You stayed in a hotel, and I came down to pick him up early. It was a Sunday morning. And I put him in the carriage and walked him up Fifth Avenue.

"And as is my style, I was pointing out, without end, everything. Taxicabs, 'bus,' 'horse,' 'three people from Iowa.'

"We stopped by many, many windows. And I'd say something like, 'Those are SHOES. When you get older, you'll need shoes. You don't need them now.' And we went on that way for many, many blocks."

All the while, my father kept trying to teach Aidan all of the words he would one day need. "Bird." "Sky." "Skateboard." "Bloomingdale's."

Aidan was always a fast learner. Yet I'm not sure that early lesson can be given too much credit. For my father said that when he finally looked into the stroller that morning, he saw that Aidan was fast <u>asleep</u>.

My father did have a great sense of humor. Last Passover – the last time members of our extended family gathered together, at my Cousin Laura's – we tried to convince him to stay over, rather than braving the long drive back in Jewish holiday traffic. He wouldn't hear of it, though.

"I feel more comfortable near my bank," he insisted. "I like to sleep close to my money." That was his favorite running joke. He was always referring to counting his money. Today, though, I think he would be counting friends and relatives instead. He'd discover that he was a richer man than he ever realized.

It's wonderful that so many of you could come today. No, actually… it's GRAND!

⁓

Dutiful daughter though I may have been, I can't claim that however many months later I jumped right onto the dismal duty of selecting a gravestone.

Between work and the daily demands of my own children, weeks passed after my brother's initial call. Still, it seemed way too uncanny to have been mere coincidence that I returned from my somber field trip to that local cemetery to find my phone ringing. This time it was Elaine.

She, too, got right to the point, rather than wasting much if any time on niceties. "Pat, did you buy the stone yet?"

I was glad to have made some effort and thus be able to report on my progress. But when I got to the part about the prospective color of the rock, she audibly blanched.

"Black!" she barked, barely containing her obvious distaste. "Sounds like death!"

Hullo? Was she kidding? I mean… seriously?

But she hadn't called me to debate the particulars. She just wanted the deed done.

And done quickly.

"Buy the stone," she said.

—❦

Most of the monuments I'd seen in my foray across town had born such terse epitaphs that the word "succinct" didn't even begin to cut it. We were talking little more than name and dates.

Date of birth. Date of death. "Wife of." "Husband of." That was it.

And maybe for most people, that would have been enough. How much can you relate on a slab of rock? And how much more is necessary? Doesn't the life itself have to speak for itself? And don't the people who will visit know the rest of the story anyway?

On the other hand, I wasn't just anyone. My father had been a man of steel. I was a woman of words.

And the words in this case wouldn't be for just anyone. They were for my father. If his actions in life hadn't earned him a place in heaven (if there were such a place), then they at least had earned him whatever it would cost to purchase one helluva headstone.

It was his money that I would use to buy it, after all, and I felt like I should get him the weighty and impressive marker that I thought he would have wanted for himself.

The question was, How to sum up his entire life in such extremely limited space?

The man with whom I'd initially spoken had indicated that I could say as much on the stone as I wanted. Some people opted to include an entire eulogy, he said. Why, I could put on the entire text of *War and Peace*, if I chose – and all of that writing would be included in the basic price of the stone.

I had since learned that this was not the case. There would be an additional charge *per letter* for any inscription beyond my father's name and the dates of his life span.

That is not to say that I was ready to stick to just the facts, ma'am. Money, to me, was still no real object in this grave objective. But the more that I tried to cram on there, the smaller the letters would have to be. And the less imposing and legible they'd appear.

My father had been nothing if not a man of contradictions, but never mind that. This was not the time, or place, for abject honesty or full disclosure. So forget about war. I would have to stick with peace.

That is, it was my job to bury Caesar *and* to praise him. Praise him to the hilt.

So I was going to have to do some heavy editing here.

The easy part was enumerating all of the familial roles he had played in life. Although he had been a devoted son, his parents were long gone, and these sentiments would serve to satisfy all of the people who would see the stone at my father's unveiling. Beloved husband, father, brother, grandfather... that would be more than enough.

But how else could I begin to sum him up in a single phrase?

And while I continued to deliberate, time rolled by and I soon came home to another answering machine message from Elaine. "Did you buy it yet? Buy the stone!"

$\backsim$

"There must be a website for this," ventured my nice Jewish friend Suzanne when I called to elicit her help in writing the epitaph.

"You're kidding," I said. But even if there were, did this website know my dad?

Even Suzanne hadn't known my dad. But she sure as hell knew me.

"What do you want to say about him?" she asked.

So I told her the words that remained stuck in my head. Too bad it was a bad pun.

That man of steel thing.

She didn't recoil at the concept. Rather, she simply felt it needed to be expanded. We needed a softer, gentler word too, to balance it out.

"Maybe there's a Yiddish word," she said, "like '*chutzpah*.' Only not '*chutzpah*.'"

"*Chutzpah*'s too cute," I agreed. Among his favorite words had been "*gonif*" and "*shtunk*," but these terms, meaning "thief" and "jerk," were ones he had applied liberally to other people, not himself. They also weren't words you would put on a gravestone.

And beyond that we drew a blank.

"Tell me more about him," Suzanne urged.

"Well... I guess he was very determined," I began.

"Steel and will?" she suggested.

I winced. "That sounds like steel wool."

She couldn't argue there. "Steel and dignity?" she offered instead.

"That sounds too stiff."

"Anyway, you really want a love word," she agreed.

Yes, a love word would be nice.

"A man of steel and tenderness?" she ventured.

Tenderness? My dad? Hardly. The guy had been tough. If he had been a steak, the great big kind that he'd longed to eat that night, then he would have been well-done.

"Steel and passion?" she proposed instead.

Sure, he had been a man of passion. Yet in this case... better not to mention that.

"What's another word for 'power'?" I asked.

"Like an energetic word?" she replied. "Maybe steel and vigor?" she suggested. "Or how about 'grace'?"

"He wasn't a man of grace!" I retorted.

She shrugged. "You think you're the first person who ever lied on a tombstone?"

I suppose she had a point.

Then again, "grace" was kind of a Gentile word. It just didn't sound Jewish.

"Steel and style?" I ventured.

"Too *GQ*."

Also too trite. Come to think of it, maybe "steel" wasn't quite right, either.

And that's when I came up with a synonym, albeit just as bad a pun.

My father had been a man of courage, spirit, and guts.

He had been a man of mettle.

Over the coming days, instead of doodling as I often did while chatting on the phone, I began scrawling the words under consideration in countless combinations.

A MAN OF METTLE, VIGOR AND LOVE.

A MAN OF METTLE, VIGOR AND ENDLESS LOVE.

A MAN OF METTLE, STRENGTH AND PASSION.

Not bad, I guess. But it still needed work.

"Mettle!" scoffed Elaine the next time she called. "Sounds like he was a robot." At least she hadn't said The Tin Man from *The Wizard of Oz*.

"What does it even mean?" she asked.

I attempted to explain – both the meaning of the word and my rather lame pun. But she cut me off.

She didn't want a word that nobody even knew. She just wanted me to get it done.

Get it done already. Get it done *now*.

"Buy the stone," she said.

‚

STRENGTH, VIGOR, AND ENDLESS LOVE.

ENDLESS...? LIMITLESS...? PEERLESS LOVE...?

Maybe let's forget about love.

ENDLESS STRIVING, ENDLESS STRENGTH...

‚

OK, so maybe his physical strength hadn't proved to be truly "endless" in the end. But his generosity had. He'd always been beyond generous with me – financially, that is. Generous, perhaps, to a fault.

"Here is my check to cover Aidan's nursery school fee starting in September," stated a letter that he had written to me a few weeks before my first-born child turned 3. "I would like him to study hard and I look forward to seeing his report card."

Yes, he was kidding.

But he was dead serious when he penned another letter, also with a hefty check enclosed, urging me to rent the larger of two houses for a short summer respite in a beach community we favored. "I think you all enjoy that very much, and getting away is a good idea anytime... In the meantime, here is some money for vacation, clothes, dinners out, etc. etc. You know how precious you are to me and how proud I am of all that you are."

Yet to my disappointment, he never once managed to visit my family at the shore, although he subsidized that trip for additional years and invariably was invited to come.

And therein, I suppose, lay the rub.

As forthcoming as he was with his money, he was not quite as giving of his time. He loved my kids and me. Of that I have no doubt. Yet he liked to do what he liked to do. And when he wasn't working, which he usually was, what he liked to do was play tennis.

Or stay home and relax. He did not like to put himself out.

He also claimed to sleep poorly in unfamiliar places.

So as often as he promised to visit my family, he declined to either stay overnight with us or book a room in a hotel. He would plan instead to drive roundtrip from New York City to Connecticut in a single day. And almost invariably, he would cancel those excursions at the last minute because it looked like rain, or snow, or he was simply too tired to drive. It got to the point at which I would never tell my children that Grandpa was coming because they would be heartbroken when he suddenly didn't.

His visits with them were limited almost exclusively to Passover *seders* and my kids' birthday parties, and the occasional time when I would drive to the city to visit him.

But it's hard traveling five hours roundtrip with small children, and we couldn't afford a hotel in the city in those days. Meanwhile my father chose to live in a one-bedroom apartment, even though he easily could have afforded a home of virtually any size, so we couldn't stay overnight with him. He visited my brother's children almost weekly, since they lived much closer to New York. But by the time he died, it would be fair to say that he and my kids were relative strangers.

Then again, he invited us all to join him for a long weekend many summers, at the furthermost tip of Long Island, where he stayed at a seaside motel called The Driftwood. Those were the best of times.

And so one day in July, barely a week before he would die, I wrote him this letter, although I knew, had I been in his place, it would have broken my own heart to receive it.

Dear Stuie,

When I woke up this morning, I began to imagine what it would be like to turn the clock back for one glorious day to a time when you were well.

I know I would choose a perfect summer day, and that we would all be in Montauk. We'd wake up early to play tennis before it got hot, hit the beach for some sun and fun, then spend the afternoon lazing around the pool.

Afterwards, we'd dress up and drive to Gosman's Dock and gorge on the freshest fish in the world. Or maybe we'd just gather on your patio and feast on hamburgers, or big juicy steaks fresh from the grill and golden ears of corn.

I'm glad that we got to do that together, not once, but many times. Unforgettable times. Ah, yes, I remember them... well.

As the anniversary of my father's passing approached, I set about getting the rabbi to type out for me the Hebrew letters that would appear at the top of the stone. There, in keeping with the Jewish tradition, would be his given Hebrew name, Shmuel, and that he was the son of his father, Frank, whose Hebrew name was Fievel. But also, in keeping with my own decidedly feminist leanings and my father's unfettered devotion to his mom, I insisted against tradition upon including her Hebrew name, Goldeh, as well.

Meanwhile, I continued to scrawl the words I was still considering, in block letters and countless combinations. The word "mettle" had fallen by the wayside by now. With my stepmother I'd never win, and this war of words was a battle not worth waging.

A MAN OF MEANS (yet sometimes mean)?
A MAN OF STRENGTH AND VIGOR...
A MAN WHO REALLY MEANT BUSINESS?
Nah.

Regardless of his success later in life, my father knew all too well what it was like to be poor. So it's hard to explain a story that my brother told me one day. A lifelong sucker for the good things in life – which to him meant mostly simple, country pleasures – my dad made it a point to go apple-picking each fall at an orchard I'd found in Croton Falls, a sleepy hamlet just north of New York City. My brother and his wife accompanied him on one such excursion, and after the festivities amid the trees were over, they were horrified to watch him conceal a shopping bag or two full of apples in the trunk of his car – which was a pale blue Jaguar – before heading back to the front farm stand to pay.

"How can you even think of stealing from these people?" my brother asked him incredulously. "Places like this barely make a living."

My father just stared back at him coldly, looking him straight in the eye. As the owner of five companies, with offices and warehouses in several cities, he'd now amassed an estate worth millions. But on some level he remained the devilish little hellion who'd once been a constant pain in his mother's behind long before he'd wiped it, and a man who continued to delight in getting away with almost anything that he could.

When he received bad service at a restaurant, he often stole a steak knife for spite. When he met someone he found to be hotter than my mother, he took her as his mistress.

And when my brother confronted him in that orchard, he callously stood his ground. And smugly closed that trunk.

"What are you, a Boy Scout?" my father asked.

―❦―

FEARLESS STRENGTH, ENDLESS LOVE.

BOUNDLESS STRENGTH, ENDLESS LOVE.

OK, enough already. Maybe I was going overboard with all the love.

In fact, maybe in the end, as is so often true, less would be much, much more. Or, at the very least, good enough.

―❦―

September 17, 1999
Fax to I.J. Morris
Attention: Monuments Department

Here is the approved sketch for my father's stone. Please let me know when the monument will be ready (a date that we can rely on for a mid-October unveiling).

Thank you so much for your help.

The phone rang late on the morning of September 21. It was the first day of fall. And before she could even get the words out in her nasal twang, I cut her off at the pass.

"Elaine! Guess what! I have great news. I did it. I bought the stone."

October 4, 1999

Dear Mrs. Levy,

The memorial work for your father is completed and set at the cemetery. You may now proceed with any arrangements.

If you need any additional assistance, please call our toll free number.

On the Saturday of Columbus Day weekend, six weeks after my son's bar mitzvah, we assembled with a sizable gathering of close relatives at Mount Hebron Cemetery in Queens. The polished gray stone with rough-hewn edges, 2 feet wide by 3 feet high, stood swathed in pale ivory gauze. But once we began, the material was lifted to reveal a small Star of David engraved on top, and the final words I had chosen at last.

STUART WEISS
BELOVED HUSBAND,
FATHER, BROTHER,
GRANDFATHER

A MAN OF VIGOR,
STRENGTH AND LOVE
AUG. 18, 1927 – JULY 19, 1998
ALWAYS IN OUR HEARTS

Seeing it before me, despite having studied a detailed replica printed to scale on a page, I could barely stand on my own two feet. Could that be why my brother draped an arm around my shoulder and gave it a squeeze? Or did he need to be steadied himself?

Whatever the case, he seemed, somehow, content. "You did a great job," he said.

Elaine, for her part, said nothing. Which was probably as good as it gets.

Moments later, we opened the miniature black paperback editions of Memorial Prayers supplied by the cemetery and began to recite the Mourner's *Kaddish* en masse.

Yit-ga-dal v'yit-kadash sh'may rabo,
B'ol-mo-dee'v'ro chir-u-tay v'yam-leech mal-chu-tay...

Afterwards, at the nearby delicatessen to which we repaired with everyone for lunch, my brother and I both ordered the cold borscht. It had been Dad's favorite and he would've loved a bowl. Sadly, they were all out. So we had the pastrami on rye instead.

October 22

Dear Dad,

There are days, even weeks, when I feel like we're all beginning to what you might call heal. Others, I'm not so sure.

Take today, for example. I had stopped into the kids' school after dropping them off when I happened to walk out of the building at the same time as another mother. This woman and I have never been particularly close, but she was muttering and sighing to herself so audibly that I felt obliged to ask what was wrong.

"It's my father," she sputtered, a pair of deep parentheses furrowing her brow. The man was driving her nuts — so much, she said, that she wanted him "out of her life."

I wondered if she regretted those words the moment they came out... not because she didn't actually mean them, but because she'd been tactless enough to say them to me. We may not be friends, but pretty much everyone knows that you're gone.

But no. She didn't come up for air for a second as she continued to kvetch about her dad. And as she nattered on, all I could think of was what happened two years ago, when I ran into a neighbor at a gas station and made a similar comment to him.

Seeing the stress etched on my face, he too asked me what was wrong, and was instantly treated to a diatribe about how anxious I was about an imminent visit from you.

The occasion had launched me into a frenzy of cleaning, although I realized full well that any attempt to make my cluttered house or life conform to your standards was futile.

No doubt I concluded with some snide, snarky remark, along the lines of my looking forward to your arrival, but even moreso to the moment when you would leave.

It was meant to come out as jocular, I guess, but my neighbor didn't even feign a smile.

"I used to feel that exact same way," he replied, "but that was before my father died. Now I'd give almost anything to be able to have him come over and criticize me."

At the time, I felt instantly ashamed, and I have thought about his chilling words at least a hundred times since. But today was the first time I actually used them myself.

"My father tortured me in his own way for my entire life," I told that muttering mother. "But right now, I'd give anything just to be able to call him up on the phone."

At this she stopped, visibly stepped out of her personal funk, and looked at me. "What would you say to him?" she asked with what sounded like genuine curiosity.

It was an interesting question, but one to which no answer readily came to mind.

"Nothing much," I replied with a shrug. "I don't really have anything special to say or to ask. It would be enough to just say hello."

To this, she managed a sympathetic smile. "Why don't you write him a letter?" she asked. "You could write down what you would say to him."

It was a nice idea. But I barely knew this woman, and it sounded a little nuts.

"Maybe I will," I said, mostly to be polite. "But where, exactly, would I send it?"

"Send it?" she asked. "You could send it to yourself. Maybe it would help you feel better."

—⁕—

Three months later, we attended a Friday night service at our temple because our daughter was singing in the children's choir. After the usual prayers had been read, we stood to see the Ark opened and the Torah ceremoniously undressed.

Off went the two ornate silver crowns and breastplate, the velvet belt that held the scroll together, and the embroidered mantel that cloaked it, fashioned from faded ivory. Then the rabbi began chanting in Hebrew from Genesis, translating as he went along.

That week's portion, called *Vayeshah*, was the first of a series focusing on Jacob and his 12 sons, particularly his favorite, Joseph, he of the famous coat of many colors.

It went on to detail how Joseph was sold by his brothers into slavery in Egypt, where he rose in stature, thanks to his knack for interpreting dreams.

The rabbi then proceeded to read the accompanying *Haftarah* – the thematically related passage chosen from the Book of Prophets that Jews recite in temple each week.

This one was taken from the book of Amos, documenting how Amos had warned the people not to treat the poor unfairly. And it concluded with an interesting phrase.

"A lion has roared. Who will not fear?"

At this, I sat bolt upright. And I thought, "A lion has roared?"

A lion has roared!

At last, the exact words I had been seeking all along.

So simple. So succinct. Yet so perfect a way to sum up my father's life.

His birth sign had even been Leo.

A LION HAS ROARED. No endless. No vigor. No mettle, for that matter.

If only I had heard that phrase before.

Forgive me, Dad. But the words I chose were good enough, weren't they?

I'd like to think so. Besides, it was too late now. They were already set in stone.

The other woman: *My father envisioned his mistress, Elaine, with her dark bouffant hair and almond-shaped eyes, as a Semitic version of actress Sophia Loren.*

The adulterer's daughter: *In January 1978, at age 23, shortly before I would finally meet my father's mistress.*

When he was young: *My father, Stuie, as a "skinny marink" of 19.*

Fool for love: *My mother, Bunnie, was one smart cookie… but the cookie would soon crumble.*

Sister act: *My Aunt Gloria (left) was considered a beauty. My mother, Bunnie, was better known for her brains — not exactly a priority for women in their day.*

Grannie dearest: *My mother believed that her mother, Grandma Mary, overtly favored her older sister, Gloria.*

A serious man: *My mother's father, Grandpa Charlie, shunned "the family business" – he refused to become a rabbi like his father and brothers before him.*

Young at heart: *My parents were already an item by age 19. "Let's not let trivial things mar this delicious love of ours," he scrawled across this photo of them from August 1947.*

Before the fall: *My parents, Bunnie and Stuie, on their wedding day in June of 1949. The marriage would last for nearly 30 years. Their love and radiant smiles would not.*

No longer a wide-eyed 5: *By the time we took this family vacation in August of 1961, there was already plenty of trouble in paradise. And at the tender age of 6, I was already painfully aware of it.*

Miss Taken Identity: *My mother took the liberty of mutilating many of my photos, including this one, from my brother's bar mitzvah in 1966.*

Brotherly love: *In 1971 with Joel, who – two years older and 7 inches taller – was literally my big brother.*

Fragile: *In high school I hung around in the guidance department, waiting for some adult to notice there was something terribly wrong.*

Birthday boy: *With my parents at a backyard barbecue on my dad's 45th.*

Hair I am: *At 19, before junior year of college.*

Moving day: *With my father on my first day of college. (Fearing that people might mistake my roommate's mother for her, my mother tore her out of the picture.)*

Love is blonde: *My parents at a rare tender moment.*

L'chaim!: *My mother, father, and Aunt Gloria at a cousin's bar mitzvah in 1973.*

My father, myself: *With Stuie in Montauk, at age 23.*

BFFs: *With my friend Lisa in 1980. "Like most men we met, we wanted one thing and one thing only. But that thing was to date."*

Friends indeed: *With Hallie (center) at her med school graduation.*

Looking for love: *At my mother's in 1981, dressed in the purple jumpsuit I would soon wear on the blind date on which I would meet my husband.*

Let there be Nins: *In three weeks we went from blind date to dating to no longer dating because we were already in a relationship.*

Strike two!: *At a Mets game soon after we met.*

"Aunt Smith": *My mother-in-law's nosy neighbor. "Believe me, my dear, you're doing something wrong," she chastised me. "Men don't want to marry Emily Dickinson these days."*

At last: *Our wedding at The Water Club in New York City, July 15, 1984.*

Father of the bride*: Stuie and me…*

and his former mistress (now wife), Elaine.

Bride and joy: *My parents, though divorced, walked me down the aisle together.*

Members of the wedding: *(from left to right) Wendy and Dick Malina, my mother, Steve Kornhauser, Grandma Mary, my brother Joel, my sister-in-law Karen, Marie Cox, Jay Lagemann, Lisa Keith Block, Harlan, me, Hallie Weiss, Betsy Kornhauser, Ellen Howe, Russ Hoyle, Chris Cox, Rick Freeman, and Gerry Joseloff.*

See ya later, alligator: *My kids, Allegra (age 3) and Aidan (age 6), in 1993.*

The three amigos: *Allegra, Aidan, and my mother-in-law, Harriet.*

"All heart": *My daughter, Allegra, at age 5 was as spontaneous and outgoing as I was deliberate and shy.*

His mistress became a grandmother to my children: *(clockwise from left) My father, brother, husband, nephew, sister-in-law, niece, Allegra, Aidan, and Elaine.*

It's a wrap: *With Allegra (age 9) in Lenox, Massachusetts, summer of 1999.*

Here comes the son: *With Aidan (age 13) at his bar mitzvah in August 1999.*

Second time's the charm: *My mom with husband No. 2 Sid at Aidan's bar mitzvah.*

Double trouble: *Elaine gave my father 30 good years; unfortunately, half of them just happened to coincide with the 30 years that he spent married to my mother.*

Family affair: *(from left) Aidan, Harlan, me,*
Allegra, and my daughter-in-law Kaitlin.

Still the one: *Celebrating our 30th anniversary back at The Water Club.*